Alberto Gonzalez provides us wi... countryside combined with impor... is an extraordinary translator, as well as an avid and colorful storyteller... Peace was fortunate to have Alberto serve as translator for almost every Friendshipment Caravan to Cuba. He, indeed, was Born to Translate Cuba to the rest of us and has done so remarkably well.

Gail Walker, Co-Executive Director, Pastors for Peace
Interreligious Foundation for Community Organization

Born to Translate Cuba provides an honest look into the history, culture, and society of Cuba. By integrating history into his personal narrative, Alberto provides a genuine and honest look at life in Cuba and the impact of the Revolution on the people who have experienced it. From the literacy campaign through the collapse of the Soviet Union to the challenges of tourism and the dual currency system, this book provides a unique perspective on Cuba from a man who truly knows it. Alberto's story personalizes the Cuban experience and will change readers' perspective on Cuba while simultaneously serving to inspire them to pursue their dreams regardless of how difficult.

Kaitlyn Sill, Assistant Professor, Political Science, Pacific Lutheran University

Alberto's intellect, his curiosity, and his determination have enabled him to become one of the outstanding interpreters of his country—even being honored to translate for Fidel Castro. A great story for anyone who wishes to learn about the opportunities the Cuban Revolution has offered its people.

Donna Neff, Friend of Alberto and of Cuba

Alberto's book rings with the energy, humor, intelligence and zest for life that he exhibits daily.

Ellen Gabin

This book captures the ebbs and flows of day-to-day life in Revolutionary Cuba, For anyone interested in understanding the "special period" and the U.S. blockade's impact on Cuban life this is a "must-read."

JB Miller, retired financial services executive

Alberto gifts the reader with a sense of both his culture and his place in the ever-evolving Cuban Revolution. He is a translator with heart, soul, and humor.

Jeanne Lemkau, Medical School Professor,
Author of *Lost and Found in Cuba: A Tale of Midlife Rebellion*

In his memoir of growing up in revolutionary Cuba, Alberto Gonzalez has woven together a rich tapestry of life's joys, sadness, triumphs, and cruelty. Keenly observed and deeply felt, Gonzalez depicts the human condition in all its glorious complexity and celebrates the resilience of the human spirit.

Jeffrey Boutwell, Pubwash Conferences on Science and World Affairs

Alberto Gonzales treats his readers to an engaging, witty, and inspiring collection of stories that illuminate the unique features of his life as well as the complex flavors of the Cuban experience.

Trevor Poag, intercultural educator

Alberto's story offers an in-depth picture of growing up within the Cuban Revolution. Alberto is more than a translator. His knowledge of Cuban history and culture make him a passionate teacher. This book provides a fascinating glimpse into the beautiful reality of Cuban life, and the hopes and dreams of its people.
           Martha Pierce, delegate to Cuba in 2005 and 2012

Filled with typical "Alberto humor," this book offers a very personal view of life within the Cuban revolution. Alberto does not shy away from describing the impact that the U.S. embargo/blockade—now in place for more than 55 years— has on everyday Cuban life. Rivoting reading!
           Mavis Anderson, Senior Associate and Policy Analyst
           Latin America Working Group

Those of us who know Alberto Gonzalez's work in Cuba have marveled at his skills and knowledge. He can instantaneously turn spoken Spanish into free-flowing English, and vice versa, while also assuming the tone, cadence, gestures, and personality of the person speaking. This warm and engaging memoir illustrates and celebrates the progress, resilience, and incredible humanity of the Cuban people.
           Dr. Susan D. Rose, Professor of Sociology and Community Studies
           Dickinson College

For Americans, Alberto offers a powerful antidote to the politically motivated misinformation and dehumanizing narratives we generally receive about Cuba. I found this book insightful, balanced and honest. Meeting Alberto and now reading this story has helped me to recognize some of the positives and marvelous achievements of the Cuban Revolution. In this passionate account, Alberto serves as a guide into Cuban life during the last 50 years.
           Peter Berres Retired Foreign Policy and Medical Systems Professor
           International Tour Group Leader and Advisor

Alberto Gonzales is a remarkable Cuban with an important story. This book is a unique account of how Alberto achieved his dream.
           Joan Remple Bishop

A somewhat ominous mystery to most Americans, the real Cuba requires translation! And translate Cuba is what Alberto does best! This book reads like a fast-paced adventure story—and that's exactly what it is. He parallels his own 50 years with the five decades since the Cuban Revolution. In ten year segments, each chapter presents both his life experiences and the maturing of the great Cuban social experiment.

Alberto's Christian journey is very much a part of his story and corrects one of the most pervasive myths about Cuba today. Despite our U.S. fears, there is no contradiction between the social and spiritual goals of liberation theology and the social and humanist goals of the Cuban State. In Cuba both work and live together peacefully.
           Judy Robbins, Let Cuba Live Committee of Maine

Born *to* Translate
Cuba

A Country Boy's Dream Come True

Alberto González Rivero

Born to Translate Cuba

A Country Boy's Dream Come True

Alberto González Rivero

Pfeifer-Hamilton Publishers
Middleton, Wisconsin

Pfeifer-Hamilton Publishers
8665 Airport Rd.
Middleton, WI 53562
www.pfeiferhamilton.com

Born to Translate Cuba: A Country Boy's Dream Come True

© 2014 Alberto González Rivero. All rights reserved. Except for short excerpts for review purposes, no part of this book may be reproduced or transmitted in any form by any means, electronic or mechanical, including photocopying, without permission in writing from the publisher.

Scripture quotations are from the Holy Bible, New International Version, copyright 1973, 1978, 1984 by Biblica.

Editor: Susan Rubendall
Cover design: Ben Rubendall
Cover photo: Sergey Arnold Martínez Alvarez

Printed in the United States of America

10 9 8 7 6 5 4 3 2 1

Library of Congress Control Number: 2014938026

ISBN: 978-1-935388-11-1

I dedicate this book

To the memory of my parents,
Avelino and Delia, my roots.
May God keep them in His Glory forever.

And to my two great treasures, my daughters,
Wendy and Betsy, my fruits.
May God always bless them.

Contents

Foreword vii

Preface x

Introduction xii

Acknowledgments xv

Maps 1

The Little Nest Egg 4

My Intelligent Country Boy 28

My Fondness for English 52

A Real School for Me 80

The Sadly Celebrated Special Period 106

Yes, I Can Do It 132

Nothing Like Personal Experience 160

I Do Not Believe in Chances 188

I Would Be a Translator Again 216

Epilogue 244

Acknowledgements 246

Cuba: A Brief History

From Columbus to Castro 2

The 1960s: The First Decade of the Revolution 26

The 1970s: A New Economy and New Directions .. 50

The 1980s: The Golden Age 78

The Early 1990s: Collapse and Rebirth............ 104

The Mid-1990s: Back From the Abyss 130

The late 1990s: Underway in a New Direction..... 158

The early 2000s: The Envy of Other Nations....... 186

The late 2000s: A Better World Is Possible......... 214

Welcome to Cuba 242

Foreword

On April 25, in the year 1987, a simple celebration was held in which the dream of a small faith-based community was fulfilled. Since 1971 members of the community had been on a path towards renewing both the understanding and the practice of their faith. We sought a biblical and theological foundation so as to "bear witness of our hope" within the new Cuban context, which started in 1959. The point was specifically to strengthen our Christian witness while reshaping a Christian identity that would fearlessly become present in a revolutionary process. We committed ourselves "To place our hand on the plowshares and not look back."

The theological choice was aimed at the evangelizing action of carrying the spirit of Jesus Christ to every single sphere of the life of our people. This community dream was embraced with full conviction, vocation, and commitment by the author of this book, Alberto González Rivero, who has translated it to thousands of US citizens. His story is closely linked to both the Marianao Ebenezer Baptist Church and the Dr. Martin Luther King Jr. Memorial Center.

During the past 20 years, Alberto and I have shared our dreams. His dream has been to become an accomplished translator-interpreter. For me and the Dr. Martin Luther King Jr. Memorial Center, it has been to continue materializing the dream of the faith community within which this pastor and his favorite translator work.

One day back in 1993, I was introduced to a potential translator for the MLK Center. I can still close my eyes and see that young man, eager to start a new stage of his life. Expressively, he told me, "I am kind of fearful, but I will try my best to succeed." Ever since, he has been translator par excellence for the US-Cuba Friendshipment Caravan of Pastors for Peace. That day, we began an adventure and a friendship with true empathy. Alberto knows my thoughts, my gestures, and also my deepest feelings and emotions. He is the only person who is able to translate my words in just the way my ideas spring up.

Likewise, Alberto may claim that, if there is someone capable of knowing him thoroughly, close to the most sacred place in his life, it is I his brother, friend, and pastor. My relationship with Alberto and his family has come to enrich the breath of life that God has given me.

Born to Translate Cuba is an autobiography, the story of Alberto's life on the occasion of his 50th birthday – as we Cubans put it, his "half wheel." As you read it, you will both laugh and cry, because it will touch your heart. Alberto's story will be a source of inspiration to youngsters searching for their own dreams, even when those may seem impossible to attain. As he has told me, "My witness is an encouragement to hope against all hopes, to the stubbornness of faith as you used to say, and to always think optimistically that the very best is yet ahead of us."

As a child of farmers, myself, this book touches me because it portrays a sector of society unknown to today's youth, Cubans who are easily and superficially called "the rank and file ones." Life was not easy for our parents, and it's important that we remember and tell their stories.

I must highlight both the responsibility and the professionalism characterizing the way in which Alberto undertakes every single translation-interpretation job. During one of the Pastors for Peace caravans, we had to visit the Pinar del Río province where we were expected to have an exchange with the managers and employees of a swine production facility. During the talk, Rev. Lucius Walker and several members of his delegation asked many questions about the raising of pigs, their diet, diseases, and a few other related issues. The answers provided were technical and used terminology familiar only to professionals in the field. Alberto translated it all fluently. When we walked out, I approached Alberto and told him, "Wow buddy, you certainly did a great job! Where did you get all that information from?" He responded, "I saw this visit on the schedule a few days ago, so I read a book about animal husbandry."

Another experience like this took place just a few days after Barack Obama's election as president of the United States. I saw Alberto holding a book in his hands. Of course I asked him what it was about.

He showed me the book: Alberto was already reading, in English, the book written by President Obama about his parents entitled *Dreams from My Father*.

When Alberto asked me to write the foreword to his own book, he told me, "I want you to know that I am finishing drafting these words with thanksgiving tears falling down my cheeks. May God bless you a lot forever for He has already blessed me much more than expected when allowing over twenty years ago for our paths to cross the way they did for the common good of both of us. AMEN!" Thus, I finish this prologue and tell him, "Alberto, to you and to your dear family, I wish the words of the Book of Proverbs be fulfilled thoroughly, "But the path of the just is as a shining light, that shineth more and more unto the perfect day." (Proverbs 4:18)

Rev. Raúl Suárez Ramos
Emeritus Pastor of Marianao Ebenezer Baptist Church
Director and founder of the Dr. Martin Luther King, Jr.
  Memorial Center
Deputy to the National Assembly of the People's Power
  (Cuban Parliament MP)

Havana, June 20, 2013

Preface

*"In the world there is a language understood by all:
it is the language of enthusiasm,
of the things done with love and good will,
searching for what is desired or believed in."*
Paulo Coelho

I entered this book as a proofreader in response to a personal request from a former student who is, today, my friend. At that time, I was burdened by duties that limited my time to read and correct, but I accepted the responsibility when allowed to work on the manuscript without rush.

Alberto's storytelling captured me from the beginning due to the simple nature of his language, its unique turns, and the deep feeling emanating from his stories. I smiled at the mischief of the protagonist and was deeply moved by some of his anecdotes, which startled and saddened me. The pleasant, conversational, and sometimes slangy style allowed me to read his life story without problems. It was told from the deeply humane perspective of a simple being who reveals his perseverance and optimism.

Alberto's story provides examples of the benefits of personal sacrifice, of what people may attain when they strive to achieve objectives. And it demonstrates how continuous studying and upgrading can help a human being to be both good and useful.

The history of our country's educational system emerges in many of the stories. This young boy living far from town found schools waiting for him and teachers with the wisdom and the kindness to acknowledge his efforts and reward his intellect.

His evolution from boy to teenager to man is reflected in his roles as a son, brother, grandson, husband, and father. Alberto describes with grace, modesty, and simplicity his adult roles as professor, translator-interpreter, and man of faith. There is no vainglory, only goals that have been reached with many sacrifices and with the firmness and perseverance of one who knows how to build up, step by step, a profession, a family, and a life which, at the age of 50, has made him proud and satisfied with his accomplishments thus far.

I see in this book Alberto's nonstop quest for his dreams. Walking towards them seemed illusory. However, human grandeur is found in the gift of dreaming about possible futures and being open with confidence to far away prospects.

Mario Benedetti, the great poet of our Americas, wrote, "How am I going to believe . . . that the world was left without utopias . . . ?"

Alberto's challenge has been fulfilled. His utopia is already a reality. The only thing left for me to do is be grateful for the opportunity I was given to write these words and to congratulate him for continuing to be the Alberto he has always been: the country boy from Managua and the professional he is today.

Ileana Domínguez García, PhD.

Havana, March 12, 2012

Introduction

It is 7:35 am, and I have just received a message on my cell phone. The text reads, "Happy HALF WHEEL! LOTS OF GOOD HEALTH. Your book will be great just like you." Today I am 50 Septembers old; some time ago, I decided to write this book as a gift to myself. Reading a few autobiographies such as *Yo vendí mi bicicleta* by Enrique Núñez Rodríguez, *Cuando pasares por las aguas* by Rev. Raúl Suárez Ramos, and, more recently, *Dreams from My Father* by Barack Obama, the current president of the United States has inspired me.

Today is September 9, 2010, and I cancelled plans to celebrate with friends and family, instead starting to materialize a dream by implementing what was recommended by our beloved José Martí, "Every man before passing away should plant a tree, beget a child, and write a book."

I was born and reared in the countryside, so I have planted many trees, and I have two wonderful daughters. I have already fulfilled these two challenges; however, although I have written a few things and have translated several books, I have not written a book of my own. Turning the famous "half wheel" is a timely moment and a reason to begin.

It is said that when we turn 40 years old, we start to live the "senior years" of our youth; when we turn 50, we start to live "the junior years" of our adulthood. Maybe that is why my daughters thought it wise to present me today with a cake on which a sign announces, "I am not turning 50; I am only 18 + 32."

If 50 years is truly half the wheel, then one should live twice as long to reach the whole wheel. There are only a few lucky ones who manage to make it and a very few who reach the amazing 120 Club. My grandfather on my mother's side had almost completed his whole wheel when he died at 96 years old.

Once, when answering a question about the secret for a long life, he confessed humbly but with great wisdom, "Eating properly and having good thoughts." I inherited many things from my grandfather Pedro. He was able to help himself, even in his nineties, with a spiritual richness, a life philosophy, a physical strength, and a mental sharpness that was just amazing. If my fate is to have a long life, I hope I may be able to enjoy the same quality of life, for he was hospitalized only once at the very end of his life, and he never became a burden to anyone.

Today, on my 50th birthday, I feel a mixture of happiness and pain, sadness and pride, both sweet and bittersweet. On one hand, I have the joy of reaching 50 years of age, having enjoyed good health and the achievement of goals, some of them unsuspected – surprises that life treats you to – such as the huge privilege of having received a priceless gift: the book *La Victoria Estratégica* by our Commander in Chief, which he autographed and sent to me.

On the other hand, tonight the tribute worship service in memoriam will be held to honor the life and work of Rev. Lucius Walker, Jr., who passed away a couple of days ago in New York City. Life is a roller coaster; it either lifts you up to great heights at a lightning speed, or it shakes you up; but we have to cope with its challenges, and be thankful to God no matter what.

From the perspective of my five decades of existence, I invite the kind reader to follow my steps, to walk along with me through the imponderable meanders of my life's river, and to share the experiences, feelings, and emotions of this adventure I am writing. I hope to reach the hearts and minds of people who, whether they like my book or not, might identify with my memories, since our humanity binds us together in this unique and wonderful experience of life and solidarity.

Because I was born in the land of Cuba and have lived my entire life here, I will begin each chapter in my book with a bit of history that will help readers understand the context in which my story takes place. The challenges faced by my family were not unique. They were common to all Cubans, and they made us who we are today.

It is my greatest desire that whatever I write in this book of my dreams will be pleasant to those who decide to spend precious time digging into my memories. Whatever their reason, if they do it, I will be more than grateful to them, knowing that my efforts were worthwhile.

Alberto González Rivero

Havana, March 1, 2014

BORN TO TRANSLATE CUBA

Cuba

Havana

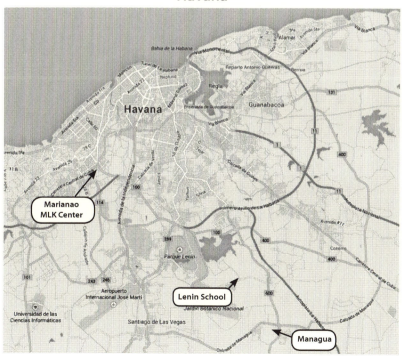

CUBA
A brief history

From Columbus to Castro

Today, when Americans think of Cuba, a multitude of images come to mind: the bearded Fidel Castro, the Bay of Pigs disaster, the Soviet-Cuban Missile crisis, Ernest Hemingway, cigars, the mafia, oppression and human rights violations, and poverty. It's strange that the real Cuba remains a somewhat ominous mystery to most Americans, since Cuba is only 90 miles from the US border, and so many US families share connections.

Cuba lies at the entrance to the Gulf of Mexico. It is the Caribbean's largest (785 miles long) and most populated (11 million people) island. Cuba remains a beautiful land, green throughout with fertile fields, rolling hills, and mountains. Its convenient harbors and beaches are both lovely and useful for international trade.

Settled in 1250 by native tribes who prospered, Cuba was conquered in 1492 by Christopher Columbus who plundered. Within a decade, the Spanish established settlements, and the first sugar cane (still Cuba's main export crop) was planted. The country struggled against Spanish colonialism, home-grown dictators, and American intervention until Fidel Castro emerged in 1959. Since then, Cuban-style socialism has molded the nation's unique and in US minds, controversial development.

In 1500, an estimated half-million indigenous people lived in small villages farming corn, yucca, yams, peanuts, avocados, and tobacco. As the Spanish established new settlements, smallpox, brutal treatment, and malnutrition quickly decimated the natives. Thousands committed suicide rather than submit to the Spaniards. By 1570, the entire indigenous population had been wiped out.

Today, Cuba's people are the most racially varied in the Caribbean. Why? Following the complete destruction of native peoples, Spain needed cheap labor for its sugar fields and mines. The first African slaves were brought to work the mines and plantations in 1522. The sugar industry grew rapidly after 1791, when French planters fled a slave revolt in Haiti and settled in Cuba. To work the fields, thousands more Africans were imported over the next 40 years, eventually outnumbering whites.

After slavery was abolished in 1886, another quarter million blacks came from Jamaica and Haiti. Eastern European Jews fleeing oppression flocked to the island in the 1920s, mostly to Havana. In the nineteenth century, more than 150,000 Chinese were imported as indentured servants to build railroads and work the sugar fields. Today, Cubans comprise a rich cultural mix of races and traditions.

By 1850, Cuba was the world's largest sugar producer, with the United States its biggest market. The US twice attempted to buy Cuba from Spain, in 1848 and 1854, but Spain refused to sell. After the first Cuban revolution for independence from Spain failed in 1878, the country's economy was destitute. US investors snapped up plantations sold cheaply by bankrupt Spanish landowners. By the late 1890s, 70 percent of the land in Cuba was in US hands, and 90 percent of the country's sugar was shipped to the US. In this way, US financial interests succeeded in purchasing Spanish Cuba one piece at a time.

In 1895, Cuba's national hero, Jose Martí, launched a campaign for Cuban independence from Spain. In 1898, the US also declared war on Spain. In July, the Spanish surrendered, and the Americans occupied Cuba. Cuba had finally gained independence from Spain, but it was forced to accept a made-in-the-USA constitution, which included a clause that gave the US the right to intervene in Cuban internal affairs and to invade Cuban territory whenever it felt the need to protect American interests. It also allowed the US to establish a permanent naval base at Guantánamo Bay.

The next five decades of the 20th century were dominated by corruption, incompetence, and increasing American control of the economy. Tourism boomed along with gambling and prostitution, as mobsters from Miami and New York moved into Havana. Meanwhile, poverty and unemployment increased, and the countryside was virtually ignored. Several rebellions ended in failure or were themselves corrupted. The situation was intolerable, and the people suffered greatly from oppression and poverty.

In 1955, rebel leader Fidel Castro gathered other revolutionaries around him, including his brother Raúl and a radical Argentine doctor Ernesto Guevara. The guerrillas established themselves with the support of peasants and underground resistance. After three years, the forces of US-backed dictator, Fulgencio Batista, collapsed.

Fidel Castro, then 33, arrived in Havana on January 8, 1959. The Cuban Revolution had finally succeeded, but the economy and the countryside were in ruins.

This is the world I entered.

The Little Nest Egg

Honor your father and your mother, so that you may live long in the land the LORD your God is giving you.

Exodus 20:12

I WAS BORN ON SEPTEMBER 9, 1960, BEFORE THE SUNRISE, at about six o'clock in the morning. Roosters were already crowing. When I saw the light for the first time ever, I was not only near those roosters but also near pigs, rabbits, dogs, and cats that were never missing in my environs. I was born in the countryside, in a very poor house with a thatched roof, wooden walls, and a dirt floor, without electricity or toilet, approximately one kilometer away from the town of Managua, on the road to Batabanó. I became the sixth and last child of my parents, Avelino Nicolás and Nieves Delia, who had decided previously to name all their progeny with the letter "A."

My parents on their wedding day

We were all born in an amazing marathon – a period of only nine years. The first two children were born within the same year without being twins. The firstborn, Avelinito, was born in February 1951 and Alicia, who seconded him, in December 1951. Right after them, and in chronological order, came Ada, Ana, Armando, and finally, in 1960, I arrived. My birth was a true miracle, which leads me to think that my existence had to materialize at all costs.

When my parents had only my five siblings, my father endured an automobile accident while working as a truck driver distributing milk in the city of Havana. Miraculously, he managed to survive, for he was trapped under the deck of his truck and crushed against the pavement for a long time before they managed somehow to lift the vehicle with a crane. By the time he was removed, he was already blackened, and there was no hope for him to survive. He was seriously ill for a long while, but eventually he managed to recover to such an extent that he was able to resume his reproductive activities. Everything seems to indicate that, with the happiness after his recuperation, he neglected to use condoms, luckily enabling me to enter this world.

I reiterate that my existence was predestined, somehow, because when my mother was already pregnant, and I was hardly an embryo trying by all means to complete my intrauterine formation, my father got sick with the mumps. His condition worsened to such an extent that it took hold of his testicles and magnified them to a painfully huge size. Before daring to reveal his cruel diagnosis, the doctor who took care of him at the first-aid post in town asked him with concern how many children he had.

Facing such a big question and rather puzzled, my father immediately replied "I have five of them now and one more that is already on his way." The physician relaxed then, knowing that there were enough children within our family setting and that one more was not really needed that badly. He categorically proclaimed, "Well, if the one who is already on his way, as you claim, manages to arrive, you will then have only six children, because you have regretfully been left sterile as an aftermath of this disease."

The forecast of that medical doctor was absolutely right. Apparently, everything happens for a reason. The accidental sterilization of our father was a blessing, a very timely contraceptive method, which prevented the continuous proliferation of the González-Riveros family. At the early age of only 30 years, my parents already had six children. Sometimes I wonder how many more of us there would be today if the paternal testicles hadn't complicated themselves in such a blessed way!

On my birthday, when our poor mother started to feel her labor pangs and I was at long last getting ready to complete the perfect sextet of siblings (consisting of three girls and three boys) my father hurried to fetch the midwife, as was then customary in the countryside. When this lady arrived on board a taxi cab from the El Anchar taxi rank, I had already preceded her, and I was the one who welcomed her. Nevertheless, to make sure that she had not wasted her time, I allowed her to cut my umbilical cord and cleanse me. Following the tradition in force, she then cut a very yellow lemon from the backyard of our house into two halves and squeezed one drop of pure natural vitamin C into each of my brand new little eyes. That must have been a very painful experience for me, but I honestly swear that I cannot remember it.

When the midwife was about to leave – gratefully, I guess – or maybe kind of frustrated because I did not let her perform her skills thoroughly, she approached my brother Armandito, who was only three years old then and asked him, "Would you like to give me your little brother as a gift?" He, rendered speechless, did not open his mouth but emphatically refused by shaking his little blond head.

When you come to think about it, however, maybe he was also feeling jealousy toward that tiny baby who had just arrived to deprive him of the family position that was traditionally known in the countryside as "the little nest egg." I was unable to understand this very well at first. Over the years, I gradually came to realize what people really meant when they met me for the first time and asked whether I was "the little nest egg."

The hen's last egg is usually left in the nest to make sure that they get into the habit of laying their eggs there only. Thus the importance of the famous and intriguing "little nest egg," a special category granted to the last laid egg until the arrival of a new one. It was only in later years that I understood I was indeed my mother's last nest egg and will continue to be so no matter what, thanks to the fact that our father's "eggs" got spoiled. Everything happens for a reason.

Practically a slave

When I was born, our father earned his living milking cows at La Madama Dairy Farm, just a kilometer away from our home.

Our mother was practically a slave, a tireless housewife, taking care of a male-chauvinistic husband, six small children under nine years of age, and a few animals, all in a house without any comforts – without electricity or a bathroom or hydraulic installations, not even a water well in the backyard. Her hands, particularly her fingernails, were literally worn out with so much housework and never-ending, tiring, day-long efforts. If I remember right, I saw my mother's fingernails polished only once, for the wedding of my two elder sisters, who got married on the same day.

The few times I saw her lying down during the day, I felt an overwhelming anguish. Every now and then, I entered her bedroom very carefully to make sure she was breathing, trying not to awaken her, even though I doubted that she would really be asleep. I was afraid she might not be alive because it was quite unusual to see her lying down during those hours. She always had so many things to do that she did not have enough time to rest, even when she was not feeling well.

Although I was still a very young boy, I realized that life was not being fair to her. I felt a lot of pity for her – always the first one to get up in the wee hours to fix breakfast for our father first and for all of us later, then, always the very last one going to bed, very late at night, totally exhausted, and very likely already thinking about what needed to be done the following day. Although she worked like a mule to guarantee the minimum well-being for all of us, I never heard her complain. Every single day, I am more convinced that my father's complicated mumps were truly a blessing for her. How much more she would have had to work had she had more children!

As was customary for many women in the countryside, and following a tradition she inherited from our grandmother, she singled out one day for each weekly task. She organized her huge household work into specific daily activities. Of course, she could never neglect the fact that she was compelled to cook every day for eight people, since there was no electricity available, and without a refrigerator, she could not save any food for the following day lest it get spoiled.

On Mondays, she started very early, tackling a gigantic mountain of clothing, scrubbing one piece at a time with her bare hands and strongly brushing them in a galvanized zinc basin. She would squeeze them and hang them in a thick rope by separating the braids of that tough cord with her finger tips. Sticking the first few pieces into the rope was easy since the rope was loose, but as the line began to be filled with clothes, it became increasingly more difficult to insert the clothes because the rope gradually tightened with the added weight of each new piece. To make sure the clothes smelled really clean, she let them dry thoroughly after being directly exposed for long hours to both the sunshine and the wind. She used long rods made out of woody trees from the forest that her father, our grandfather Pedro, provided to lift her clotheslines as high as possible.

Tuesday was the day to starch all the khaki school uniforms as well as my father's work clothes. She used homemade cassava starch, one of the many items that she made herself.

On Wednesdays, she devoted herself to spraying all the clean laundry with water, so it would be ready on Thursdays, when she would cope with the worst job of all.

Thursday was the day to iron that huge bundle of clean clothes, using either a flat iron heated over charcoal embers or an old gasoline flat iron, which produced a blistering blue flame right under her fingers. She endured unbearable heat and stood for long hours on end. For her ironing board, she used the large dining-room table, lined with an old blanket covered by a bed sheet.

Friday was reserved for mending, fixing, sewing clothes, and other necessary household activities.

Saturday was the day for general cleanup which sometimes included washing the dining-room chairs and removing spiders' webs from the ceiling of the thatched roof.

For this task, she used one of the longest rods of the clotheslines, to which she attached a duster at the very top. She swept the house daily but saved Saturday to mop the floors with a lot of water. She also swept the outdoor yards with the palmiche broom sticks that my grandfather brought her.

Sunday, allegedly the day to rest, she spent in the kitchen cooking homemade desserts, usually made out of fruits. My father was very fond of enjoying some dessert right after meals, no matter how small it might be, and she did whatever it took to make sure that treat would not be missing, even within our very limited resources.

Then, another Monday would arrive. The whole cycle started again, over and over, endlessly, while she was wearing herself out with so many household chores. Adding to her trials, she had to cook with vegetable charcoal, firewood, or kerosene at best, which created an everlasting and useless struggle against soot and grime, which stuck relentlessly to the pots, jars, and frying pans. And she was the one in charge of washing all the utensils with sand, ashes, and natural scrubs. As my sisters grew up, they started to help with some of the chores, such as house cleaning and washing the dishes, which unquestionably was a great relief for the heavy burden on our sacrificed mother.

Like father, like son

Avelino and Delia in 1970

My father, every inch an islander offspring, was an extremely hardworking man, friendly, formal, and hospitable, demanding much of himself and each of his children. He was authoritarian and domineering, displaying a lot of bad temper that generated in us – particularly in me – an excessive respect that would occasionally be almost fear. My father had an uncommon natural intelligence. Despite the fact that he was almost illiterate, in terms of formal instruction, and had not even completed elementary schooling, he learned many different trades almost perfectly simply by observing attentively how others performed them. His sheer intuition, unleashing his common sense and his desire to succeed in finishing things properly, helped him learn. He knew how to accomplish everything. He was a perfectionist par excellence. He would not accept doing anything poorly and hated sloppiness. He either did things well or did not do them at all. That was his maxim, and he abided by it. More than once, I witnessed him break a piece of furniture in his rudimentary carpenter's shop when he was disappointed, frustrated, or not pleased with the quality of his end product.

His father, our grandfather, Nicolás Clemente González Hernández, whom I never got to meet, died in 1951 in a tragic accident that left him virtually beheaded. He was born in the Port of Garachico in the Canary Islands. Searching for a better life, he came to Cuba when he was hardly 17 years old on a ship that brought him to the Port of Cárdenas. He met our grandmother, Avelina Rupertina Medina González, whom he married later in 1927, and settled down in Bejucal, her hometown. There they had six children: three boys and three girls. Amazingly, our father emulated him a generation later, for he had the six of us with exactly the same gender ratio. My grandfather died without having obtained his Cuban citizenship, although the paperwork was in process.

Gradually, over the years, our father managed to modestly improve the conditions of our housing. He dug a septic tank and built a bathroom with a toilet and fibrocem roof tiles, made a cement floor in the house, and most importantly, he got help to drill a water well in the backyard of our house. The manual water pump's handle had to be pulled a million times (or so it seemed) in order to fill a couple of tanks placed on top of a big triangular structure supported by three hardwood pillars. Undoubtedly, having water available inside our house, with pipelines installed in the bathroom and the kitchen, was a turning point for our poor rural family.

Once water was in the house, our father got the happy idea of building an artisanal cooler with a coil in its upper part, on top of which a block of ice was placed every morning. This enabled us to cool the water in the small tank above and to have the great luxury of drinking cold water at least at meal times. The homemade desserts cooked by my mother were stored over the ice blocks inside the cooler.

Back then, our father began practicing carpentry with just a few tools that he managed to acquire. This enabled him to perform the small repair jobs occasionally needed everywhere in our household.

When the Ejército Rebelde Dam was being built, the former town of La Chorrera was totally demolished, for it was sitting right within the boundaries of the planned hydraulic engineering work. Thanks to the demolition of so many houses there, my father managed to get a truckload of good quality dovetailed boards. With them, he was able to repair the whole façade of our house with bars in the windows and jambs in the doors. He also managed to get a truckload of cana palm tree fronds from the Pinar del Río area – much more lasting and of better quality and aesthetics than those of the royal palm trees that we had prior to that point. With these, he thatched the gabled roof of the front part of our house, and covered both the living-room and the two bedrooms on each side of it. Our house was then completed with a porch made of tin tiles all along its facade, in front of which there was always a modest garden where roses, jasmines, mantles, crotons, malanguitas, 10 AMs, Saint Joseph's sticks, aralias, and little witches added cheer and welcomed our visitors. Later on, three pine trees were planted in a straight line along the peripheral fence, which provided pleasant shade and a cool ambience.

The famous ceiba tree

In the yard around our house grew fruit trees such as lemons, both sweet and sour oranges, mangoes, custard apples, guavas, bananas, plantains, and avocadoes. But without a doubt, the major landmark was a gigantic old ceiba tree, completely hollow inside, surrounded by several royal palm trees that escorted it with dignity as faithful guardians. Its roots were huge, starting at a height of about one meter above the base of the humongous tree trunk and forming cubicles in between them that we used as our outhouses. No wonder that, during almost all my childhood, I suffered from intestinal parasites that rendered me without appetite. My mother was worried and used to take us to see the doctor, who would prescribe medicines and the unforgettable B Complex Syrup that I had to take for years on end to recover my appetite. Parasites would not give me a break, of course. When I turned my back to my mother, I often pretended I swallowed those bitter pills that tasted like shit. I spat them out on the grass shortly afterwards when she wasn't looking.

Armando and I on a cieba tree branch, 1968

But if those pills were bad, it was even worse whenever my siblings and I had indigestion from swallowing orange skins or eating too many green mangoes sprinkled with salt. Then Mama would take us to town, to the house of an old lady by the name of Pastora, who used to heal us by anointing our abdomen with cooking oil and aggressively rubbing our stomachs with her hands. That was such a painful experience that many times, instead of going to her, we would try to hide under the beds and needed to be pulled out and dragged by force. When a visit to Pastora was clearly upcoming, we would refuse to go, knowing ahead of time what we would endure.

Two bus lines passed right in front of our house: numbers 38 (Víbora-Batabanó) and 59 (Víbora-Güines). Even though there was not an official bus stop there, because ours was the only house along that stretch of road, every bus driver would stop right in front. Everyone used to refer to our place as La Ceiba, because our majestic tree, truly huge and imposing, could be seen from afar and never went unnoticed. Whenever we were on board the bus and were approaching home, it was enough for us to shout out "La Ceiba!" and the driver would stop.

Eventually, the celebrated ceiba tree became a potential danger. One day when I was still very little, I was playing on the grass near my mother who was doing her customary weekly laundry. I was there with a couple of medicine flasks bound with a stick (my imaginary oxen with their yoke), dragging a little cardboard box full of grass (my sugar cane wagon). Fortunately, my mother called for me to eat the crust of a custard dessert she had made. (I used to quietly scratch the bottom of the large iron pot with a teaspoon, taking advantage of my siblings' absence; otherwise, they might get jealous of the little nest egg.) At the exact moment when I entered through the kitchen door, a turkey buzzard, startled by seeing me run towards the house, suddenly flew away. The momentum of its takeoff provided the huge branch on which it was perched the very last push it needed to be totally detached from the tree trunk. It tumbled down noisily, landing right on top of my makeshift toys. That homemade chocolate custard saved my life. If I freaked out, I can only guess what it was like for my poor mother – as if she hadn't more than enough stress already!

Many times I heard people claim that they have not met anybody who has dared to cut down a ceiba tree. Most fear the unlucky consequences that doing so may bring about for the one bold enough to do it. Well, our father gathered the courage it took and cut that tree down, despite all the well-intentioned warnings against it from people who, extremely concerned, predicted appalling things and tried by all means to talk him out of it.

The ceiba tree was already in intensive care, so to speak. Every now and then, it would drop a piece. Inside, it was completely hollow, and it became a lodging for owls and a privileged perch for turkey buzzards. After the big branch fell, my father decided once and for all to ignore well-intentioned pieces of advice. He enlisted the help of several men who showed up one afternoon equipped with hatchets, ropes, wires, winches, and a Caterpillar bulldozer. After analyzing how to knock it down effectively and safely, they attached strong cables to the bulldozer, which pulled powerfully from the pasture range beyond the back of our yard. After being shaken and pulled several times, the huge ceiba tree collapsed.

The onlookers suffered great stress. First, there was the potential danger that, given its huge size, the tree might wobble and squash our house. Second, there was the possibility that it might hurt or kill someone when it fell.

After a few years had elapsed, several people attributed our family's misfortunes to the cutting of this tree. They reinforced staunch convictions that ceiba trees are sacred and that nobody may cut them down and get away with it unpunished.

That ceiba tree was a witness to all our childhood games. It freaked us out at night, and it appealed to us during the day. Very near our house, the road curved and rose over a hill. When cars drove down from its summit at night, their headlights were projected from afar, going through the hole on the upper part of the ceiba tree and illuminating its hollow section inside. So many evil things were said about ceiba trees that when, in the midst of darkness, it was lighted in this manner, it certainly appeared spooky, particularly to our highly impressionable children's minds. During the day, however, the effect of the ceiba tree was just the opposite. Under its shade, we used to unleash all our ingenuity in order to cope with a lack of toys. We did not have commercial toys bought at the store because we did not even have enough bread and cassava to eat, so we had to come up with alternatives for toys, which turned out to be quite interesting at times.

It is amazing what necessity triggers in the human mind. I am not surprised at all to witness the development attained by the National Association of Innovators and Rationalizers of our country, because it is something that we Cubans carry in our blood. In the countryside, we used to say that necessity makes baby boys be born. An equivalent proverb in English claims that necessity is the mother of invention. I still remember very clearly, for example, that when my three sisters did not have dolls to play with, they resorted to several alternatives in keeping with the availability of natural resources that were found in our setting, according to the season of the year. When corn was harvested, they made dolls of the largest, healthiest, and most beautiful, tender corncobs with exuberant blond, chestnut, or red heads of hair, dressing them with pieces of patterned fabric. They combed their hair, made them hairdos, and gave them haircuts. These were their short-lived dolls. When corn season was over, they resorted to picking fragrant flowers from trees that lined both sides of the road, a variety of acacia with petals shaped like human strands of hair. When these started to wither, they represented the little head of a blond doll with which, sharpening their imagination, they were able to play hairdressers. When the green corn ear and the acacia flowers were depleted, my sisters used empty perfume or little medicine bottles. The caps became the heads of the dolls, which were dressed with little pieces of fabric with a hole cut in the middle. Their imagination, fortunately, was never lacking. My sisters used to play jacks with 12 pebbles and a small green orange or lemon, and when they were a bit older, they made their first rustic dolls by themselves, using rags and cardboard paper.

We boys created makeshift toys out of unimaginable things. During the mango season, we would stick dry twigs in the mud, building pigsties for our pigs, which were dry mango pits. The larger and hairier pits were the farrowing sows, which we arranged by placing them sideways for them to be able to "nurse" the smaller pits that were our baby pigs. Arranged vertically, one right next to the other, they would suck perfectly well in that pigsty before their scheduled weaning time. The bottles of *Bebito eau de toilette* or medicines were our oxen or draft horses. They transported the trimmed grass, mango leaves, small pebbles, pieces of broken glass, dirt, and snails that we used to imitate objects from our daily life. With seashells from the ocean sand and the noble snails, we arranged long queues, lined up by order of size and spaced out evenly. We were emulating the students' lineup in the schoolyard, keeping the right distance in between each student, just as was demanded from us on a daily basis before walking into our classrooms. The round shells were the girls; whereas the cylindrical ones were the boys standing side by side in the next parallel line.

We made our own kites out of grass stems or sugar cane flower stalks, paper, a glue made of cassava starch, and pieces of tied and waxed thread, discarded at a nearby dump by the shoe factory of our nearest town. By using those very same sugar cane flower stalks and the rods of coconut fronds, we made cages to trap birds, which were abundant in the bordering forest. With pieces of branches of any tree whatsoever, we made bird snares to capture wild pigeons, using thistle seeds as bait. If we did not have real marbles, we played with little round pebbles that we found in the nearby creek. When we were compelled to play indoors, with a couple of condensed milk or talcum powder cans and a stretch of cord, we could improvise a telephone in the blink of an eye.

My father used to make rustic hardwood tops for us, blunting the tip of four-inch nails. Most of the time we had homemade slingshots available, made out of old bicycle inner tubes and twig forks taken from the tree branches in a "V" shape, which we would call arrows. With them, we would, unfortunately, become the bird busters in our environs. Even though it hurts to admit it, and I do not take any pride in this other hobby at all, to be totally honest, every now and then we would play surgeons. For our patients we took the unlucky and helpless lizards and frogs that lived in the wide pasture cattle ranges with a lot of living fences in the back and on both sides of our house as well as in the thick woods in front of it. Having also so many banana plants, we never ran out of handy frogs.

The large pasture ranges of the omnipresent grass called *pangola* gave us a safe place to fly our kites when the strong Lenten winds started blowing in April. We ran barefoot most of the time over that grass, which was full of *mimosa*, a sensitive thorny plant also known as *dormidera* (sleepy). If touched, it suddenly takes a defensive posture, closing up its tiny leaves, isolating itself for several minutes, then opening again when guessing that the danger is gone. It goes without saying that thick calluses formed on the soles of our feet, which made us practically invulnerable to them.

Our maternal grandparents, Pedro and Aguedita

Once, when I was at the home of our maternal grandparents, Pedro Rivero Vasallo and Águeda Zamora López, my grandpa held one of my feet in his calloused hands, examining it as patiently as a lab technician would. He concluded categorically with all the authority of his farmer's experience, "Mice are eating your feet over night!" I thought he was teasing, but I was wrong. He checked my brother Armando's feet, too, and found the traces he was looking for. In our feet, just around the edges of our heels where the skin became rougher, there were indeed some little holes resembling those you would see in a yellow cheese slice. The point is that sometimes we would go to bed after having been barefoot in the kitchen, where there were pork lard stains on the floor. It goes without saying that living in a thatched roof house, without electricity, in the middle of the countryside and surrounded by trees of all kinds, mice were an intrinsic part of the night life and teemed all over the roof beams. My grandpa claimed that the damn rodents would blow when biting, and that was why it hadn't hurt us when they nibbled the calloused skin with pork lard flavor. We were terrified by our grandfather's conclusion, and from then on, we would tuck in the mosquito net's brim thoroughly by wedging it with the thin, individual, padded mats we rested on. It was not nice at all to be aware of the fact that while we were soundly sleeping, those filthy rats were, literally speaking, eating our feet.

We used to look forward to the coming of the month of May and its lush springtime. It was a real festivity for us to witness the arrival of our new natural toys, fireflies, which we would pick in large numbers and place in glass jars. In a house without power, hardly lit by the kerosene lamps, jars with the green light of those unfortunate lightning bugs were really something, particularly for children. We used to get up every morning with black sticky nostrils due to the smoke released by those rudimentary lamps.

Our grandparents on the hill

Going to Grandma's house on the hill required a long walk, which I enjoyed a lot. We were always accompanied by our dog. We needed to cross several cattle ranges, wade the creek, go through a few fence gates, and finally climb the hill along an old fence made up of rocks and mouse pineapple, before we arrived at the big, old, colonial, wooden house, with a high tin roof, surrounded by the largest collection of medicinal herbs, ornamental plants, and fruit trees, as well as root and green vegetables that I have ever seen. My grandpa was every inch a farmer, almost illiterate, but with a work stamina that had no match. In spite of the fact that his small piece of land was rocky and rough, for it was on the slope of a hill, he kept it impeccably clean and tidy all the time. It was free from weeds, and he thoroughly exploited even its most secluded corners. If my grandfather were still alive, his yard would surely be paradigmatically labeled a "national reference patio." I have no questions about it at all.

Grandpa Pedro was a tireless working machine, likened only to the Amish, with a very special combination of an unbearably bad temper and a peculiar sense of humor. He loved jokes. He had a strong faith in God and in spiritualists or mediums. He frequently visited Iluminada, his psychic friend who lived in La Palma. Grandpa was a man with a gold heart, extremely loving and kind. His golden rule, which he always instilled in us, and the one he preached by setting his own personal example all along his lengthy lifespan of 96 years was, "Do always good, disregarding whom." He was quite moralistic. Never ever did I hear him curse. He was also very tidy and thoughtful for all his things. I learned a whole bunch of good things from him, and to a large extent, I even owe him my own faith. After noticing my interest in reading, he was the one who bought me my first short-story books and magazines. I also enjoyed very much whenever Grandpa Pedro asked me to milk Chacha, his she-goat, under the ceiba tree in the backyard, filling a whole canned pear container with her warm, thick milk in a matter of just a few minutes.

My grandmother Aguedita, in turn, was a withdrawn woman, who spoke very little. She used to walk very slowly. She would not get mad at anything or anyone. She always had a cigarette hanging on her lower lip. She smoked quite a lot but did not inhale the smoke. When we arrived, she would treat us to salty crackers, which she kept in an airtight can inside a bedroom cupboard, where they would stay crispy, just waiting for the arrival of any of her grandchildren. Without the slightest doubt, I may categorically affirm that Grandma made the best black bean soup and the best rabbit fricassee that I have ever eaten. She was also my baptism godmother. I was happy whenever it rained cats and dogs while I was visiting my grandparents. The river would overflow, so I would have the best of pretexts to stay overnight at their house, sleeping under the delicious sound of tapping rain on the tin roof. My grandparents occupy a privileged place in the altar I keep deep down in my heart.

It was a great blessing to have that creek, one of the many tributaries to the Almendares River, just 300 meters from home. It provided us with great opportunities to have fun, healthy recreation, and it was even a source of food and water on many occasions. I learned how to swim in it when I was still very young. There were a couple of ponds we used to frequent too. The largest and deepest of them were El Charco del Brinco and El Guamá. There, we used to bathe ourselves stark naked. If by any chance an unknown person got close or a woman passed by, we immediately plunged into the water.

In the river, we fished with rods made out of bamboo and nylon cords with a lead weight in the hook and a bottle cork as bobber, which would float and let us know when the fish were biting. As for bait, we used red, pink, and iridescent purple earthworms that we took after digging with a pick right behind the pigs' pen, where we knew we would find the biggest ones. We would always arrive home with a hook, usually made out of wild guava branches, on which we would carry the *biajacas* we had caught, threading them on the guava hook through their red gills. Fried *biajacas* marinated with a homemade lemon juice dressing was a feast that depended on our luck and our expertise as fishermen, so we sometimes lingered by the river for long hours, making sure that we caught enough for our whole big family. Occasionally, we were lucky and caught a turtle, but we never killed them to eat them. We took them home as one more toy, and when we got bored playing with them, we took them back to the river. By the creek, there were also wild mango, plum, and honeyberry trees, which delighted us when their fruits were in season.

My mother often sent us to gather firewood for boiling water. We went with jute sacks slung over our shoulders, scooping up dry twigs and branches dropped from the trees along the living fences made up of acacias, carob trees, cedars, *piñones, atejes, guásimas, almácigos* and many other botanical species of the area. We took advantage of this great opportunity to entertain ourselves by hunting lizards and sticking them into jars. They provided plentiful raw material for surgical practice at our natural outdoor operating room under the backyard almond tree. Likewise, we scoured the tree branches searching for pigeon nests that, once identified, would be systematically surveyed to make sure we could capture the baby birds when they were learning how to fly. We were just as cruel and as happy as we could get.

Are they twins?

Because my brother Armando was closest to my age, he was my playmate, my accomplice, and my defender on many occasions. He was over three years my senior and therefore would unilaterally take the right of deciding many things on my behalf, trying long and hard to dominate me at times and to fool me at others. Despite the age gap between us, we were of the same size and physically resembled one another quite a lot. To avoid jealousy, we were usually dressed in similar clothing; therefore, people who did not know us thought that we were twins. Unfailingly, whenever somebody asked "Are they twins?" Armando would twist out of rage, while I silently enjoyed the reply that either of our parents provided to clarify the facts, "No way! This one is three years older than that one!" It was a selfish and sweet, though silent, retaliation that, at least in physical appearance, I matched my brother.

Armando trimmed the grass much faster and better than I did, so each time Daddy told us, "Tomorrow when I come home from work, I want to see the yard trimmed," my brother took the unilateral liberty, as a relentless foreman, to organize our job in keeping with his whim. He loved to start very early to take advantage of the cool hours. During the summer months, with downpours almost daily, the grass grew rapidly. It was convenient to cut it first thing in the morning because, with the overnight dew, it was soft and wet at daybreak, and the machete would slide over it way better than later in the day. Armando always told me, "I cut the grass; you throw it away and clean the yard." That division of our work was very convenient for me. I was supposed to pile the trimmed grass using a rake, place it on top of a jute sack, then pick the sack up by both ends and dispose of the grass. Or I could fill an old wheelbarrow, push it along the road, and dump its contents by overturning it in the ditch by the roadside.

In order to make that job more bearable, I put our dog on top of the grass heap and gave him a ride. On our way back, I brought him as my only passenger, sprinting with the little wheelbarrow as much as I could. Thus, the work became a game and big time fun. When said like that, everything seems to indicate that those days of trimming the yard were very fairly arranged. However, don't trust appearances. What you see is not what you get. More often than not, there was a fist fight between us. We rammed each other like two lizards claiming their respective territories. Grandpa Pedro had to intervene several times. When he arrived at our house in the midst of a fight, he rushed to split us up.

Over the course of years, I convinced myself that my future could not be linked to the tough work of the countryside. There had to be other choices available to me. I knew very well that in school I was admired, loved, and respected for my academic scores, which made me stand out in the opinion of students and teachers alike. I knew by intuition that I would not end up milking cows like my father or working in the fields like my grandfather. Nor would I drive a tractor as my eldest brother did. I did not host the slightest doubt about this. It would be up to me to find a different path despite the fact that I was reared in a family setting without books or newspapers or intellectual relatives. Everywhere I turned, I saw only hard work, ignorance, and a lack of interest in the world outside our community – an endless cycle in which life became overwhelmingly boring. That was not what I wanted for myself or for my future family.

Only once a year

Despite all the sacrifice and effort entailed in the raising and keeping of pigs, in our place there were always a bunch of them. My father, assisted by other neighbors, would harvest the fruit of the royal palm trees and bring the bunches of ripe *palmiches* to feed our pigs. Those red and purple dates were the favorite food of our pigs and guaranteed that their meat would have an exquisite flavor for the Christmas Eve and New Year's Eve suppers. He delivered milk from El Lucero, the pasteurizing milk factory in Mantilla. His customers provided him with garbage to feed the pigs and regularly purchased pork when he slaughtered them.

That process was illegal, but it was necessary to raise a little extra money to provide food, clothing, and footwear for his six children. Every time he was going to distribute the pork bundles, he took several of us along, particularly the little ones. He filled the green Pontiac 48 – the car borrowed from his friend and neighbor Cándido Breto – by placing the bundles painstakingly under the seats and covering them thoroughly with a carpet of innocent children, accomplices of their father in crime. We had an interesting ride and helped avoid suspicion in the event that, for some reason, the police stopped us. It was indeed a great risk he had to run, but it paid off. It was a wonderful opportunity that we never turned down to see a bit of the city and – as it is said in the people's jargon – to remove our *ariques* – that is, our awkwardness and clumsiness.

We all looked forward to welcoming Christmas Eve, except for my mother, for her workload multiplied with preparations for the feast plus the special general cleanup of the house. Our uncles, aunts, cousins, and a few friends always showed up, including at least twenty children. That day, all the tables were taken out into the yard. Road lanterns were hung from a cable stretched over the tables. In later years, Chinese lanterns were used, casting a brilliant white light. They had woven silk bulbs, which were lit after pumping them several times and preheating them with a little bit of alcohol. They were the same lanterns that came from the People's Republic of China and were used during the National Literacy Campaign back in 1961.

We children were served our food first. As the cowhide chairs were not enough to go around, my father improvised makeshift, rustic benches with long cedar boards, which he placed on crates of beer or soda bottles; thus sitting around the table was easily solved. My mother usually made cassava doughnuts with syrup and wild guava shells for dessert. For that date also, using our ration card, we were able to buy delicacies, such as hazelnuts, apples, pears, grapes, peaches, raisins, plums, jellied quince bars, nougats, cans of fine sweet cookies, and other snacks that were a true oasis in the desert, for we enjoyed them only once a year. No wonder that we waited for *Nochebuena* (Christmas Eve) with so much anticipation!

Men do not cry

When I was still very little, three or four years old at most, I climbed on a kitchen chair to find out what was cooking. It was a pea soup that my mother was tenderizing without benefit of a pressure cooker. My curiosity led me to spill the peas, and I ended up getting burned. Thus I claimed the first burnt-skin experience of my life. It is rightly said in English that "curiosity killed the cat."

Unfortunately, however, that was my first, but not my last, serious burn. When I was five years old and not yet attending school, I experienced an intense second-degree burn. At home, we used to take a bath with warm water even in the summertime, unless it was too hot. Since we were very little, we had gotten used to bathing ourselves by squatting in front of a plastic washbasin, scooping water with a bucket and a little mug. The process was to heat a water container in the backyard. We used firewood as fuel, so as to save the charcoal and kerosene that were prioritized for cooking.

One day, some friends of my father brought a Chinese piglet to our house. It was pitch black with a couple of "little bells" on its neck – protuberances like little teats that dangled whimsically from its throat. We had never seen anything like it before. I thought it was a hybrid of some sort obtained from crossbreeding a pig with a goat. Goats have those "little teats" hanging from their necks. My siblings were still in school when I first saw that exotic piglet, and I couldn't wait to be the herald of that sensational information for my elder siblings when they got home that ill-fated afternoon.

My sister Ada had already arrived and was getting ready to help our mother in the kitchen with the day's dinner and household chores.

I was impatiently waiting on the porch, keeping an eye out for my other siblings' arrival, so I could give them the happy news, take them all to the pigsty, and show them with due pride the new and exotic acquisition. At long last, the troop arrived, and the commotion and stampede started. I bolted into our house to make sure that nobody arrived at the pigpen before I did. Unfortunately, I didn't get to show them the piglet.

At the exact moment that I shot through the kitchen door, my sister Ada came in holding a big jug of boiling water with which to prepare a warm bath. I did not even give her time to dodge me. My head slammed against that metal jug, and all the boiling water was spilled over me. Ada, poor little thing, panicked and tried to the best of her ability to wipe my face with the skirt of her school uniform because she thought it was my face that had been burned. My mother, who was in the kitchen at that moment, tried to remove the threadbare white cotton T-shirt I was wearing, and when she did, everyone panicked and began to scream and to weep. At that point, I thought I would die.

When taking off my T-shirt, they realized that my skin had peeled off and was clinging to the shirt just like a lizard's or a snake's when they change their skin. I don't know whether it was due to my fear or to the impact of such a severe burn over my neck and most of my right shoulder and torso, but I began to shake uncontrollably. I was covered with a thick blanket and placed on one of the beds while they tried to reach my father and tell him at all costs to find a car that could take me to see a doctor. The big green-and-white duck-tailed 1960 Chevrolet Impala owned by Humberto Cortón, a friend of my father, took a good while to arrive.

First, I was taken to the polyclinic of Managua. When the seriousness of my burn was diagnosed, I was referred to the clinic in Mantilla, where better resources were available. The nurse who took care of me, a very pretty young mulatto woman, scratched all my scourged skin thoroughly, which had corrugated like papier-mâché. After that, she anointed me with a yellow cream that had a very strong odor and then dressed my burn with long gauze strips. I still remember her wiping away her tears while she removed those sticky skin strips. She even told the physician who was standing next to her, "I know that what I am doing to him hurts a lot, but it is for his own sake, and when he grows up, he will be grateful, because I want to make sure that he won't have many scars left."

She was absolutely right. Never before that day had I stood such intense pain, but I refused to cry. I could not do it. My father held my little hand when we entered the emergency room – very likely trying to strengthen me and to cheer me up, but I took his words very seriously and followed them to the letter. He told me, "Remember that men do not cry!" And I did not let him down at all. In fact, I did not cry out of my eyes but out of my lower body – and a lot, by the way. The pain was so excruciating that I could not help peeing in my pants profusely.

I do not want to die

It is amazing how news gets distorted through human networks or by the "Thick Lip Radio Station" as we used to say in elementary school. Once, looking at me with a very sympathetic face, my teacher asked, "Tell me honey, was your little brother, the one who died after getting burnt, younger or older than you?" I was taken aback by that question, but then I realized what she was talking about. I was slightly afraid to think that somebody thought me dead when I was still so little. When I arrived home that day, I immediately told my mom about the incident. Still feeling a bit apprehensive, I confessed to her my deep concern, "Mama, I do not want to die, and I do not want you to die either." Smiling, she looked at me and said, "We all have to die eventually, but you don't need to worry about it, because that will be when we grow very, very, very old." It was at that point in my life when I became aware of the fact that I would have to pass away eventually. Such an idea, when one is scarcely six years old, cannot be digested easily.

One night, a few days after this disturbing revelation, our cousins the Montenegros came to our house to visit us with their parents, Olga, my aunt on my father's side, and Vicente, my uncle-in-law. The adults were playing dominoes at the dining-room table while I was holding tightly in my little right hand a big firefly that I had caught a few minutes before on the rotten roots of the ceiba tree. All of a sudden, I felt a shooting pain in my hand, an intense prick. When I screamed, opening my hand quickly to find the cause, we all realized that a big hairy spider had stung me while trying to attack the firefly. My mother washed my hand, dabbed it with Mercurochrome, and wiped my tears. Totally unaware of my emerging trauma, my cousins started to say things like, "Oh my God, now your guts are going to spill out over there, and you are going to die!"

This untimely phrase reminded my mother of my comment about death, and she shared it with my father and my aunt and uncle. Papi, as I used to call my father, tried to discredit my apprehension about death. In order to cheer up our guests a little bit with the euphoria of the passionate dominoes game – and obviously without thinking too much about the impact that his words might have upon my mind – he categorically asserted, "Don't you worry, because here nobody will be left as seed. All of us are going to die, and one day, all our skeletons will play dominoes under the cemetery."

I did not try to say or do anything at all after that appalling verdict. The only thing I still remember clearly is that I started to visualize, over and over again, a picture of our whole extended family playing dominoes six feet under the ground. I pictured my tiny skeleton keenly watching how the other bigger skeletons of my relatives were playing. That was more than enough for me to start throwing up everything I had eaten that evening.

It was such a traumatic experience that, even now, I can remember what I projected against the floor at the threshold of the door to our bedroom. It included pieces of chicken, noodles, potatoes, and tomatoes from the soup I had eaten half an hour before. Perhaps my family thought my stomach had been upset because that stupid spider had startled me, but deep down, I know for a fact that it was triggered by that creepy image in my mind. My dad was not trying to traumatize me, but that was the undeniable impact that his words had. The road to hell is paved with good intentions.

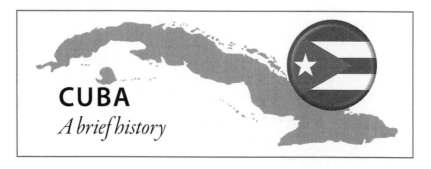

CUBA
A brief history

The 1960s: The Challenging First Decade of the Revolution

The day Castro entered Havana, a large portion of the Cuban people were illiterate. Most had not been educated beyond a few years of grade school because they were destined to be field laborers serving large corporations, most of which were owned by US interests. Most of the population was desperately poor, subsisting on the bare necessities. The country's economy was in turmoil.

Castro's revolutionary victory brought great hope and pride to the majority of Cubans, but it created anger and fear among the elite, wealthy, corporate landholders, who started leaving en masse for the United States. Castro defied US interests and began to redistribute the wealth to the poor majority. He decreed that Cuban land could be owned only by Cuban citizens. He nationalized the factories and seized foreign-owned properties and businesses. The entire economy was placed under control of the revolutionary government and redesigned to serve the entire population.

US interests were furious, and US policy and military forces began a series of ongoing efforts to overthrow the new revolutionary government and regain control of Cuban wealth for the deposed US financial stakeholders. To punish Cuba economically for its socialist policies and expropriation of US businesses, the US government established an economic blockade and cut off diplomatic relations. Travel to the island by US citizens was banned. The US supported many separate efforts to overthrow Castro. As Castro strengthened his hold on power, the US expanded the trade embargo on Cuba.

The Cuban economy was in a tailspin, and resources were in short supply. Recovery and growth could not occur in isolation. Once the US made the importing of Cuban goods illegal, Cuba needed allies and trading partners. The Soviet Union, seeing an opportunity to support the establishment of a communist government in the Western Hemisphere so close to the US border, stepped in with support in the form of subsidies: oil, the purchase of sugar, and military support.

In October 1962, the US discovered that Soviet missiles were being installed in Cuba. After a tense confrontation with the US, Soviet Premier Khrushchev agreed to withdraw the missiles, and the US agreed not to invade Cuba. This crisis brought the world to the brink of a nuclear war. Although resolved diplomatically, it provoked even more Cold War hostility from the US and pushed Cuba firmly into the Soviet camp.

Nevertheless, in the midst of all this turmoil, Castro managed to implement a massive number of country-wide, humane policy changes designed to improve living conditions and opportunities for all Cuban citizens.

All schools were immediately nationalized, and all military barracks were turned into schools. Education became equally available to all without charge from kindergarten through university. In 1961, two hundred thousand young volunteers were sent to every corner of the countryside to teach peasants how to read and write. The results of this successful literacy campaign were astounding. Within twenty-four months, the Cuban literacy rate matched the highest in the world – virtually 100 percent.

A universal social security system was established that ensured every family could fulfill their minimum living needs. The ration card issued to each family provided the basic social safety net for all citizens and limited price gouging on basic goods via the black market. This card authorized each family to purchase a quantity of 30 different products each month from bodegas (government grocery stores) at subsidized peso prices. This program immediately began to equalize opportunity for all, regardless of income. To further increase equality and opportunity for all, racial discrimination was abolished; rents were slashed; and salaries were increased.

An innovative and free national health-care policy was designed and quickly implemented. The population was divided into units of approximately 250 families (1,000 people). A clinic, established in each local neighborhood, was staffed by one physician and one nurse who were responsible for continuing care of all within their jurisdiction. Augmented by specialty clinics and regional hospitals, this coordinated system of care resulted in infant mortality and life expectancy rates comparable to those of the most developed countries.

During the 1960s, Cuba was radically transformed. Despite the fact that improvement would take time, people of all ranks across the country glowed with hope and a new pride in being Cuban. The changes did not immediately trickle down to our family during the first ten years of my life. We remained dirt poor. I am, however, a product of this decade. And during the next years, I was to become the beneficiary of the revolution's innovative policies many times over.

My Intelligent Country Boy

*Trust in the LORD with all your heart
and lean not on your own understanding;
in all your ways acknowledge him,
and he will make your paths straight.*

Proverbs 3:5–6

As I was the little nest egg, and all my siblings attended school, my father decided that I did not really need to go to kindergarten – that my elder siblings could very well teach me at home all those "pieces of nonsense" that were taught in preschool. And so it was. I started school just a few days before I turned six years old. I was happy to know that, even though I had not gone to it before, I was not illiterate. By that time, my five siblings had already been in charge of teaching me not only preschool concepts, but also many others typically taught in first grade. I already knew how to read and write, even in cursive letters, when I joined the Adolfo del Castillo elementary school on September 1, 1966. No wonder that my first school teacher, Josefina, an adorable elderly lady who would finish her long tenure as a teacher that school year, claimed that I was her intelligent country boy. The school principal, Haydée, held me the first day and lifting me up with both her arms, said emphatically, "The last González. Let us see how this one fares!" The reputation gained by the previous González children was not very good; thus, I was a jack-in-the-box.

I liked school a lot from the very beginning. Our teacher was like a sweet and loving grandmother who kept an assortment of table games, boxes of marbles, story books, and other toys in an old wardrobe. She would lend them to us every now and then as a reward for good behavior and successful performance in school. She always had many initiatives available to awaken our interest and keep it alive and to encourage us to focus our attention. My favorite book was *Once upon a Time*, a well-known collection of classic children's short stories. During my free time, I always asked my teacher for it, and she lovingly gave it to me, tapping my head gently with her hand and smiling at the same time, for she really enjoyed witnessing that her children were interested in reading. I read that book so many times that I ended up knowing all the stories by heart. Whenever I visited my cousins Jorge and Carlos Arévalo González, my aunt Irma's sons, who were a few years younger than I, they sat on both sides of the armchair where I settled, so I could tell them all the stories that I already knew by heart.

That is precisely why I will never forget that happy day, while I was sick with the mumps during my summer vacation, when I received my first storybook as a gift. It had been sent by my dear teacher, who was already retired. She had learned about my disease and was thinking how I could use my leisure time in a didactic way. Luckily for me, she decided to dedicate with her own handwriting the book that she knew for a fact was my favorite and that she had lent me so many times. What she wrote in it was rather short, but it was there in her flawless and beautiful penmanship:

> *For Albertico, my intelligent country boy,*
> *from his school teacher who loves him*
> *and will never forget him, Josefina.*

Getting that book was, for me, the greatest acknowledgment that a child might ever get. I felt big and important, filled with desire to go on learning new things and read much more. My teacher, Josefina, may God keep her in His glory, will forever occupy a very special corner in my heart. On a Friday afternoon in 1967, halfway through my first school year, before the bell rang for our exit, she said, "Albertico, bring a photo next Monday for the classroom Honor Bulletin Board." I had been chosen that afternoon as the vanguard student of my class. It took me a few seconds to think about it, and then I told her with great sincerity and some embarrassment that I did not have any photos at all, that I had never had my picture taken. I meant it, because it was the naked truth. Although I was already six years old, no one had taken any pictures of me.

Me at age 6

Thanks, then, to my beloved teacher, Josefina, my father took me all the way to La Palma, where the closest photographic studio was found, and so at long last, I managed to have my first six ID photos, when I still had my milk teeth and the traditional haircut that, out of respect for my father, I kept until I got into the university: the legendary *malanguita*, with the parting on one side and the natural way on the back but no type of straight outlining on the nape of my neck.

Most of the children in my class lived in the town, within much smaller families. They had more and better resources compared to those my family had available. Many of my classmates were only children or had only one other sibling; therefore, materially speaking, they lived with much more space and had many things that I never had. Most of them were brought snacks from their households during the breaktime in the mornings. That was another moment of controlled infant envy, wistfully wishing deep down in my heart to have fewer siblings and to live in the town with electric light, a TV set, a refrigerator, and either a grandmother or a mother bringing me snacks at 10 o'clock every morning just like most of the other children around me.

Little by little, however, I realized that, although it was true that I did not have what others enjoyed, I was able to excel in terms of knowledge; and by so doing, I could somehow compensate for many other things that made me feel unhappy, particularly when classmates were cruel and boastful. They didn't hesitate to display their belongings with pride, showing off before those of us who had just a little or almost nothing at all. I am not talking about special items, such as bicycles, wrist watches, and such. I am referring to the objects that were owned by the overwhelming majority but which I lacked due to my social background and precarious family situation – things as simple as a humble schoolbag, which I could never have. I had to carry my books in an old and worn-out plastic bag, which I tied with a knot at the very top so as to better hold it.

Even though I loved to participate in class, I thought twice before going to the blackboard because, not having any briefs, I was embarrassed when my pants stuck in the crack of my butt. This made me the target of relentless mockery from other children, who made fun of me by saying things such as, "Your beans are getting burnt" or "The goat is eating up your garden."

To save my self-esteem

I envied my classmates who enjoyed having a bedroom just for themselves, who had their pictures taken when they were babies, and who talked enthusiastically about the television programs they had watched the night before. It is true that not each and every one of them had a TV set at home, but they could go a neighbor's to watch, which in my case, was absolutely out of the question due to the distance separating us from the town.

Nothing is worse for a child than to feel humiliated before his or her peers. With my excellent academic performance, I was able to compensate in school, but I hated feeling that I was inferior to my classmates, and I longed for access to the TV adventures at 7:00 and 7:30 PM, Monday through Friday, that were the delight of the city children. I had no choice but to resign myself to listening to others tell the details of those famous episodes, so I wasn't totally ignorant of what everybody else knew.

I tried to arrive at school early to listen keenly to the children who gathered every morning in small clusters to chat about the TV adventures from the previous night. I listened intently. I was a huge ear dressed in a school uniform, so to speak. In order to make sure that I grasped every single detail, I memorized them thoroughly, so a few minutes later, when I approached new arrivals, I could tell those blessed adventures just as if I had watched them with my own eyes. I developed such an ability to imagine, memorize, and visualize that I surprised myself incredibly and enjoyed deep down the success of my new strategy for school survival. It was the ideal resource to save my self-esteem. It was thus that I was able to "watch" TV through the mouths of my companions.

Lunch for students in the semi-boarding system began to be delivered in our school. It was intended for the children of working mothers; however, we, the González-Riveros, were also entitled to have it because we lived far away from school. This was a great relief for our family, not only because we did not have enough time to go home for lunch and return to school for the afternoon session, but also because there were not enough food supplies at home to provide lunch and dinner for all of us on a daily basis. It was only one meager salary – my father's – which had to be stretched like chewing gum to provide for the basic necessities of eight people. The fact of having lunch at school led me to think about another possibility of which I could not avail myself up until that point. All of a sudden I saw the gates open!

One of my classmates, Rafael Rafca Morales, lived near our school on Independence Street, the main street of the town. His parents were both professionals and lived in a comfortable house with all the amenities, including, of course, a black-and-white American TV set. His father was originally from Syria in the Middle East and had been based in Cuba. He had only an older sister. Their grandmother, who lived with them, brought a hearty snack to school every morning and had a nice lunch ready at noon when the children returned from school. Rafael always ate lunch sitting in front of the TV set because, right at that time, a series of cartoons were shown. Thus, he would always talk with friends at school about Donald Duck, Felix the Cat, Betty Boop, Mickey Mouse, Yogi the Bear, the Two Magpies, Porky Pig, and many other celebrated characters from the unforgettable casts of US cartoons.

My first grade class at the Adolfo del Castillo elementary school in 1966.
I am the third boy from the left in the third row.

At 5 o'clock in the afternoon, there was another round of cartoons on TV, but at that time, I was already on my way back home, and I could not be late under any circumstances; therefore, that option was ruled out right away. If I wanted to have the privilege of enjoying the cartoons first hand, without anybody disturbing me, I had no option but to do without lunch and go hungry for a while every day – this obviously, without letting my siblings or my parents learn about it.

However, as was so rightly stated by our beloved José Martí, there are certain things that need to be hidden in order for them to take place. Everything that we really care about in life entails a quota of personal sacrifice, and I was willing to pay the price of an empty stomach so I could watch the cartoons, pretending before the insistent questions of Rafael's grandmother that I had indeed eaten lunch in school already. The point is that one is a child only once in a lifetime. Childhood is short-lived, although at that wonderful age it seems to be everlasting to us. I could not afford to wait. Either I did it then, or very likely I would never do it, and it is very important for a child to watch cartoons.

Sometimes Rafael's grandmother looked at me suspiciously – incredulous, maybe – because she noticed how, despite the fact that the cartoons on the TV screen drew my attention powerfully, every now and then, I could not help but glance at Rafael's lunch plate. He stuffed himself with french fries, chicken drumsticks, pork chops, meat balls, or whatever was provided each day. It made my mouth water, and for them not to realize that I was drooling like a dog, I had to swallow the accumulated saliva ever so slowly. No wonder my poor mother was always concerned. In spite of the B-complex syrup and the antiparasitic tablets, I would gain not even an ounce of body weight, and my belt coiled around my waist almost twice.

Sometimes, when I arrived home at 4:30 PM, totally starved, I asked my mother to please let me dip a little piece of bread into the beans or chicken soup that she was cooking. She would ask me, "Didn't you have lunch in school today? Do not fill yourself now because then you won't eat later at dinner time." To this I would always reply, "Mama, it is just a little bit. I promise you that I will eat all my dinner." Those little makeshift sandwiches, morsels made out of whatever was available (sometimes only kitchen tomatoes and salt) tasted like glory and stirred my hunger even more, but I had to play to forget about my raging appetite, that roaring lion I had in my belly until dinner time. I could not eat before or after that time, for supper was every inch a family ritual we could not fail to participate in for any reason but illness.

Everything was very poor

We had dinner approximately at the same time every day, between 7 and 7:30 PM. The eight of us sat on the same seats around the large rectangular wooden table, under which there must still be all our childish graffiti. It was totally prohibited to write on the walls, and heaven help whoever dared do it! On one side of the table, a bench was placed on which Alicia, Anita, Armandito, and I sat, in that order, from left to right. The others sat on *taburetes*, the chairs made out of wood and cowhide. Our parents sat across from us four, and on each end sat Ada and Avelinito.

At our table, everything was very poor. There were no tablecloths or forks or knives, only spoons. I did not learn how to eat with a fork properly until I started boarding school at the university when I was already 16 years old. The first time I took a fork to my mouth, as I was not used to doing it, I bit the tip when miscalculating the size of the morsel I was placing in my mouth, splintering one of my lower front teeth. There were no crystal glasses either, only aluminum jars and condensed milk cans to drink water with. One such can usually had hot cooking oil for us to add on top of our food to our taste. I will never ever forget the day that I choked on a piece of fried sweet potato. With the distress and the sudden coughing spell that followed, I took the wrong can, and instead of water, I swallowed a mouthful of hot cooking oil, which made me throw up like a drunkard.

We had to eat all our food, and we could not play with it. It was absolutely prohibited to burp at the table or to speak with a mouth full of food. The dessert, if any, was evenly distributed by our father, and woe to the sweet-toothed ones who tried to eat more than their own share! None of us wanted to go through the unforgettable and unpleasant experience that Anita endured for being greedy. One day, our father showed up with a can of grated pineapple dessert in syrup. That was something completely unheard of for us all, and we were certain that we were going to like it a lot. Anita, always a big eater, was gluttony itself in the flesh of a girl with curly blond hair. That evening, since the moment when Daddy took the can out of the cooler and started to open it using the tip of a knife – because we did not have more appropriate can openers to do that job – she held out her plate and expressed her gastronomic fantasies, "Yummy, yummy, how nice! If I could, I would certainly eat it up all by myself!" She and her big mouth! She chose the wrong time to say so. Here is what happened next.

My father tried to use her as a dramatic warning against gluttony and extreme selfishness. His reaction did not take long to appear. Very quietly, he told Anita, "Don't you worry because you will eat it all!" Then he finished opening the can. He overturned all its sticky and gooey contents on her plate, tapping the bottom of the container and slapping it several times with his hand until he had drained it to the last drop. Then he took off the thick buckle belt that he always wore and, like a relentless executioner, stood by her side to witness everything that happened next. We all thought for a split second that this was just a nasty joke and soon we would all eat that appetizing dessert. Anita, however, fully convinced that it was really serious, thought instead about the great feast she was going to have all by herself. She ate the first three or four spoonfuls very slowly, savoring them in front of the silence, the envy, and the panic of us all. She licked her sticky lips with obvious glee but did not succeed in doing that for very long. She could not finish even half of the can. Our father, uncompromising, shook his belt threateningly and forced her to swallow every bit of that dessert, which was an infernal torture for her and for all of us, as well. Anita virtually choked on the dessert while puking and weeping, thus adding one more legend to the family saga.

Our father joined the sugar cane harvest every year through the trade union cell at his workplace. That is why he used to spend several months away from home, in faraway provinces. Our mother stayed alone with the six of us, in the midst of the countryside, without electricity, having to deal with many difficulties. Contributing to our finances by working the sugar cane harvest provided a strong incentive for our stoic father, who excelled as a great sugar cane cutter and stood out from the beginning as a leader as well, undertaking responsibilities as a brigade leader first and as the camp director later on. He took great pride in joining the famous 10 Million Ton Harvest in 1970. Being involved in the harvests, despite the sacrifice that it entailed, not only for him personally, but also for our mother and for us all, meant the possibility of storing accumulated noteworthy merits so as to be able to apply yearly for the highly coveted electric appliances that were distributed by trade unions all over our country.

Thanks to his sacrifice for the sake of our family's well-being, we were able to enjoy the first Soviet TV sets that were granted through the unions. It was during the early seventies that he won his TV set: an *Electrón 2*. The TV set was a real blessing for our whole family, particularly for Mama, who enjoyed the classic programs of those times so much. I rarely saw my mother smiling and laughing, which is why I enjoyed so much watching her sit in front of the TV set and enjoy all those shows. TV provided a true recreational oasis in her enormous desert of daily work. Hard as she tried to hurry dinner-related activities so she could watch *Palmas y Cañas* on Sundays at 7:00 PM, most of the time, the relentless clock, ticking away, betrayed her. Often, I compelled her to sit down in front of the TV, removing her plastic apron and wearing it myself in order to finish doing all those dishes. Otherwise, she would have to wash the dishes herself because my sisters had married and were living in other places. As a victim of the prevailing male chauvinism, I did not like to be seen doing the dishes, but I was ashamed that my mother did not have a break at all, that she could never rest, even more so without the assistance my sisters had provided when they were still single.

They were married when they were still very young, as was customary in the countryside back then, 17 or 18 years old. Their boyfriends had to court them first, visit them at home, and "ask for their hand" afterwards. They were also compelled to abide by the weekly pattern of scheduled visits at the days and times set by our father: Wednesdays, Saturdays, and Sundays from 8 to 10 o'clock in the evening. My sistes were not allowed to go out with their boyfriends unless they were escorted by a chaperon, a role I had to play more than once and which brought about a lot of jealousy.

The first girl I fell in love with, when I was in fourth grade and nine years old, was named Marta. She was very feminine, thin, and rather shy. She had straight blond hair and very fine features. I was always looking for a pretext to be included on the team she belonged to and to sit as close to her as possible. Once, trying to impress her, I wrote her a love letter complete with proverbs. I thought it would be a secret to be kept between the two of us. I was wrong. She was so amused by what I did that she decided to share the letter with her mother, who refused to believe that such a young boy could have written such a serious letter, so well drafted. In order to verify the authorship of the love epistle, she brought it over one day and showed it to my older sisters who recognized my handwriting. Bingo! There was no doubt about it. Their youngest brother had written it. They knew my calligraphy quite well and identified it right away. I wanted to impress Marta, not her mother, but my efforts backfired. These are things that happen even in the best families.

A dog in another life

My father was dreadful when he was angry. As I said before, in our household, there was always at least one dog. One of the biggest pets we had was a female dog with lush cream fur. As she had so much fur, we decided to call her Pelúa (Hairy). She was a lovely animal, extremely gentle and playful with all of us kids. She was a hybrid, a mutt, obviously with some vestige of a nice breed, about the size of a German shepherd.

It was very hard for me to accept some of my father's orders. Although, of course, I would obey them to the very letter without complaining, lest he might label me as weak. Whenever the dog had puppies, he got rid of the newborn females, grabbing and lifting them by their tiny tails one at a time, carefully double-checking that they belonged to the sex that was doomed to death, before crushing them with one blow against the hard bark of the avocado tree trunk. He then dropped them, one on top of the other, in an old bucket or pot. When only the males were left alive, he asked Armandito or me to throw the bodies far from home. He justified that unfair female "caninecide" by saying that they did not feel any pain when dying like that and that this process was better than throwing them all away when they had grown up. Despite his cruel logic, sometimes I felt like protesting and asking him to please not do that, no matter how much he needed to. Still, I dared not do it.

Whenever cows were found in the corn fields after breaking through a fence, my father would urge the dog to chase them away, and she would immediately spring into action, running swiftly towards the cattle ranges, barking at the top of her lungs, and driving the cows away unfailingly.

She was also a great sentry. One evening, when we were getting ready to start eating dinner, the eight of us seated around the table, my father realized when looking into the distance that several cows were eating in a corner of the green cornfield. He stood up abruptly and commanded our dog to fulfill her mission by chasing those transgressing animals, which were rapidly ruining that priceless crop. It was not even ours but belonged to the dairy farm where the small lot we lived on was located.

Our poor Pelúa! It was dinner time, and she was obviously hungry, having been patiently waiting for the leftovers that would be served to her at the end of our meal. She tried to please our father the best she could, poor little thing, so she ran to the fence, barked a little bit, and then wagging her tail returned nervously to our dining-room. Obviously, her top priority at that point was to be fed. She repeated this procedure several times, making our father increasingly more furious. Our wrathful father became such a beast that he grabbed a piece of metal tube and began to chase her all over the yard. The dog, totally terrified, tried hard to hide in every single corner she found along her path, but unfortunately, my father would not give her a chance.

All of us stayed put, standing petrified around the table, with our food already served. We didn't flinch but looked at one another in silence and expected the very worst. When she reached the dining-room and saw us all still gathered there, Pelúa tried to find shelter under the table, among our legs. Before she got there, however, we all witnessed the first blow. It was awful. Our father bumped clumsily against the table, and several of our plates, including my own, broke into pieces with the impact of his blow, spilling the kidney bean soup that filled them. It goes without saying that I lost my appetite immediately, but that was not the worst. Pelúa bolted from the room, wailing from pain, in a final attempt to preserve her life. Our father was so beside himself and so maddened that he hit her hard, landing that metal tube upon her helpless body several more times, which brought about her death right on the spot.

How sad and grieving we were when, shortly afterwards, slightly more calm, our father entered the house and ordered Armando and me to dump the dead dog far away from home, in the cattle range just beyond the fence. I will never forget those everlasting minutes, walking in sepulchral silence while fighting back tears. With tight knots choking our throats, we dragged the still warm, blood-smeared, dead body of our faithful and unforgettable pet. It was truly traumatic. As a result of one of the blows he had given her, he had fractured her skull, making her eyes bulge out of their sockets. That night I could hardly sleep and felt that something very important was fading inside me. I swore then and there, deep down in my boy's hurt consciousness, that from that fateful moment on, I would become the staunchest advocate of dogs. That is very likely why I have felt such a strong attraction to these adorable animals ever since.

After that tragic and bitter experience, the respect I had felt for my father changed its name; from then on, it became fear. I was never able to understand why he killed such a good dog in that wild way. It was not fair, but we had to swallow the pain, sadness, inner rage and huge frustration that such an attitude inspired in us. Pelúa had not been the first animal my father had slain in such a brutal way just because it had refused to obey him. When he was young, for the same reason, he killed another dog, his own pet, by beating him savagely. He left him for dead under a tree in the back of a grove in his home's backyard. Little did he know what awaited him when, feeling guilty, he returned to that place a few hours later and heard a noise in the dry leaves on the ground where his dog was lying almost motionless. It was the tail of that poor little animal, faithful until his death, who, recognizing the close presence of his owner for the last time ever, thanks to his amazing sense of smell, mustered strength out of nowhere and was happy to see him, greeting him the best he could, maybe even forgiving the barbaric deed that was to put an end to his own life. Having such a personal background in his own record, I could never understand why he did not hesitate when doing what he did to our poor Pelúa. One thing I know though is that – at least that night – I hated my own father and felt a stabbing pain in the deepest part of my soul.

The tragic end of our beloved Pelúa left us all aghast and highly concerned for the unhappy fate that our future pets might have. Maybe that was why, from that sad moment on, whenever our dogs passed away, we buried them somewhere and occasionally even planted flowers on their makeshift tombs. We grew to love each of them so much that we could not stand the idea that they would end up being eaten by the scavenger turkey buzzards that were always lying and waiting.

If it is true that one has many lives and that our soul is incarnated in other human beings or animals, I have no doubts at all that I either was or will be a dog in another life. I feel a very strong chemistry with all of them, wherever they may be and regardless of the situation they find themselves in. I feel an urgent need to communicate somehow with them, as well as an irresistible drive to offer them my loving care. Many people have criticized me because, even though dogs may be sick, wet, and dirty, I always find a way to attract them to me; to speak to them with affection, as if they were understanding me; and to touch their head, providing them with a circular massage right on the spot located in the middle of their foreheads, slightly over their eyes, corresponding to the *ajna chakra* (the seat of the mind), in keeping with the science of yoga, which was born in faraway India.

The long night walks

When I was little, I had to struggle against two disorders that affected my speech and made me feel very bad. I used to stammer except when I was reading and thus developed the habit of speaking as fast as possible to avoid getting stuck. As if that were not enough, I also had problems with the sublingual frenum, so it was difficult for me to pronounce "R" when multiple or strong. I also hated the pronoun "que," which means "that," "which," or "who," because it was a stumbling stone whenever I used it. It became a tag, a pet phrase, for I had to repeat it many times to be able to resume my ideas. I tried to avoid it at all costs, but I soon came to realize that it was almost out of the question to speak without using it. I hated it, particularly when my sisters asked me to cheer up Daddy so we could go out. Being the little nest egg, I was the one most likely to successfully talk him into taking us all out to town in the evening to visit Grandma Rupertina, his mother.

Whenever that happened, I was immediately embarrassed. I stood in front of my father and started my speech well up until the moment when I pronounced the monosyllabic "que." At this point, I always got stuck. I stamped my foot on the floor, trying long and hard to loosen myself, which triggered my father's laughter. This, in turn, caused my outrage and made me disappear from the scene without completing my statement. He, of course, already knew the nature of my request and that I was nothing but the envoy of my sisters, who wanted to leave the nightly boredom in the countryside to walk a couple of kilometers to our grandmother's house in town, where they had electric lights. Most of the time, my father would consent, and in a matter of minutes, right after dinner was over, we headed out. We walked in a family procession that drew the attention of all those who saw us pass by. Our parents walked in front, and the six of us followed right behind them like chicks, chit-chatting the whole time and, as was customary in the countryside, greeting all the people who met us along the way whether we knew them or not. We were very fond of those long night walks, particularly when there was a full moon. The nonstop clicking of so many heels, mainly those of the female shoes, along the shoulder of the paved road, was like music to our ears. Many times, we synchronized our steps as if we were the military on parade to make them sound in unison. By so doing, we had a lot of fun on our way back home.

Other nights, those long walks became even more interesting because we went to visit Aunt Olga, my father's sister, who lived about two kilometers behind our house in the middle of the woods, surrounded by rolling hills and undergrowth. We had to climb up and down a few hills and cross a creek. We especially liked to go there during the winter months when the cold temperatures invited us to warm ourselves up by walking through the country under the moonlight and the stars. We had been told that God lived in the moon, and sometimes, if I tried hard, I managed to see him, a hunched elderly man with a very white beard and long hair, squatting inside it.

We should never trust in the apparent naïveté of children: I am saying so based on my own personal experience. During my childhood in the countryside back in the 60s, it was quite common for women not only to give birth right in their own homes with the help of a midwife, but also to have clandestine (and even illegal) abortions performed. During the first few years of the Revolution, the family doctor primary health-care system, emphasizing both promotion and prevention, had not been implemented in the way that it is fortunately carried out at present. It goes without saying that the prolific countryside families used to have too many children. Jokingly, it is said that, without electricity or any other better entertainment available, sex was both the best and the only choice left. Aside from the universal *coitus interruptus*, practically the only contraceptive methods available were renowned preservatives or condoms. Yet due to male chauvinism and all the biases derived from it, these methods were either seldom used or expired or of a very poor quality. The point is that *guajiros* (peasants) reproduced like guinea pigs.

A two-fold wedding

My two eldest sisters, Alicia and Ada, got married on the same day: a twofold wedding on April 25, 1970, an unforgettable day that was an unprecedented event on our family tree. It was the very first family wedding that I would witness and, as if to make sure that I would never forget, it was two at the same time. The preparations began several months prior to the event when my sisters' boyfriends, Orlando Guerra Camacho and Cenén Hernández Oliva, who would marry Alicia and Ada respectively, agreed upon celebrating their weddings on the same day. The ration card would provide twice as much food, plenty to go around for the invited guests plus more for others who were not invited.

The fact that there were twenty beer crates was a hook sufficiently powerful to beckon many people. Our father, excited by the fact that his first two daughters were going to exit our house properly married, totally clad in white, and meeting every social expectation, managed to find some oil paint and painted the façade of our house yellow with red trim around the windows and doors – very Caribbean. My brother and I, of course, were in charge of grooming the yards so they were flawless. Believe it or not, we were so happy with all the turmoil that, miraculously, we did not fight that one time.

Unfortunately, I seem to have been predestined not to fully enjoy the good things about life, such as that wedding. My sister Alicia, to whom I had been quite attached since I was very little, presented me with a bracelet, a little wrist chain, to remember her. It was the first piece of jewelry I'd owned, though I was already nine years of age. I was so thrilled with such a special gift on that unique occasion that I spent the whole day trying to find a good pretext to walk in front of the dressing table mirror in my parents' bedroom so I could see myself wearing the new jewel around my skinny wrist. Unfortunately, happiness in the poor man's house is short-lived. Mine lasted not even a full day, hardly a few hours. When leaving the town's civil registry after the wedding ceremony, I lost all my happiness and all my interest in the wedding – the snacks, the food, and everything else – because I came to realize that I had lost the little wrist-chain bracelet that I so dearly loved. My sadness for not only that loss, but also the farewell of my newlywed sisters when departing for their honeymoon, and the sheer awareness, that from that moment on, they would no longer live with us, made me feel a very big knot in my throat. Because men do not cry, I began to run before letting the first tears roll down my cheeks. I hid behind the pigpens, and then I unleashed my deepest feelings, bitterly crying all by myself, surrounded by the darkness and the stench of pigs.

Those wonderful opportunities

School uniforms are one of the best things that have ever been invented. I swear that I would love to make a well-deserved monument to them – an everlasting tribute. I, at least, will be eternally grateful to them for all the suffering I avoided because of them during my childhood and my teenage years. Whenever an extracurricular activity was announced, I would hope deep in my heart that it would require us to wear our uniforms because, if that was the case, I would not have to endure feelings of inferiority because I lacked the clothes my classmates wore with pride. I wouldn't have to decide how to dress. I knew it perfectly well ahead of time.

Whenever I take a mental trip in hindsight and travel back to my childhood, I have flashbacks in which I see myself dressed in two different ways only: either wearing our school uniform, may it be forever blessed, or wearing the only dress outfit I owned: some black pants and a light blue long-sleeved shirt, which was practically another uniform itself, because whether I liked it or not, it was all I had to wear. Thus, if by any chance whatsoever there was a scheduled activity going on either in our school or away from it, for which we were expected to wear civilian clothes, the whole world already knew what I would wear. The other choice I had was not showing up, and even though that happened a few times, it used to hurt me deeply. Joining all those scheduled excursions organized by our school was a great opportunity to get to know places and do things that, with my family, I would have never had the opportunity to do at all.

Thanks to all those timely and never sufficiently appreciated school outings, I was able to go to the national zoo park, the aquarium, the movie theater, the beach, Lenin Park (under construction at that time), and the *Coppelia* ice-cream parlor. Once, we even got to participate at the *Buenas Tardes* live TV show, when the unforgettable duet of Mirta and Raúl, as well as the young singer Leonor Zamora, were enjoying the peak of their popularity. The school provided me with all the opportunities that my humble parents were unable to give me. I will never forget the anxiety I felt whenever I arrived home to ask them for permission to participate in special activities and the great joy I experienced when my father, who always had the last word, granted his consent. Truthfully, I do not recall having been denied any of those wonderful opportunities to learn a little bit about the world that existed beyond our austere family setting.

I never went to church; however, I knew that my uncle Pedrito and my grandmother Aguedita were my godparents and that both had been with me at church when I was a baby. My family only attended a requiem mass dedicated to somebody who had passed away. The church was far away, and at home there were always too many things to do. In spite of that, my mother had faith in God and got very upset when my father cursed using God's name, which he did whenever something went wrong with what he was doing. This, by the way, happened frequently. When we heard him curse, the best thing to do was to stay put, behave properly, and not approach his carpenter's shop at all.

During a school recreational activity, held at the church square where we had taken part in sack racing and other sports competitions, some of us entered the church out of curiosity. I never understood why our teacher, Ramón García, almost pushed us out of the church, visibly mad at us because we had walked into the church wearing our school pioneers' uniforms. I did not see anything wrong with what we had done, but in our teacher's eyes, we had committed a very serious crime.

This left me quite concerned. My friend Rafael had invited me to join him in entering the church. I did it because I wanted to know what it was like inside. He told me that there were many saints, candles, and flowers. The only thing I knew for sure was that the so-called day of my saint was my birthday, and that was more than enough to arouse my curiosity. Why was it so wrong to go inside, into God's house, wearing our school uniforms? Was it by any chance that God did not like bandannas? Who was there to know?

Talking about churches and priests reminds me that on Sundays, when I was about eight years old, my mother used to send me to the bakery to buy our ration card bread. Usually, I went there barefoot because I did not want to wear out my school shoes; nor did I want to wear my dress shoes. It was an austere saving plan that I had set for myself despite my youth. Besides that, to tell the truth, I was fond of being barefoot, and I was used to it. Those were the times when, lacking pants from the store, we had to wear rustic pants made out of white linen flour sacks from the bakery. Marina, our seamstress, would use her ingenuity to make sure that the indelible red ink seal identifying the *Flour Production Industry* would be placed on the right back pocket, suggesting that it was an ornament or a brand label.

One day, when I was waiting at the bus stop, holding my bread handbag and bored because it was taking the bus forever to arrive, I decided to hitchhike. I flagged down a small white VW, hoping it would give me a free ride home. I was lucky, for it stopped to pick me up. The driver, an old, fat, bald gentleman, dressed all in white, with a large silver crucifix hanging from his neck, asked me if I was traveling far. I immediately realized that he did not speak the way we Cubans did, and that startled me. It was a bit too late for me to give up, however, for I was already sitting in the passenger's seat right next to him – very proud to be riding in one of those Bugs or Beetles for the first time ever. I was already thinking how envious my siblings would feel when I arrived home with our two loaves of bread (which was what our family was entitled to by the ration card) and told them of my good fortune. I explained to the driver that I lived just two kilometers away in the outskirts of the town. On the way, he told me that he was a Spanish priest living in Havana and that he came every Sunday morning to participate in the mass of the Catholic Church in the town of San Antonio de Las Vegas, 12 kilometers further south.

The next Sunday, right at the same time, the white Beetle appeared. Slightly less embarrassed, I flashed him down for the second time. Nevertheless, I was ashamed when the priest stared at my bare feet and then asked, "My boy, don't you have any shoes?" I clarified that I had some but that I would rather wear them only to go to school because, by so doing, they would last longer. He kept looking at my feet, sizing them up while he was driving. Every now and then, he looked back at my feet as though calculating something that I didn't understand.

It is said that the third time is the charm, and in my case that was true. On the third Sunday, I did not even have to make the universal hitchhiking signal, for my Spanish friend knew me already and picked me up at the same spot, at the same time. When I got ready to open the car door and thank him for the ride, he grabbed a paper bag from the back seat and handed it to me, saying laconically, "Here you are; they are yours; I hope they will fit you." I thanked him even though I did not know what I was carrying in the bag. I was dying of curiosity. My mother was startled by my excitement, for I arrived home running and jumping and hollering. I dropped the bread handbag on top of the dining-room table and immediately opened the blessed brown paper bag to discover a beautiful pair of tennis shoes. That charitable gentleman had done a great job calculating my feet dimensions, for the shoes were just my size. I didn't even wash my feet before trying them on. That unexpected gift was just too good to be true. It had fallen from heaven and right on time!

The first day of each month, unless it happened to be a Sunday, I accompanied my mother to the grocery store to buy our monthly quota of groceries. As there were eight of us in our family cell, and back then the allotment was plentiful and varied – enough for the full month – the groceries were too heavy for her to take home all by herself. I used to tag along with her, pushing a wooden cart made by my father with bearings as wheels. A long queue formed, and people patiently waited their turn while their groceries were packed in paper bags of different sizes. Whenever I returned home with those bulky cartloads, tired and sweaty because the return trip was slightly up hill, my mother rewarded me with either lemonade or the juice of a sour orange with water and brown sugar, both of which were a real treat.

Bath time at home could be a real concern – at least, it was for me. At one time, there was only one towel available for the eight of us, which meant that those taking a bath after the fourth turn, far from drying themselves with the towel, would rather stay wet instead. It was already quite threadbare what with daily washing followed by hanging on the clothes line exposed to the wind and sun. Because I had three sisters who usually took their baths before I did, that towel was impregnated with all sorts of smells by the time it was my turn to take a bath and wipe myself with it. I tried to use only the corners because they stayed dry longer.

Because we did not have electricity at home, our radio was powered by six large batteries. In order to save them, we used it only at very specific times, such as to listen to *Radio Reloj* first thing in the morning, to synchronize our alarm clock at bedtime, and to listen to some specific shows. When I was ten years old, the electric light arrived at our household for the first time. The light was made, as the Bible claims, and it was good! That was an event that turned our life upside down, inside out, and around and around, humanizing everything that was done afterwards. What a pleasant sensation it was on the very first night, when we could at long last see the whole house as if it were daytime! Those incandescent light bulbs brought us all much closer to civilization. It was like being blind for a lifetime and recovering your eyesight suddenly. That was really awesome! Those who have been lucky enough to enjoy the benefits of electric energy since they were born will never ever be able to appreciate the feeling that such an event generates. It is a euphoria that overwhelms you, that extends deep into your bone marrow, that leaves you sleepless, and even makes you laugh, not knowing why you are doing it. Only those who have witnessed that unforgettable experience in their own life will be able to fully understand what I mean.

Good-for-nothing

Although my brother Armando was my size, he was more than three years my senior. From when he was very little, he excelled in the skills of agricultural work. He handled both the machete and the hoe with amazing expertise and would leave behind him many skillful full-grown men when it came to hoeing a whole cassava crop. He milked cows with outstanding natural ability. He was always praised because of these skills, and even I admired him for his dexterity. However, I hated in my guts to be compared with him to my detriment, particularly when strangers were present. He, obviously, was fully aware of his skills with the machete or the hoe in his hands and did his best to impress his admirers.

I still keep, like a painful weight in the bottom of my smashed self-esteem as a country boy, the verdict issued by our father one afternoon. We, along with my brother and several visitors, were at the dairy farm where my father used to work. Armando and I were trying to cut a sackful of toad-grass for our rabbits, which was plentiful in that place. One of the men, after our father had introduced us, exclaimed, "The apple never falls far from the tree. Your kids work really hard!" My father, without thinking too much about the negative impact that such a pejorative assessment would have on my already damaged self-esteem, responded,, "Well, not really. This one (Armando) is a wild beast working; he is fire. However, this other one has turned out to be a pod" (good-for-nothing).

That was the very first time I heard that word with a meaning other than the one I was acquainted with – namely, the beans or the flamboyant pods – but I knew for sure that what my father said was not praise at all. I thought that in my father's eyes, I was a helpless, lazy, good-for-nothing, and it seemed crystal clear that he preferred my hardy brother, who made him proud with his devotion to work, over me. Those words of his shook me very deeply, and even though I did not utter a single word, I felt overwhelmingly ashamed, embarrassed deep down to my very bones, for being introduced in such an unworthy manner. It was especially hard because I had such a mighty adversary in my brother, who was absolutely impossible to match, let alone overcome. I guess my discomfort was mirrored on my face because one of those strangers, when realizing that I had bowed my head out of shame, told my father, "Don't you ever forget, Avelino, that the five fingers of the hand are all brothers, and none is alike." I did not quite understand what that stranger meant, but I appreciated the fact that he had spoken for my sake.

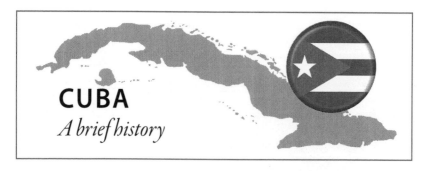

The 1970s: A New Economy and New Directions

In 1970, in a burst of revolutionary exuberance, all of Cuba's arable land was devoted to sugar production under a plan that called for a harvest of 10 million tons of raw sugar that year. The entire nation was mobilized; the world would watch the Revolution produce another miracle.

Unfortunately, when everything was counted up, only 8.5 million tons of sugar were harvested. This shortfall and the general chaos of the economy caused a complete reorganization of the Cuban financial structure on more rational lines. Although Cuba and the USSR had many trade ties, and Cuba was filled with Soviet advisers, the revolutionary government pursued a foreign policy that was often at odds with Soviet aims.

This was the era of détente, and Moscow did not want to upset the delicate relations between the superpowers. On the other hand, Cuban leaders were the idols of revolutionary movements around the globe, and they saw no reason why they should not spread their ideals.

In the 1970s, there was also a surprising opening to the United States when President Jimmy Carter eased Cuban travel restrictions that had been in place since the Bay of Pigs. This continued until the election of Ronald Reagan. Cubans saw their exiled relatives for the first time in almost two decades and were shocked: the Cuban Americans had prospered.

During this time, many schools were constructed, and a system of boarding schools was instituted, which assured that all children would be able to attend school. The number of children in the labor force decreased and then dropped to zero as the availability of schools led to dramatic increases in enrollment.

Dependence on Moscow increased in the 1970s as Cuba adopted the Soviet model of authoritarian central planning and bureaucratization. Conditions improved slowly during the 1970s as a new generation of technicians and managers dedicated to the Revolution graduated from school to replace those who had left the country. Cubans began to live more comfortably due to burgeoning trade with the Soviet bloc. This dependence, however, was to cost the country dearly.

The 1970s are remembered as the heady days of the Revolution. Fidel Castro became the spokesman for Developing World causes, traveling to South America, China, Vietnam and Africa.

In 1972, Cuba joined the Council of Mutual Economic Assistance with the eastern European socialist countries. It sold sugar, minerals, and citrus fruit and bought foodstuffs, raw materials, fuels, and equipment. The number of doctors grew from 6,000 to 25,000. The government also paved roads, built low-rent apartment buildings, and eradicated illiteracy. Cubans felt proud.

In 1974, Soviet premier Leonid Brezhnev visited Cuba and publicly endorsed his Caribbean comrade. The following year, 1975, the Organization of American States lifted its sanctions against Cuba, and many Latin American countries resumed ties with the country. Although Cuba's political system was redesigned to mimic the Soviet model, Castro remained very much his own man, particularly in terms of foreign policy. He saw Cuba as part of the non-aligned movement. Capitalizing on Cuba's Afro-Cuban heritage, Castro also aligned himself with the Black Power movements in Africa.

In 1975, Cuba sent several thousand troops to Angola to help it fight against US-backed South African troops. In 1976, a third Cuban constitution was drawn up and approved by referendum. The new constitution canonized Marxism-Leninism, and Castro's position as head of state became constitutional. It added eight more provinces and a special municipality to the original six inherited from the Spanish. It also created the assemblies of the People's Power, governing bodies of elected officials who delegated power at municipal, provincial, and national levels.

In 1978, gradual dialogues with the Cuban community abroad began, trying to normalize relations with all Cubans in the diaspora.

But, the revolutionary emphasis continued. Cuba sent troops to Ethiopia; while in the Americas, Castro befriended left-leaning leaders in Jamaica and Grenada. In 1979, Cuba hosted the annual conference of the non-aligned nations, and Castro was elected as its president for a three-year term. That same year, Cuba supported the socialist revolution in Nicaragua that brought the Sandinistas to power.

My Fondness for English

*For this very reason, make every effort
to add to your faith, goodness;
and to goodness, knowledge; and to knowledge, self-control;
and to self-control, perseverance; and to perseverance, godliness;
and to godliness, brotherly kindness;
and to brotherly kindness, love.*
                                            2 Peter 1:5–7

Beginning junior high school in September 1972 was a very important step in my life. Out of my five siblings, only one, Armando, had managed to reach junior high. Many things were completely alien to me, including a new school uniform made up of a white shirt and blue pants, which was premiered that school year. Unlike elementary school, where there were one or two teachers teaching us everything, we had one professor for each subject, along with the famous TV classes, the first English lessons, the mobilization during 45 days to a camp in the countryside, the daily bus ride with my friends, the onset of puberty, and high school sweethearts. It was a new world, which was appealing and intimidating at the same time.

When I got to junior high school, I fell in love several times. First it was with Ileana, a sixth grader from the elementary school next door. My classmates used to call her the pussy cat because she was very elusive and surly. To conquer her, I had to catch her by chasing her several times along many blocks. It was because of her evasive attitude that she was given her well-deserved nickname. When I was in eighth grade, my girlfriend was Martha Daisy, another country girl. When I was in ninth grade, however, relationships started to be more complicated. First, I became Marisol's boyfriend, though she was barely in seventh grade.

I still treasure the first Saint Valentine's gift she gave me on February 14, 1975. She was only 12, and I was her senior by a couple of years. I was hardly 14 years old myself. I fell in love with her beautiful light green eyes. She was very short and so was I. We were both the first in our respective classes' queues when we lined up in our schoolyard every morning. She had just joined our school and was a seventh grader, the first grade in junior high, whereas I was a ninth grader, and that would be my last year at that school, for even when junior high comprised four years back then, tenth grade was not available there; so, I needed to take it somewhere else as I eventually did. People just thought we made a cute little couple, and we thought so ourselves. As an endearment, people called her *cachete* (cheek) because her cheeks were chubby and made her unique among many teenage girls her age. They were her most distinctive face feature, which she undoubtedly inherited from her father.

A couple hours after we broke up during the morning break, I connected up with María Antonia at the bus stop. She was a year my senior and twin sister to María Luisa. I was able to tell them apart thanks to a little mole that María Antonia had on her face. My classmates used to tease me, claiming that I had traded the cow for the she-goat, because they believed Marisol was prettier and made a better couple with me than María Antonia did. Out of spite, one is capable of coming up with anything whatsoever, even getting yourself a new girlfriend in a couple of hours.

When I was in eighth grade and learned about the opening of an English language interest club, I signed up on the spot. My only experience with English had been when I was in fourth grade. Sometimes in the afternoons, two high school girls, Mayra Rancel and Amarilis Cortina, came to our classroom. They dramatized for us the dialogues they had learned in their English lessons. That struck my attention powerfully, though I would not be able to explain why. They asked us to repeat after them several sentences in that foreign language, which was completely new to my ears. I immediately realized that, unlike other children, it was relatively easy for me to grasp it. That is why, as soon as I heard about the English interest club, I signed up excitedly.

Marisol Rodríguez, a pretty young woman with light eyes, was my first English teacher. She taught us the basics of the language in that super-timely interest club. I was envious when I saw and heard the ninth graders reading the English dialogues from their textbooks and doing the written exercises in their complementary workbooks. I waited anxiously to reach the long anticipated ninth grade, just so I could start studying English officially. Back then, according to the curriculum in force, the study of foreign languages started out in that grade.

An everlasting nonconformity

As soon as the school year started in September 1974, I realized that English was what I wanted to study in the future. I did not have to struggle or hesitate as many teenagers did because they did not know what they wanted or because they liked many different things at the same time. Luckily for me, I never had that problem. Since the first day, I felt a magnetic attraction towards the English language that was almost pathological. It was a true obsession that I enjoyed immensely. It was love at first sight, a delicious daily vice to which I dedicated a great deal of my time both inside and outside of school. There were those who prophesied that, if I went on as I started, I would certainly end up as a psychiatric patient. There were even a few who made fun of me by singing an old refrain that went like this, "Mazorra is asking for crazy people, and Alberto is almost there." (Mazorra was the name of the Havana psychiatric hospital.)

In junior high, due to the long distance from home, I was again provided with lunch in school. In my free time after lunch and before physical education class, I used to go inside any empty classroom; once there I was delighted that without anybody bothering me or mocking me, I could learn by heart every single dialogue we had studied in class, down to the very last word. I wrote them on the big blackboard. Then I double-checked them in the textbook to find any spelling or grammatical mistakes that I might have committed. If I found any, I erased the whole thing and began all over again. My own class, knowing me as well as they did, chose me as their English monitor, a role I accepted happily and willingly.

I recall that my skills never went unnoticed, amazing my classmates and even our English teacher, Armando Rojas, who, in order to increasingly challenge me publicly, dictated to me the instructions for exercises from his desk. I wrote them on the blackboard, under a certain amount of stress, without committing mistakes. I used to enjoy it when, after I finished taking his dictation, I made eye contact with him, waiting for his assessment about my performance, and saw him smile widely as a token of his approval. This would immediately trigger a round of applause from the whole class.

My fondness for the English language reached such an extent that whenever my mother saw the tractor towing the trailer from the military unit enter the road leading to the landfill, I willingly volunteered to go there immediately. This meant pushing an old small wheelbarrow to fetch the leftovers that the soldiers dumped. Thanks to that food, we could feed our chickens and pigs without any cost at all. I did it very gladly with a twofold purpose in mind. First and foremost, I was helping my family, particularly my mother, who was in charge of feeding the poultry. But I also took advantage of my round trip to the landfill to practice my emerging English, which was growing speedily with my pathological obsession. If by any chance, somebody approached me along the way, I would be quiet so as not to be labeled as crazy, but as soon as I saw myself alone, I resumed my repetitious drill like a parrot, reciting all the latest dialogues we had learned in class, the days of the week, the months of the year, occupations, trades, and professions, the alphabet, whatever I had recently learned in the English lessons.

The English teacher used to encourage me a lot, predicting a promising future for me if I decided to study English. He told me he was fully convinced that I had what it took to become a good translator-interpreter. I believed that deep down in my heart, and from then on, there was no vocation whatsoever for me other than studying English like a workaholic. I did not need to decide what to do at all. I had done that a long time ago in my own humble way. I daydreamed about the faraway day in which I would be able to hold a real conversation with a foreigner, read a book in English and understand it thoroughly. That sweet utopia pushed me towards an everlasting dissatisfaction with the knowledge I had already attained and an unquenchable cognitive appetite. I knew it all depended on me, on my personal endeavor, and on my constancy.

Learning English became not only a means to an end, but an end in itself. The progress I was making was the greatest spur toward succeeding in the goal I had set for myself, which I was trying to approach slowly but without missing even one minute. Deep down in my soul, I was convinced that eventually my dream would come true. When dreams are that extra large size, what is seemingly unattainable is not really out of the question. How long it would take me to reach it, I did not know. I was certain, however, that one day, sooner or later, it would happen. I had a gut feeling that I only needed to strive to achieve it, even if I was labeled a crackpot.

Too good to be true

I still keep in the back cover of my last English notebook from the year 1975, a handwritten remark by one of my classmates, María Teresa Pérez, who was a student leader in our school. She predicted in writing, "If you keep on having the first record, you will climb the Turquino Peak this year." That forecast encouraged me a lot. I was aware of the fact that I had very good grades in each and every subject, but never had I imagined that my school performance would have such a huge surprise in store for me. Just a few weeks later, my class was going out when the last period of classes was over, and I was walking down the steps of the hallway across from the principal's office. I was puzzled and could not give credence to what my ears were hearing directly from the mouth of our principal, José Raúl. He pointed me out with his index finger and told Margarita Artigas, our physics professor, "There he is, the best academic record in our school!" For a split second, I thought it was a joke or that he was not talking about me. I looked around and, bowing my head, slightly embarrassed but dying of curiosity, I asked him silently by pointing at myself with my right index finger in a signal that can be translated as, "Do you mean MEEEEEEE?" He then grinned widely and shook my hand effusively, confirming it when I passed in front of him, "Yes, sir. YOU, yourself. Congratulations!"

During the morning school lineup the following week, it was officially announced that I had been selected to climb the Turquino Peak that year, representing the region of San José de Las Lajas, as a member of a contingent made up of the 500 best students in the whole country. I could not believe that I was granted such a special gift. Never before had I traveled to any other province, and now I would go all along the Central Road, up to the easternmost Oriente province. I would also climb the highest summit in Cuba, located at 1,972 meters above sea level. That was too good to be true. It was one of the deepest and most gratifying emotions in my whole student life.

I never told her anything

When I was in ninth grade, I began to study the subject that I liked the least: chemistry. Fortunately, Elenita Roque, who taught it in ninth grade, was a magnificent professor who did her best to teach excellent classes. I never knew why, but when that school year was almost over, whenever she arrived at our classroom for the fourth class period, right after the morning break, I became very restless and could not concentrate at all; therefore, it was difficult for me to be able to understand her explanations well. One fateful day, something very weird started to happen to me that scared me a lot, but that I never dared tell anybody. I did not want to be labeled as a crackpot because, with my English addiction, I had more than enough of that already.

Each time I made a mental effort trying to understand her, I started to visualize in my head something very similar to current video clips. It was always the same terrifying scene in which I would see my mother, wearing the orange dress that she used to wear a lot – one of the very few she had – lying on the road right in front of our house, a crowd all around her, raising their hands in despair and screaming at the same time. It was quite clear that she had been the victim of a tragic accident in which she had lost her life. That picture was repeated over and over again in my mind, and I could do nothing other than ask God that such a thing should not happen. It seemed to me that if I did not repeat that prayer constantly as a mantra, then it would become true. That was something that was unbearable and was driving me crazy whenever it happened.

No wonder I could not understand the subject and rejected it deeply in my own guts, hating it in my bone marrow. When the class period, which seemed to be never-ending, was over, I would leave the classroom with an anguish that I would wish not even to my worst enemy. I had to walk six blocks to the bus stop. I would not dare sit down even if there were empty seats available. This vision was a psychological distress that devoured me relentlessly. The 12 kilometers to my home were the longest in the whole world. When the bus approached the hilltop just before the bus stop across from my house and began its descent, my heart would start to race; the palms of my hands would sweat; and I was afraid to look into the distance, thinking the worst – that I would witness the materialization of that hair-raising image that had tortured me so many times before.

Only God knows the unfathomable sensation of relief that I used to experience upon arriving home and finding that everything was quiet, normal, in peace. Nevertheless, I would not calm down totally until I managed to assure myself with my own eyes that my mother was safe and well. Very often, whenever that happened, I would find her in the kitchen, busy fixing lunch, and then I would hug her strongly and stamp a hard kiss on her forehead. I remember that she would smile and say to me, "Hey, what's the matter with you? Why are you so caring today?" I would shrug my shoulders and laugh as if it were just a prank. She already had too many concerns of her own for me to increase her quota even more with my piffle. I never told her anything at all.

Right on the target

In San Antonio de Las Vegas, I was enrolled only through ninth grade even though junior high school comprised four years. In that school, tenth grade was not available, so I had to transfer to another school in Mantilla, the Pablo de la Torriente Brau Junior High School. When I arrived in that school, I gained the sympathy and loving care of my English teacher, Silvia Valdés. I won a municipal contest in her subject, and she awarded me with a book on English grammar, *A Guide to Patterns and Usage in English* by A.S. Hornby, in which she wrote, "Alberto: May your tenacity enable you in a short time to use this book, a true treasure for any scholar of the English language. Try to be the best."

During that school year, 1975-1976, the fifth contingent of the Manuel Ascunce Domenech Pedagogical Detachment was being shaped up all over our country. This was due to the upcoming demographic explosion of high school students and the shortages of professors to meet the teaching needs that this social phenomenon was generating. Even though my illusion was to apply for training as a translator-interpreter – the dream of my life – reality was being depicted in another color. Things are not always the way one imagines them to be. The pre-university level, senior high school, would require three more years, and I did not have the assurance that, upon completing it, I would be granted what I had requested. There were priorities for training translators, but in other foreign languages and dialects, and my obsession was English. I was afraid that after so much sacrifice, I would end up being given another language. Facing that dilemma, the available alternative presented to me was highly appealing – becoming an English teacher. It was my decision. I was not supposed to hesitate too long about it because I could easily lose, as we Cubans put it, *güira, squash and honey.*

Teachers were so greatly needed that we were practically begged to step forward and embrace the call issued by our homeland. If I made a decision to be one, I would enjoy some advantages that were not to be belittled at all. First, I would immediately start being trained in the English language – intensively. That was my greatest motivation; it was right on target. Second, I would not have to go through the pre-university level. Instead, I would join the university right away though I was only 15! I would not have to study chemistry any more either! Besides, it was a great temptation to know that I would start earning a monthly stipend of $45, which would make a huge difference in our family income. Also, I would not be required to spend three mandatory years in the General Military Service because I would automatically be exempted from that obligation. And in five years, being only 20 years old, I would be every inch a professional, a full-grown university graduate – the very first of all my big extended family, as well as the first and only González Rivero who would hang his diploma on the wall with great pride. For a poor country boy like me, it was too great a temptation to be looked down upon. *A bird in the hand is worth two in the bush.*

Your mother had an accident

On Wednesday, April 21, 1976, I was in the classroom in the afternoon session when tenth graders were taught. I had taken a bath before having lunch at home, the leftovers from the previous evening meal, which my mother had warmed up for me. I said goodbye to her as was customary, with a kiss on her cheek, which I would always give her both when leaving and returning home. I left her sweeping the front porch, and I walked out to take the bus wearing my blue school uniform pants and my white cotton T-shirt with the image of Manuel Ascunce Domenech across my chest, showing that I was a professor–to–be. It was already the second class period in the afternoon, and at that point, we were working in teams. I was the student leader of our class. All of a sudden, the teaching deputy director stood at the door and, with a strange expression on his face, asked me, "Albertico, you live in Managua, don't you?" I limited myself to a nod with my head. Right after that, he said, "Please, come with me!"

When I reached the classroom door, he looked at my empty hands and commanded me, "Bring your books along!" I did not know what he was up to, but I sensed that it was not good at all judging by his unusual attitude. When we were heading towards the principal's office, he flung one of his arms around my shoulder and gave me the most appalling piece of news in my whole life, "Sonny, your mother had an accident, and someone has come to pick you up."

How difficult it is to assimilate a message of that nature. I started to run, to scream and to cry, all at the same time. I cannot describe what I really felt at that point. There are no words capable of conveying the pain, the fear, the anguish, the sadness, the despair that I felt when Lulu, an elderly neighbor of my uncle Pedrito, came in a taxi cab to pick me up upon his request. She was extremely nervous, totally stressed out. What an errand my uncle had given to that poor old lady when sending for me!

When grilled by my questions, first in the lobby of my school and later in the taxi cab, she would only tell me that my mum had an accident. She had been run over by a tractor, and that was it. I pictured her in a hospital with plaster casts and bandages and IVs and probes and devices of all sorts – even smeared with blood stains all over – but alive. My mum could not die on me like that! The ride back home was an unbearable torture all the way. I was freaking out, in despair, in total shock, panicking, screaming at the top of my lungs, crying, sobbing, gasping, asking and beseeching God desperately to please, please save my mother's life. It was drizzling lightly when the taxi cab approached the crossroads and the red flashing traffic light at the entrance to my hometown. There were only two more blocks to go to arrive at the polyclinic when the driver emphatically demanded that poor old Lulu tell me the truth. Only then, she could not hold back her tears any longer, and in the midst of her sobbing she told me, "Sonny, you are already a little man. You have to be strong, my boy. Your mother is dead!"

She had to hold me really hard because my very first reaction was to open the car door and jump out. Upon arriving at the polyclinic, I saw a crowd of people who looked at me pitifully. My grandfather was there weeping; he hugged me very tightly. It was then, when looking to my right, that I saw her. She was lying on her back on a metal stretcher, stained with blood, with a few bruises on her face and dirty tire tracks all over her chest. There was a white enamel bucket almost full of blood right under her gurney. My poor mother was still soft and warm when I touched her. I held her head in my hands and lifted it so as to kiss her lovingly for the very last time. I was moved when I felt how heavy her lifeless head was now. That was indeed the worst minute of all. I went completely mad with so much pain. I stormed out of that ER, hitting and kicking everything along my path. I even got burnt by the hot sterilization autoclave when, in my despair, I leaned against it inadvertently. I told my grandpa that God did not exist. Why would He allow such a dreadful thing to happen if He really existed? I was so out of control that a nurse had to give me a tranquilizer with a shot in my buttocks. Then Lulu took me to her house, just a block away from there, and asked me to please lie down on a bed.

When the sedative effect wore off, I was taken to the funeral home and there, little by little, I began to learn the details about her death. She was waiting for the bus at about 2 o'clock in the afternoon, standing in the shade of a big tree by the roadside – that acacia whose scented flowers had been my sisters' makeshift dolls. A couple of soldiers without a driving license, after having stolen a tractor to escape from their military unit, got very nervous when looking at her standing there. They lost control of their vehicle and accelerated instead of putting on the brakes. They ran her over, smashing her with one front and one rear tire. In addition, they destroyed two fences, finally coming to a stop after hitting a pillar of the front porch of our neighbor Agustín García's house.

The video clip that I had watched in my own head so many times the previous year had come true. My mother had indeed died, run over by a vehicle right in front of our house, and what was even more incredible, as if that were not more than enough, she was wearing her orange dress that day. It goes without saying that her tragic death, with all those antecedents, marked me forever in an ineffaceable way, and that it left me suffering from a whole sequel of exacerbated anxiety under stressful situations along with severe sleeplessness that has lingered until the present.

When we returned home right after her burial, the saddest day in my whole life, we came across the unfinished meal that she had started to cook for our dinner the day before. She had left it half cooked, so she could go to the town's leather store to buy some shoes that she needed badly. Right there, over the *Pike* Korean stove, she had left a black bean soup that she had already tenderized, always concerned about getting her work done as soon as possible in her eternal eagerness to serve others. On top of the kitchen counter, she had also left a papaya that was almost ripe. She had scratched it with a fork, getting it ready to make sure we would never lack some dessert on our table. That is how my poor mother left this callous world, worried and busy until her very last minute for the sake of our wellbeing. May God keep her in his glory for ever!

After our mother's death, my elder sisters, Alicia and Ada, began to take turns weekly to stay at home with us. They did their best to do the tasks that Mum used to do up until that ill-fated day, mainly cooking, washing, and cleaning – the work that was supposed to be a woman's job, according to the male chauvinistic, patriarchal mindset prevailing in rural areas back then. The vacuum that Mama left behind when she was gone was huge and very painful. I kept on dreaming of her for several weeks in a row, the same old dream over and over again every single night. I would be elated when I saw her coming, excited and happy. She would get off a bus in front of our house just as she used to do regularly whenever she returned from the grocery store, wearing her orange dress, and I would run out to welcome her home, relieved to know that everything had been just an awful nightmare. She, in turn, would hug me very tightly and kiss me all over, telling me to take it easy and not worry because everything was alright and nothing was wrong.

The joy I felt was so intense that I always woke up right at the spot of that amazing euphoria, just to realize in a matter of seconds that the true nightmare was the tough situation I was facing. Mama's death was a sad reality that I would have to get used to eventually, no matter how much I resisted that idea. My sisters would fix me warm herbal infusions at bedtime; they would sleep cuddled up with me; and when they saw me restless in my dreams, they would do their best to comfort me, to caress me, to weep along with me. Those were very hard, unforgettable, and sad days that have left their imprint deep in my soul forever and ever.

Before my mother died in such a tragic and fateful accident on April 21, 1976, Marisol and I had broken up and were not together any longer. She was still in the same school in San Antonio de Las Vegas, whereas I was in the Pablo de La Torriente Brau in Mantilla, completing my fourth and last year of junior high school. As soon as she learned about my mother's passing, she immediately showed up at the funeral home in Managua to show her sympathy. I can still recall her, with tears falling down her cheeks, among that sad crowd in our town cemetery, right after my dear mother had been buried and her eulogies told. That meant a lot to me and showed me that she really cared about me.

My boarding school

Alberto, age 15

A few months later, in September that very year, 1976, I went to a boarding school when I officially was enrolled in the Fifth Contingent of the Manuel Ascunce Domenech Pedagogical Detachment. I bore a gigantic load of sadness, because I knew that my late mother had been very happy with the decision I had made. I had been waiting anxiously for the first day of my weekend leave, in which I would arrive home wearing my full uniform, including the elegant neck tie. Now I could never share that joy with her. Her memory, however, inspired me to move on, even during the most difficult times, and honoring her memory, I committed myself never to let her down. I had to graduate at all costs – not just for her, but for Daddy as well, who would occasionally complain about the fact that none of his children had ever brought home a university degree, despite all the opportunities available now to study and to become somebody, as he used to say. I was fully aware that I was the very last hope that he had left, so I wanted very badly to claim that immense spiritual satisfaction. Being able to present my father and my mother's memory with a university degree was a goal of paramount importance for my own self-esteem.

My brother Armando, who was still in the military service, decided to get married without a celebration a few months after Mama's passing, so our sisters would not have to come so often to take care of us and our house. Our aunt Irma, who was a notary public, came over and conducted the legal ceremony right in the living-room of our house. That was not totally fair, particularly for Marta Barrios, my sister-in-law, who though very young and newly wed, was compelled to undertake our household chores overnight, caring for her husband, her father-in-law and two brothers-in-law. If this was not enough, my brother Armando, recently married, was sent to Angola to fulfill an international military mission that extended for 28 very long months.

When I entered the boarding school after my mother's death, surrounded by young people from all the municipalities of our capital, my inferiority complex was exacerbated because the differences separating me from my classmates were now very evident. Up until that time, I had been simply one country boy among many others, since all my classmates lived either in the countryside, like me, or in a rural town. In boarding school, however, at age 16, in the prime of my youth, I was the only country boy among the capital city boys and girls. For all of them, the mere fact of living in a rural town was synonymous with backwardness, lack of culture, clumsiness, sloppiness, poor taste, stagnation, ignorance, and illiteracy. To sum it up, they thought I came from a second or third category world at best.

I was aware of what was spoken and thought about country people, so upon arriving at that school where luckily nobody knew me, I limited myself to saying that I lived in Managua, so everyone would think I lived in the town. That did not make any difference at all in their way of thinking, because I qualified as a country boy either way, but I was ashamed to think that they might get to see the thatched house where I lived. Very likely, no city girl would pay attention to, let alone fall in love with, a country boy like me, who lived in a secluded place and in poor conditions. That is why on Fridays, when I came home on the school bus, I never got off in front of my house as I should have done. I waited until the bus reached the main square of the town, and only then did I ask the driver to drop me off. Then, I walked all the way back for a couple of kilometers with my bag slung over my shoulder. Being so young, I was very sensitive to the assessment of others, and I really needed to be accepted and liked by them all. I did not want to be less than anybody else. *Everyone has their own little heart.*

My boarding school, the Pedro Sotto Alba Pedagogical University branch, which was located in the outskirts of Melena del Sur, was, from many different perspectives, a true turning point in my life. Even though I had taken part in the mobilizations to agricultural camps for four consecutive years in junior high school, lasting six weeks each, now things would change. Many of the young people were stragglers. There was such a pressing need for trained teachers that the gates were wide open for anyone willing to join in. The mere fact of getting a monthly stipend encouraged many young people, who were not really interested at all, to get enrolled so as to take advantage of those social benefits. In my class, for example, the I-4, there were students who were already 24 years old, whereas I was still 15 at the onset of our training.

We had our classes in the afternoon session; in the mornings we went to work in the fields. We went home every Friday afternoon right after finishing our classes and returned to school on Sunday evenings. That first year, trying my very best to adapt to so many new things was hard and seemed never-ending to me. Fortunately, I was pleased to have Miriam Pérez Rolle as my main English professor. We all already knew her very well and admired her a lot because she had taught the TV English lessons in junior high school. Her English was flawless because she had been raised in New York City when she was a little girl. She was by far the greatest motivation I had there, which undoubtedly helped me immensely in terms of putting up with other adversities.

It was in boarding school that I learned how to dance salsa, which we Cubans call *casino*. I was taught by my classmates, which I appreciated a lot, although I felt guilty dancing after the tragedy of my mother's death. They helped me get out of that black hole of despair, step by step, serving as psychologists when I most needed support. Some weekends, they invited me to spend time with them and their families, so instead of returning to my house, they took me to theirs.

That first year of my training as an English teacher was very hard for many different reasons. Being far away from home was partly good and advisable, for it took me away from the environment that reminded me of my mom. Every single detail of our home was associated with her. When I was there, I began to suffer from anxiety; the palms of my hands started to sweat; I felt butterflies in my stomach that made me lose my appetite; it was very difficult for me to fall asleep, and when I did, it was very lightly.

When I was at home over the weekends, at 6 o'clock in the morning,

I was already up, searching for freshly made coffee in the kitchen and thinking about what to do next so as to entertain myself when everybody else was still soundly sleeping. If I stayed lingering in bed, it seemed like my chest was going to explode because I began to feel an uneasy pang, a stabbing discomfort right under the right side of my rib cage.

One day when I was naked, wiping myself with a dry towel after having taken a cold shower upon returning to school from the morning agricultural activities, I noticed a white spot on my skin, quite small, the size of a penny. At first, I did not pay much attention to it for it seemed to be harmless. Every now and then, however, when getting undressed, I would check it out, and thus I observed that it was growing gradually, increasing its diameter little by little. Then, I really started to worry about it. The physician who took care of me at the polyclinic referred me to a dermatologist at the 10 de Octubre Hospital, where I was seen by several specialists.

After a biopsy, the dermatologist in charge of my case, Dr. Benítez, let me know that my diagnosis was scleroderma. It was the very first time that I had heard that word. He prescribed a treatment based on vitamin E and Triamcinolone in a cream. He also suggested that I should avoid exposure of the affected area to the sun and to hot temperatures in general. Even though he never told me that it was something bad, judging by the name it had, I did not like the idea of being the bearer of such a thing. The closest word to that intriguing term that I knew about was "arteriosclerosis," and I did not like it at all because my grandmother Aguedita was suffering from it, and I knew very well what it was about. *Sclero* had to do with atrophy, hardening, clogging; whereas *derma* was obviously the skin. Was my skin being atrophied? How much more would that invasive spot grow? Those were questions that harassed me all the time.

With all the concerns that were already overcrowding my mind back then, now this one was being added – a weird, enigmatic, not very common disease, which had whimsically decided to choose me in which to develop. In spite of the fact that I was following the treatment to the very letter, the stain – far from stopping or vanishing – continued to grow relentlessly and became darker, brownish, developing an irregular outline in the shape of a paramecium or a foot sole. I asked many people if they knew anything about it. Nobody knew a thing. Seemingly, I was the only freak who had that damned disease. Fortunately, although the patch never disappeared, it continued to grow very slowly and has never been more than a nuisance.

A stranger in my own house

At some time during that school year, I came to realize that my father's behavior was kind of unusual. I would see him bathe early on Saturday afternoons, get dressed, dab on some perfume, and leave, claiming that he was going to visit a co-worker who was hospitalized. That became a routine, and it soon was clear that his outings had nothing to do with any hospital. He was involved with a new partner and he either did not have the courage to admit it or was ashamed that we might learn about it. We were all very upset with that situation, especially me, because I was the only one left at home. My brother Armando was fulfilling his internationalist mission in Angola, and his wife, Martica, was the one who lived with us; but she used to stay with her parents over the weekends.

One Saturday afternoon, my father again dressed up, wearing his Sunday best, to go to the "hospital." While he was tying his shoe laces, he asked me to do him the favor of sealing the envelope and mailing the letter that he had written to Armando. I felt deeply curious about the content of that letter, for I somehow guessed that I would find in it what I had been suspecting for a long time but that my father did not dare tell me face to face, obviously because he was afraid of my reaction. Sure enough, when I entered the bathroom to take my bath, I took that letter along with me, and before sealing it, I sat down on the toilet bowl to read it carefully. Bingo! Right then and there, I confirmed the suspicion I had all along. It really hurt me a lot that Armando, far away in Africa, would get to know before I would, at least officially, about our father's new love affair. He told Armando about Natalia Díaz without sparing any details. She was a divorced co-worker with three children of her own from her former marriage, who lived in Arroyo Apolo. What outraged me most was that he was planning to marry her. Never before had a letter made me feel that mad. I even thought about tearing it up, burning it, throwing it away, you name it. It was a wound that cut me deeply to the very core of my inner feelings.

From then on, the psychological torture that almost drove me insane began. I did not know what to do or whom to heed. Every time I came home on weekend leave from boarding school and went to see my grandmother on my father's side, Rupertina, she tried to convince me that my father was old-fashioned and that he did not know how to do anything in a household She said that it was not only about the bed and sex issue, but that he was not used to being alone, that he needed a woman. She spoke to me at length, trying to help me understand all the reasons why my father really needed to have a new partner.

Returning to school in 1976

Had everyone said to me the same thing, it would have been far easier for me to understand the whole thing, to digest it, to assimilate it, though not necessarily to like it. However, other family members, acquaintances, neighbors, and friends filled my head with ideas that were diametrically opposed to those of my grandmother. Mother as she was, she couldn't help advocating for her son. They told me that we, his children, should not allow our father to be involved with another woman so early on, when our mother was only recently buried in the cemetery. They said we had all the right in the world to demand more respect and consideration from him and to tell him that he should still be mourning. They placed me between a rock and a hard place, and I did not know what to do. Any decision that I made was sure to upset one of the two factions in that ongoing debate, and I, obviously, wanted to be at peace with both God and the Devil.

My father remarried on July 9, 1977, just a few days after I completed the first year of my training. In spite of everything I was going through, I had incredibly managed to score very good academic results. From that moment on, I felt like a stranger in my own house. I was uncomfortable even when opening the refrigerator to get a drink of cold water when I was thirsty. I tried by all means not to stay at home. Whenever there was a chance, I took my bike and vanished, making sure that I did not return until it was very late and everyone was asleep. If I stayed at home, however, I locked myself in my bedroom either listening to music or reading a book and came out when nobody was left at the table, and I felt that there was a wild and hungry lion eating up my entrails and roaring in my stomach.

An English teacher at the age of 17

Most of the students with an English major would not start their teaching practice until their third year, so they would know the subject better, particularly in terms of the vocabulary that was necessary for us to master to be able to teach high school students. However, due to the great need for teachers, as soon as I finished my first year, I and a few others were chosen to complete the demands of the following school year, and it was thus that I started to perform as an English teacher at the age of 17. This was a huge challenge. I had to cope with an understandable amount of nervousness and fear because we were given a great deal of responsibility, especially considering our youth, and I wanted to succeed in fulfilling the high expectations of my teachers.

I was designated to work at the People's Republic of Mongolia Junior High School in the Countryside, one of the first ESBECs in the municipality of Batabanó. I was charged with a couple of classes of eighth graders. In the mornings, we went to the pedagogical unit on one of our school buses. Ours, the Bernardo O'Higgins, was located in Santa Rita. We returned to our ESBEC for lunch, and in the afternoon we would face the classrooms again – three times a week in class periods of 45 minutes each. I was very frustrated when I walked out of the classroom the first time I taught. Just by chance, it was precisely on September 9, 1977, my 17th birthday.

Abiding by every single methodological guideline to the very letter, I tried to speak in English the whole time without resorting to Spanish at all, supporting myself the best I could with pictures and gestures. I had to repeat everything several times because I realized that most of my students were not understanding me. Forty-five minutes was not enough time.

I left the classroom even more nervous than when I had entered it. But at least I knew that I had impressed the students with my English, and with that, I had already scored a good point in my favor. Although that first experience was not totally good, it could not turn into debut and farewell. Even if the students had not understood a thing, they would have to do so eventually. I was just paying for been a rookie.

In order to impress my students even further, whenever I arrived in their classrooms and realized that they were restless, I tried to catch their attention immediately by addressing them in a loud voice, always in English, allegedly reprimanding them for their lack of discipline. What I was really doing was verbalizing by heart long dialogues that I knew top to bottom from my own training in the previous year's lessons. To make them sound more authentic, I changed the tone of my voice a little bit and varied my inflections. I ended up surprising myself with the outcome that such a strategy brought about and with the skill I gradually developed by doing it so many times. The human mind uses amazing resources to cope with the challenges it faces. It was a trick of mental agility that obviously bore fruits and thus was worth implementing. As the Bible claims, "I had to be meek as a dove but shrewd as a snake."

My fondness for the English language was further intensified by my teaching practice. The fact that I had to prepare myself properly in order to teach those lessons motivated me to do a good job and to do it to the best of my abilities. I felt that the classes I was getting at the pedagogical unit Monday through Friday were not enough. I wanted to learn more and more as soon as possible. As I did not have anybody to turn to, I determined that I needed to find self-taught, personal, unilateral alternatives, to meet that pressing need of mine. In February 1977, the bimonthly magazine *Somos Jóvenes* was published for the first time and quickly became quite popular. In its last few pages, there was a section called "Amigos" in which there was a list of names and addresses of young people my age from all over the world who wanted to correspond with Cuban youths. That juvenile magazine was also sold in Europe. In a flash, I thought this would be a great opportunity to practice and thus further improve my English, to expand my vocabulary, and at the same time, to learn about other parts of the world and make new friends in faraway countries.

I also began listening to the program *The Voice of the Americas* in special English, in which the native speakers would read the most important news from the whole world in English, but at a slower pace, to benefit many people like myself who were interested in learning and understanding what was said in America. In order to take better advantage of that activity, as soon as I managed to purchase my first radio-cassette recorder, a SANYO, I recorded that program whenever I could, and in my free time, I transcribed all that oral information onto paper. By so doing, I systematized my oral training. I developed and improved my spelling as well as my inference skills when I had no choice but to make my best guess about how words were spelled. This was because I could only listen to them, but did not see them in writing. For me to check if I was right, I needed to resort to the famous "donkey-killer," as we Cubans call dictionaries. It was indeed my sidekick, which gave me a lot of satisfaction whenever it proved me right each time I hit the nail on the head. I learned a great deal of vocabulary that way and was updated not only about whatever was going on all over the world, but also about scientific discoveries, celebrated characters, historical places, cultural events, and so forth.

The songs in English of my generation fulfilled a double purpose in my case: they were entertaining, and they were also a never-ending source of new words and phrases in English. In that regard, my favorite group was the Swedish quartet ABBA. My obsession with their songs did not have a match. I was also very fond of the Jamaican Boney M, which was based in Germany, the famous Bee Gees, Barry Manilow, Barbara Streissand, Neil Diamond, Kenny Rogers, the Beatles, Elton John, Billy Joel, Lionel Richie, Steve Wonder, Michael Jackson, Olivia Newton-John, Air Supply, and so many others. I always kept an eye open in my constant search for the lyrics of all their songs, in which I found much more than the benefits of the language itself.

Throughout my third year (1978-1979), I taught English to seventh graders at the Democratic and People's Algerian Republic Junior High School in the Countryside, also in Batabanó. My students were a year younger than the previous ones, and the program was easier, so, with a year of experience, I felt way more comfortable teaching them, and my vocabulary had increased a lot.

The girlfriend's hand

It is said that where there is smoke there was fire. When I was in that third year of my training, at the age of 18, I began to date Marisol Alvarez, who had attended my mother's funeral. She was one of my junior high sweethearts. Those were still times in which the girlfriend's hand had to be requested and "cards were checked," as we used to refer to the formal, frequent dating. Her father, Reyes Alvarez, a lieutenant-colonel of the Armed Revolutionary Forces, had a reputation of being severe and uncompromising. To make our relationship official, I had to speak with him to request his daughter's hand. In addition, she happened to be his firstborn child, and it goes without saying that he was extremely protective of her.

Nothing took place as I had hoped. The day I requested Marisol's hand, I could not possibly have presented myself as a more ridiculous figure. We had gone to Guanabo, where my classmate Carlos Franco lived, to spend the whole day on the beach. The worn-out T-shirt I was wearing had been torn, so Carlos lent me one of his shirts, which was pretty large for me when the fashion was just the opposite. We wanted to return home early before her father arrived so as to keep him from seeing me in such inappropriate clothes. To make matters worse, our bus broke down, and, as *he who does not want broth is given three bowls*, what I expected the least happened. Upon arriving at her home, I was red as a ripe tomato from the sunburn on the beach, with hair that looked like rope. I was also soaking wet because it was raining, and I was wearing that extra large borrowed shirt and shoes without socks. I could not have made a worse presentation.

To go to request a girlfriend's hand, one was supposed to look much better than the way I did during that unfortunate and unavoidable occasion. I will never forget the way Reyes looked at me, sizing me up from top to bottom when we were introduced. I was ashamed that he might think that his daughter had fallen in love with a shabby, dirty, rough-looking guy. He asked me to be seated on the sofa across from the TV set, and when I let him know about my intentions, he provided me with a speech that lasted for what seemed like hours on end. He finished his dissertation by saying that I should not promise him anything at all. He said that he would not believe in promises and that only time would have the last word in terms of what I wanted to let him know.

The best years of my student life

Upon completing my third year in our pedagogical training, due to the pressing needs for English teachers in the capital, from the next school year (1979-1980) on, we studied at the Salvador Allende Teachers' Training School in Havana in order to complete our two remaining years. These were by far the very best years of our whole training. Our stipend was raised from 45 to 90 Cuban pesos per month; we were now in the middle of the city; we could arrive at our boarding school up until 2:00 AM every day; and the boarding conditions were excellent: wonderful dorms with innerspring mattresses, hot showers, large classrooms, sports facilities, swimming pools, a huge library, plentiful food and snacks – everything, and yet, we used to complain about many things. *Nobody knows what they have until they lose it.*

For those of us who lived in the countryside, being in a boarding school in Havana for a couple of years, enjoying all those prerogatives, was a blessing that would be appreciated for a lifetime. It allowed us, the small cluster of country boys and girls, to know the amenities of the city little by little. We used to take advantage of our free time as much as possible, and we went to many different places at night. The public transportation system was pretty good during those years, so we could afford to go to the movies, the theater, restaurants, sports activities, concerts, the National Library, and the *Coppelia* ice-cream parlor. Or we could just walk down the streets or have a walking tour along the ocean drive, the Malecón seawall. We would return late, sometimes on the last bus available.

I took advantage of each opportunity that came my way to practice my English with native speakers, for that was the only chance I had to do it. That is why I always encouraged the rest of the country boys to join me and go to the small cozy theater hall of El Sótano (The Basement), on K Street in El Vedado. As it was so near the main hotels of our city, it was always frequented by tourists, particularly Canadians. They were my favorites by far because, even though Europeans spoke English as their second language, nothing compared to those who spoke English as their first language. I just loved to clash against truth, as we used to say every now and then. That is why, although I was slightly shy, I would patiently wait for the intermission of the plays and then would always find a way to approach English-speaking foreigners and strike up a conversation with them, no matter how simple it was. I always learned something new, no matter what, even if it was the subtlety of improving or correcting the pronunciation of a word poorly learned in class or self-taught. Going to the theater and talking with English-speaking people was for me a great incentive that encouraged me to go on striving to reach ever higher levels in my unceasing linguistic upgrading.

From the viewpoint of the teaching practice, these two last years of our training were quite intense and varied. In the fourth year, I was placed at the Pedro María Rodríguez junior high school in Wajay and afterwards at the Raúl González Diego junior high in Calabazar. In the fifth and last year, I did my first semester at the Rubén Martínez Villena Animal Husbandry Polytechnic Institute in Rancho Boyeros. For the second and very last semester, I was chosen as a student-teacher and stayed in our own school, where I taught an intensive training course in the English language to a class of professionals from all over our country. They were preparing for an international mission in Ethiopia. Those were intense times, but the best years of my student life by far. They will be longed for, but they will never return. I used to be actively involved in each of the activities that were scheduled: the theater plays, the university sports games, the research works for the scientific-pedagogical events, the patriotic marches, the political rallies, the camping sites, et cetera.

When I had almost finished my last semester, I went to the offices of the teaching secretary one morning to submit a report from my class, because I was a student leader. I was flabbergasted upon reaching the threshold of the principal's office. The provincial ranking list of our English major had just been publicized on a bulletin board supported by a tripod. It comprised all the students from Havana City, Havana province, and the special municipality of the Isle of Youth. I was expecting to be within the twenty top places because I knew that I had accumulated a good academic record throughout the five years. Obviously, in an enrollment of almost 150 students, there were a number of other students with very good academic grades. I was aware of the fact that I was a good student, but I was also aware that I was not the only one.

I was rendered speechless as I stood frozen in front of that board. I could hardly breathe out of emotion – my full name occupied the second position, with the highest score of all the graduates. I shared first place with my friend Carlos Alberto Franco, whose name was at the top of the list. We had both obtained 4.85 points. As the two of us could not be placed in the first ranking position, despite having both the same average, they decided to abide by the traditional solution and use the alphabetic order of our family names. His was *Franco* while mine was *González*. It was the only time in my whole life that I would have loved to change my name or wished that the letter G would come before F in the alphabet. Truthfully, Carlos deserved that first ranking position as much as I did, or maybe even more, for he was an excellent student: bookish, flawless, studious, and sympathetic. In any event, it was crystal clear that I was occupying a place at the very summit of that list, which I honestly did not expect to reach, although, of course, I longed for it from the bottom of my heart.

How I wished to have my mother still alive to share my unfathomable joy. How happy and proud she would have been! At times of such deep emotion, we can't help but recall those we most love, those with whom we would like so much to share our experiences and who would rejoice the most with us. Oftentimes joy is turned into sadness, becoming a bittersweet sentiment that is hard to reconcile – but life is the way it is.

Graduation celebration in 1981

We graduated in July 1981 and went to the Salón Rojo of the Capri Hotel for our graduation party. The following day, a group of the *guajiros*, who got along as real brothers, held a party at my house. A few days later, we gathered at our school theater to receive job assignments for the social service required of us for three years. It was organized in keeping with the order obtained within the provincial ranking list. Most of the available choices were found in other provinces. Fortunately, as I was number two in the ranking, I was able to choose one of the few available in Havana province: the Tomás David Royo Valdés Technological Institute in Batabanó. It was an excellent option because there was a school bus that would pick me up at 6:30 AM right in front of my house. However, I would rather have gone to a high school in the countryside because technological institutes did not enjoy a good reputation in terms of the quality of their students and their technical English program.

CUBA
A brief history

The 1980s: The Golden Age

Our system survived on Soviet subsidies, which helped build an impressive social-welfare program. But underneath, the economy was sputtering and frustration was growing; dissent and criticism were stifled. Opportunities for economic advancement were limited, and corruption was spreading – bringing with it both cynicism and disillusionment.

On the surface, the 1980s were by far the golden decade within the revolutionary period. Every year was better – at least, that's the way most people saw it. The Cuban economy was successful. Sugar production increased at a 40 percent rate. Nickel exports became strategic. Cuba became a major citrus exporter.

On the surface, things were looking up for Cuba in 1980. The Soviets not only agreed to delay repayment of the Cuban debt, they also increased subsidies. More goods rolled in; and gasoline was nearly free. Due to cheap energy from plentiful Soviet oil, sugar production jumped from an average of 5.6 million tons in the 1950s to 7.5 million tons in the 1980s.

Then a small tear in the envelope protecting Cuba turned into a gaping hole. A group of dissidents broke into the Peruvian embassy in Havana, demanding asylum. When the embassy refused to turn them over to the Cuban authorities, Fidel made the mistake of removing the guards as punishment for the embassy's intransigence. Then, thousands streamed into the embassy, hoping for asylum and entry into the United States. Fidel allowed them to leave, permitting small boats from Florida to pick them up at the port of Mariel. Nearly 100,000 left on that huge boatlift.

During these years, the economy was dependent on Soviet Union support. Sugar exports accounted for around 40 percent of export earnings. After the Revolution, a deal had been made with the USSR. The Soviets paid five times more than the world price and arranged a sugar-for-oil swap that cemented Cuban's dependence on sugar exports. In the mid-1980s, Fidel Castro tried to loosen the rigid Soviet model, but with US President Ronald Reagan's anti-communist crusade in full swing, there was little room to move.

Cuba was not underdeveloped due to a lack of resources but rather to the hostility of the United States, including a decades-long economic blockade, illegal economic measures, violations of the sovereignty of other countries, and violations of international laws. As a result, Cuba was compelled to dedicate a great part of its budget and human and other resources to defense. At the same time, there was also a continuing migration of people to the United States.

Yet progress continued. Health care improved beginning in 1983 when primary care was transformed by the arrival of the "family doctor's home office program." Doctors were provided with a home, an equipped medical office, and the assistance of a nurse. They conducted primary care and primary prevention activities in rural and urban areas alike. Today they cover most of the island, even in the most secluded areas. Family doctors in communities were linked to neighborhood polyclinics, which provided more sophisticated care and access to specialists.

The educational revolution opened up new opportunities. Scientific research and technological applications enabled Cuba to be among the first ranked in several fields. However, technology was inefficient, resulting in a great waste of fuel.

While the US maintained neither diplomatic nor commercial relations with Cuba, other countries took advantage of the opportunity to positively engage with our island nation. Cuba re-established diplomatic relations with 164 different countries and was an original co-signer of the General Agreement on Tariffs and Trade. Cuba is also an original member of the World Trade Organization.

At home, the mid-1980s were relatively placid. But from abroad came rumblings that the future was not so certain. In 1983, the socialist regime on the tiny Caribbean island of Grenada self-destructed when its Cuba-supported leader, Maurice Bishop, was killed by radicals in his own party.

Two years later, Mikhail Gorbachev became leader of the Soviet Union, and the empire began to totter. When Gorbachev finally arrived in Cuba for his first state visit in April 1989, everybody knew that change was in the air. By the end of the year, the Berlin Wall had fallen, the East Bloc regimes were on the run and Fidel Castro knew that aid would soon be reduced to zero.

The good times were ending. There was little room to move, and with the collapse of the Soviet Bloc in 1989, Cuba lost five billion dollars worth of support almost overnight, which meant 85 percent of our foreign trade. The Golden Age had ended.

A Real School for Me

For this reason a man will leave his father and mother and be united to his wife, and they will become one flesh.
Genesis 2:24

When in September 1981, at the youthful age of 20 years, I arrived as a new graduate at the technological institute in Batabanó, which was located right behind the pencil factory, I already had four years of experience in the classroom thanks to my previous teaching practice, which undoubtedly made a lot of things much easier. I recall that when I was observed for the very first time as I was teaching a class, the teaching deputy director congratulated me when assessing, "You don't seem to be a new graduate but rather an experienced professor." There was no head of the English department; the only professor who was teaching the subject was not a graduate. I was immediately bestowed with the responsibility of that post, and I was compelled to cope with the reality that almost nothing had been done previously. The English being taught was meant only for the first two years. The students were being trained as high school level technicians on Wood Mechanical Manufacture.

In keeping with the methodological guidelines for Technical and Professional Teaching, the second-year students were supposed to receive technical English according to their specialties so as to develop the skill of reading comprehension by means of many exercises that were aimed at that goal. As there were a variety of technological and polytechnic institutes all over the country, the Ministry of Education could not guarantee specialized texts for each and every one of those centers; thus the respective heads of the English departments were asked to create the required materials. Upon arriving in that school to do my social service, such texts were non-existent, so I immediately consulted the staff who taught the technical subjects so as to become acquainted with the nature of the texts with which the students worked in their respective majors. I searched for, chose, translated, typed, and mimeographed all the necessary texts to meet the needs of the syllabus. I also created the reading comprehension exercises to use in class. It was a modest effort that provided a practical solution to a long-standing demand.

Some time later, an elderly professor by the name of José Casanova Fraga showed up at our school. He played a very important role in my professional performance and provided encouragement and inspiration in my constant obsession with the English language. Casanova had been raised in the United States. His English, of course, was impeccable. He provided me with an unending source of reliable tutoring and systematic learning, which I will forever appreciate. He was concerned about my training on a daily basis. He cared a lot about it, making sure to teach me new things, give me books, and share with me pieces of poetry and old songs that he knew by heart. To sum up, he became a real school for me.

He used to address me in English at all times, and every single day, right after lunch, we sat in the balcony of the third floor, in front of our English office, to talk at length for a whole hour. We were hanging out in English, a social gathering that became a habit. Occasionally, he encouraged me to translate things that he read in Spanish into English, providing me with rudimentary consecutive interpretation training. That became an expected routine, which I enjoyed thoroughly and looked for anxiously. Those were my very first little steps or tiny attempts, when I was just toddling language-wise, in the exciting art of interpretation.

One day, when finishing one of those daily practices, the professor kept on staring at me. He then spoke as a prophet, predicting with an awesome certainty that sounded funny at the time, "Never quit studying. I am sure that eventually you will translate for Fidel Castro himself." Getting to translate professionally was a dream that appeared only on a far horizon. I trusted, however, that with my constant upgrading, I would eventually succeed in attaining it. But to think that I would one day translate for Fidel was indeed science fiction. He told me that several times while I laughed and thought that he did not have to exaggerate with such a forecast. Nevertheless, it was nice to know that he trusted me and that he encouraged me to move on, because as he himself would assert frequently, "he who perseveres, overcomes."

The attitude of my students

If I had to recall the most memorable moments of my stay in that technological school, I would think first of the attitude of my students, from whom I gained, since the onset, their loving care, admiration and respect. I used to talk with them a lot, particularly when I was on guard duty and stayed in the school overnight. With some of them, I established relations of true friendship that have endured even to the present. Such is the case of Vladimir Lázaro González Vega, my great friend. Thanks to his first place finish in a provincial contest in my subject, my salary was raised the following school year. Being the professor-tutor of a student who won an award at the provincial or national level provided a financial reward within the salary brackets. It was one of the incentives that existed to increase our salaries.

I will not be able to forget that day when I arrived very early on the school bus that transported us, the professors. I dressed much more formally than usual because I knew that I would be visited in a demonstration class by the English methodologists from all over the country, who, together with the national methodologist, would watch my lesson and analyze it methodologically afterwards. Andrés, my methodologist from Havana province, had asked me to prepare myself after explaining what was to be expected from me and my students. We were expected to show that it was indeed possible to teach the class thoroughly in English, from one end to the other, making sure that the students were understanding everything. That was undoubtedly a real challenge, taking into account the fact that most of the students in technological schools were prone to get rather low academic scores. This was especially true in my subject, which many of them could not care less about. Most claimed that to be a carpenter, it was not necessary to know foreign languages. English teachers all over our country were frustrated by that unhappy reality. They complained before their respective methodologists that it was almost impossible for them to teach their classes completely in English as was expected.

I have always firmly believed that one cannot give what one does not have. *The elm cannot be asked for pears.* Had I not gradually developed the skills in my students up until that date, I doubt that they would have been able to perform successfully. I was very nervous witnessing the scope of that large group of visitors, made up of fifteen methodologists, some of whom were already prejudiced and skeptical. They believed that with the type of students I taught, the goal of teaching entirely in English could not be attained. I was fully aware of their skepticism, so my palms were sweaty out of anxiety upon arriving in school. Very discreetly, I wiped them with a handkerchief. I knew that I had prepared myself properly and that I could not let down my methodologist, who had placed so much confidence in me. Still, I could not help being jumpy.

I had always felt a special loving care for my students, but never as much as on that day when I arrived in the classroom and witnessed everything they had done to make sure that our lesson went well. I do not exaggerate at all when I say that they were more worried and nervous than I was. They grew up before my eyes and occupied a very special spot in my heart from then on. I knew that they loved me, but I could not have guessed how much they were willing to do for my sake. That history-making day, they demonstrated it to me big time. They had not gone to bed the night before, but spent it painting their classroom with whitewash and looking for flower pots and ornamental plants to decorate it. They had done a thorough cleanup, washing the glass panels over the windows, sweeping the ceiling, and removing the cobwebs. They covered their notebooks and bare books with cardboard jackets, flat-ironed their school uniforms, and even wore their neckties and bow ties that day so as to dress up to the best of their abilities.

I had trained my monitor, Noel, very well on how to introduce our class and welcome our distinguished guests with all due respect. He did it in English as a perfect master of ceremonies. The lesson was based on the grammatical analysis of a text that summarized the structures that had been studied up to that point within the syllabus, highlighting the comparison of adjectives in English in their different degrees and irregularities. The students did a great job. Even the least capable of them managed to respond both in the short and the long way, just as I had trained them. All of them raised their hands and stood up properly whenever they interacted with me. As the class began to unfold, I started to relax and enjoy harvesting those fruits that with so much patience, I had achieved in my students by implementing my favorite method: the repetitive-continuous-systematic-progressive one, as I used to call it jokingly. They did so well during our exchange that some of them ended up surprising me. Never before had I been as proud of my students as I was that day. Our lesson was over right on time and not a single word in Spanish was spoken.

The bell rang just as I finished explaining the instructions for their assignment, or homework, as it is better known. The visitors congratulated the students for their skills and climbed the stairs to the conference hall next to the teaching deputy director's office, where they would discuss the recently visited class. When all of them were inside waiting for me to join them and I was getting closer along the external hallway, I overheard a phrase that filled me with optimism. I was hopeful, even certain, that I had done a good job, but I could not wait to know the opinion of those experts, who were obviously the ones who would have the last word. Having fifteen specialized people watch the same process, I was certain that not everything had been perfect. Because he who searches will always find something, I could not celebrate my victory yet.

When I was almost at the threshold of the door, I overheard, "The guy really hit a home run!" Being a good Cuban, I knew the semantic implication of that blessed exclamation very well. It was just the prelude to all the other praise I got afterwards. That activity was undoubtedly a turning point in my professional performance as a teacher. It gave me prestige in the eyes of my superiors and colleagues alike. Almost a new graduate, I had passed my first trial by fire and had succeeded greatly. As we country people say, "I didn't have room for a birdseed" when I arrived home that afternoon in a state of total bliss and wholesome pride. Nothing compares to the deep spiritual satisfaction of having fulfilled one's duty in the right way, particularly when it comes to what you are fond of.

Getting home with the university degree

For some reason, the diplomas with our degrees were not ready the day of our graduation ceremony. In order for us to have our pictures taken properly and not to affect the quality of the ceremony, we were handed a rolled up certificate bound with a ribbon that did its job with enough dignity. We received the true diploma – the parchment scroll of our degree with Gothic letters and a raised dry seal embossed over the waxed see-through paper, accrediting us as high school English professors – some time later, when we were already working and had enrolled for two additional years of the so-called enlargement. Training courses, held every other Friday at the Maxim Gorki School, would lead to the degree of *Licenciados* in Education, issued by the Paul Lafargue Higher Institute of Foreign Languages. I received this degree in July 1983.

Returning home with the university degree was, ironically, one of the hardest moments during my youth. I felt a deep mixture of joy and pain, satisfaction and nostalgia. As usual, my father was in his carpenter's shop when I arrived home. Smiling widely, I unrolled my diploma in front of him so that he could read it on his own. I knew how important that moment would be for him and for me, of course. Of all his six offspring, only the very last one, the little nest egg, achieved what none of the five others had accomplished. Thus, I was his last hope, his last train, his last bus, his last shot – and I had not let him down. He looked at me in a very unusual way, gave me a hug, and congratulated me. I got a lump in my throat, and my chest was very tight after fighting back tears for so long. I locked myself in my bedroom and sat down on my bed. Looking at my mom's framed picture on the wall with the fresh garden roses that were never missing, I could not hold them back any longer. I felt that I would explode if I did not cry. So many images of her came to my mind, so many special moments, such as when she would call me "my little black boy" while caressing my head lovingly as I sat on the floor and leaned against her knees while she sat on a dining-room chair. I thought about our many conversations in which we projected ourselves into the future and spoke about the day of my graduation. It was now a reality, but one which, unfortunately, she could not enjoy.

In my house at that moment, my father lived with his new wife, Natalia, and Marlene Cubillas, her youngest daughter from a previous marriage. That afternoon, when realizing about what was going on, Natalia approached me and said, "I know very well why you are crying. Do not be ashamed. Your father is crying in the carpenter's shop, too." Those words intensified my pain even further. My father, extremely male chauvinistic, every inch a macho man, would not show his feelings easily. In fact, the only time that I had seen him cry was when my mother died, and it was not even in public. The fact that I had made him cry with my university degree meant that I had touched him very deeply in his very entrails. At that minute, I fully realized the impact that my accomplishment had upon him. A few days later, he made me a beautiful cedar wood frame in which to hang my diploma. He varnished it and placed it with pride on one of our living-room walls, very close to the main door, where all those arriving could immediately see it. The very first university degree of all the Gonzálezes was required to be shown with pride. It was unprecedented in our family and, therefore, worthy to be boasted of.

Those who get married want their own house

I spent several years going to date my girlfriend by bicycle. It was roughly three kilometers from my house to the Frank País neighborhood where she lived, in which the military prevailed back then. In 1982, four years had elapsed in my relationship as her fiancé. We were both working and earning salaries, and because we were no longer a burden for our respective families, we decided that it was about time for us to get married. The problem was where to live from then on.

Dating Marisol, 1978

I did not really want to settle down at my in-laws' household after getting married, let alone at my own, where I did not feel comfortable at all.

In August that year, I had a very serious conversation with my father in order to find a solution to my problem. He suggested that we could get married and come to live with them. I was thankful for his willingness to help me out, but clearly that was not what I wanted. When Natalia got home that day, my father told her about my concerns, and she claimed that we could all live together, highlighting that we only needed to get along nicely. The crux of the matter was precisely there. In terms of living together, there had already been serious issues between her and my sister-in-law Martica, which ended with the unfortunate divorce of my brother Armando, who had a newborn baby boy – his firstborn, Armandito. I did not want to become the second chapter of that soap opera. After I declined their kind offer, my father brainstormed about the issue, and one afternoon a few days later when I got home, he asked me, "If we fix the roof of the carpenter's shop a bit, would you be willing to live in there?" My reply took not even a second, "Surely we would, even if it is in a cardboard box, but completely independent."

He made me very happy with a solution nobody had thought about. He asked me to talk it over with my father-in-law, who worked in a military unit in San Francisco de Paula, and requested that he provide me with some discarded wooden crates so as to avail ourselves of the boards, the shingles, and the nails they had. I also bought paint, as well as sand, cement, and gravel for the floor. Using tar, I fixed the leaks on the tin roof. In order to insulate it a little bit and to avoid excessive heat, I purchased some wood-cardboard planks and lined the whole ceiling with them. We painted that small cabin orange and painted the doors white, along with the windows of Persian blinds that my father had made. It looked like a train wagon. It did not even have a bathroom or toilet at the onset, but that was not the most important thing. We would be all by ourselves in our own little place no matter how humble and small it was. Those who get married want their own house. As a surprise, when we returned by taxi from our honeymoon, my father was about to complete a small counter, which he had improvised in one of the corners of our little wagon. It would qualify as our kitchen. Luckily for us, we did not have to live in anybody else's house – not even for one day. Nothing compares to what you own.

We were married at the Víbora Park Wedding Palace on December 3, 1982.

We were married on December 3, 1982, the very day that the Ameijeiras Brothers Hospital was dedicated, and we did everything at the Wedding Palace of Víbora Park in our municipality, Arroyo Naranjo, including the toast reception. It was a very simple ceremony but quite joyful. At the Capri Hotel in El Vedado, we spent the first half of our honeymoon. We completed the second half at the Riviera Hotel in a room on the seventh floor overlooking the sea. For anybody living in the city, that would not have any relevance, but for a country boy like me, who was from way out in the middle of nowhere, that was every inch a special event.

On May 31, 1983, during a diagnostic test applied to all the teaching staff in the technological institute where I was doing my social service, besides taking dictation, we were required to draft a composition of our free choice. I still keep what I wrote on that occasion:

> Her eyes, light as emerald. There are many light eyes in the world, but those are exclusive. Her way of looking, her apparent simplicity, and her unique figure make up a whole worthy to be loved. To complete, an aestival name: Marisol.
>
> I will never be able to forget when I met her. She was still a girl, and even though I was not a full grown man myself yet, I fell in love as such. I take pride also, in having conducted her properly, in teaching her many things; anyway, in making her happy.
>
> We have already got married and our plans are many. We want to consolidate our marriage based on mutual assistance, understanding, and respect. Afterwards, later on, children will come who cannot be missing. A home without children would be something like a garden without flowers.

While I was working in the technological institute, newly married, I dreamed about the possibility of having our own house, one with all the basic comforts, in which we would raise our future children, instead of the humble little hut made out of wood boards and old rusty tin roof tiles without hydraulic installations or toilet furniture.

My father saw me one Sunday morning, soaking wet in my own sweat, all by myself with a pick and a shovel, digging a small septic tank at the very end of my little house. It was squeezed against the bottom fence where I planned to build a rustic outhouse. He felt awkward and told me not to dig any further. Why was it, he asked, that I who was already a full-grown, respectable professor, a university degree holder, was going to be solving my needs in an indecent outhouse. As the proverb goes, "everything happens for a reason" because we ended up making a larger septic tank with the works, with a stone mouth made out of large rocks, a concrete deck for its cover, and its corresponding and necessary vent pipe, inside which frogs would inevitably find their lodging. That motivated me to buy a set of toilet furniture and some boxes of white ceramic tiles with which my brother Armando and our father built a small, but very comfortable bathroom. It became the best-equipped room of our modest dwelling, which was now enlarged with a larger bedroom. What had played that role up until then became a small living- and dining-room combo. From then on, it did indeed qualify as a house – tiny, but quite cozy.

Some time later, Raúl Henríquez, a friend of mine from Santiago de Cuba who was a planner-draftsman, assisted in turn by his friend, architect Vivian Díaz, drew the blueprints for our future house, which was to be built next to my father's home if I got both the opportunity and the required authorization and if I managed to gather the necessary resources to build it. If that ever happened, I would not need to wait for blueprints. My dream had been to welcome my children in that planned house, provided everything worked out as originally conceived. That was not the case, though.

I decided to search for other horizons

Happy as I was at the technological institute – I enjoyed very good prestige before students and professors alike, and the transportation provided for the staff picked me up right in front of my house – as soon as I completed my required three years of social service time, I decided to search for other horizons. Unquestionably, the technological school had advantages, and I could have stayed there as long as I wanted, but I had other ambitions. I needed to get closer to the capital, where there were better choices and where I could submit my knowledge to the test in a more demanding school. This would challenge me to go on upgrading myself all the time. That was why, before I finished the last school year of my social service in 1984, I submitted myself to the competitive examinations at the Vladimir Ilich Lenin Vocational Training School in Arroyo Naranjo, the municipality where I lived, just 8 km away from home.

Each year, all the candidates applying for vacant teaching jobs were required to pass an English grammar written test and to teach a lesson as part of the competitive examination. As the Lenin School was the very best school in our country in terms of the quality of its students and its teaching staff and was the first of its kind in the whole island, working in it was a highly coveted goal for many teachers like me, who were looking for better working conditions and higher salaries. Fortunately, I passed both requirements without difficulties at all, and I was granted the first job available that school year, 1984-1985. I started out at the Unit 3, teaching six classes of eighth graders because, at that time, the school was intended for the whole range of the high school level – namely, from seventh all the way through to twelfth grade. I used to go there by bike, because the daily physical exercise back and forth was good for me, pedaling eight kilometers first thing in the morning before the sunrise and sweating profusely in the afternoon on my way back. My new students, younger than those from the technological institute, were quite exceptional. Just for their sake, any sacrifice whatsoever was worthwhile. The selection process for admission of the students was quite demanding. They were brilliant, talented, bookish, and concerned – everything a professor expects from and appreciates in his students.

With those vocational school students, I achieved amazing things, and I was mistaken when I underestimated them. I demanded more and more of them, always raising the rod to a higher notch, demonstrating to them and to myself the unquenchable potential we have available if we manage to explore it.

Every year, I took part in the Pedagogical Meeting that was held in our school – a scientific-pedagogical research event organized by the Youth Technical Brigades. During this event, I shared everything that came to my mind in terms of initiatives to improve the quality of the teaching-educational process in my subject. I created many didactic games, primarily adapting well-known table or board games, such as Parcheesi and Bingo. Using them, the students not only played and had fun but also consolidated and reviewed the content of the three major objectives of our subject: reading comprehension, vocabulary, and grammar.

The English classes became a big workshop in which creativity was unleashed to its fullest. I used to gather my monitors and a few other advanced students in brainstorming workshops during which we reached common agreement on the rules of games suggested by the group. The students helped me with great enthusiasm to make everything that we needed, and they would amazingly come up with great ideas to get whatever was missing with the timely support of their parents.

At the end of each unit, a lesson was devoted to doing research about a specific issue related to the topic addressed during that unit. The students split up into teams to carry out the necessary research, and at the end of the unit, they made highly creative oral and written presentations in English, trying by all means to surpass the work of all the other teams. Those sections were called "In Point," and they soon turned into a real amateur festival in which there was a little bit of everything, including pyrotechnics. The parents of some students even rented costumes and disguises that were needed for a dramatization that lasted only fifteen minutes. The students disguised themselves, learned long and complicated speeches in English, acted, danced, sang, recited pieces of poetry, cracked jokes – you name it, they did it. Sometimes they invited the teaching deputy director and the general head of the English Department to witness and enjoy these shows, which became famous within the setting of our school.

Every single year, I tried to enroll in a post-graduate course in English. I will forever be thankful to my beloved professor, María Leticia Pérez, who taught me the subject of Extensive Reading in the fourth year of my training. I owe to her my love for reading in English and the subsequent habit that I developed in that regard. With her and with Professor Juan José Díaz – also known as JJ – I took several oral training courses for English teachers, which were organized by the Enrique José Varona Higher Pedagogical Institute. The first of them required students to read an assigned short story in English and then prepare for a debate in which we went over the plot, the characters, and the setting of each story. Thanks to wise pieces of advice, mainly from Leticia, who encouraged us constantly to cheer up and read in English, today this is indeed my favorite hobby.

My wife and I enjoyed our life as newlyweds fully, celebrating our wedding anniversaries at a hotel in a different province each year. We went to Pinar del Río, Varadero, and Cienfuegos. We could even afford to return home from those faraway places by taxi. We dreamed about a future that looked increasingly more promising. With our salaries, we could save enough money to also go every single year on one-day excursions as national tourists, enjoying the choices available in our country. *Know Cuba first and other countries next* was the slogan that was in fashion. We used to buy our tickets at the travel agency on the ground floor of the Habana Libre Hotel by 23rd street, and thus we went to places such as Viñales, Guamá, and Varadero.

Every month, we bought a bottle of rum and another of wine or liqueur so as to make sure that we always had something to treat visitors with – a welcoming drink for friends. Once a month, we went to the farmers' market and would always arrive home overloaded with everything that we needed for the whole month, without having to worry about food supplies up until the next. In those monthly purchases, there never lacked a good leg of lamb, a couple strings of garlic and onion, and a large bunch of plantains – a little bit of everything. At the so-called "parallel market," there abounded a huge assortment of canned goods and preserves of all kinds coming from the former Eastern European Socialist countries with which Cuba used to keep mutually favorable trade relations. Even though ration cards still existed – both for groceries and for clothing and footwear – it was relatively easy to get what one wanted because there were choices available. But undoubtedly, the most important thing was that Cuban regular money was valuable, and it was the only currency circulating back then. Yet in spite of everything, we used to complain. Who would have imagined at that point in time that things would change overnight after 1989?

The great news that I would be a father

In 1986, when I was already working at the Lenin School, I was given the great news that I would be a father. We waited during four years after getting married before planning our children, for we were still quite young and did not feel sufficiently matured yet. Nor did we have the minimum material conditions available to cope with responsible parenthood. During the first few years, Marisol took contraceptive pills, but she gave them up for a while because we decided that our home needed the active presence of a child.

Marisol sporadically suffered from renal colics, and she had to be taken to the E.R. of the polyclinic whenever she went through one of those awful crises. She was then working at the radio-assembling factory right next door to my school. One day, she felt one of those pains and was seen by a physician, who suspected that it might be an early ectopic pregnancy. In order to rule that out before prescribing pain killers or antibiotics that might compromise the health of the alleged baby, somebody saw fit to recommend that she have the famous "rabbit test" performed. It consisted of an innocuous urinalysis by means of which it would be known in a rather short period of time whether she was or was not pregnant. I personally carried her sample to a clinic in the area of El Vedado. The day I went over there, overwhelmed with anxiety, to claim the lab results, the experienced nurse who was sitting at the reception desk looked at me over her doctor's eyeglasses and smilingly said, "Tell her to start getting the little clothes ready." It was hard for me to decipher that answer. I was rather expecting a laconic "Yes" or "No" instead. To my blank face, she smiled again and repeated the same thing, but louder and more slowly, to see if I finally landed into reality. I got so nervous and so happy to be the very first person to know such wonderful news about my imminent paternity that, with all the fuss, I ended up taking the bus in the wrong direction.

The trip back home seemed to be endless, much longer than usual. I could not wait to get home and announce such a great piece of news. I was daydreaming all along the way, thinking of a million things, reaffirming the self-esteem of my fertility. Even though one never admits it, the fear of being childless is lodged deep down in one's bone marrow until the time when the uncertainty is cleared as it was now.

I was trying to guess whether the baby would be a boy or a girl. What would it be like? Would the baby have light green eyes like its mother? We needed to think about names, too, although we had already spoken about that specific issue and had even reached certain agreements in that regard.

As is common for many young couples, we wanted to have only two children; preferably, a boy first and a little girl as soon as possible afterwards so as to get over with the heavy work once and for all. However, deep down in my soul of souls, I longed for and asked God for, in my own humble way, that should both babies be of the same sex, I would rather like to have a couple of girls. I knew that opposite poles attracted and that girls were usually more attached to their fathers.

In September 1986, when Marisol was already pregnant, I had to submit myself to surgery that could not be put off so as to put and end to my chronic tonsillitis. It was becoming increasingly worse and had developed an amazing resistance to antibiotics. Dr. Alexis Benítez, an E.N.T specialist of the Diez de Octubre teaching and clinical surgical hospital, was the one who undertook the surgery. Dealing with the constant chalk dust and having to project my voice all the time, it's no wonder my throat complained every now and then with the infectious crises that were already making me worry a lot. I would have preferred to wait for my vacation time so as not to stop working. My E.N.T. specialist, however, intimidated me by claiming that my case could no longer be solved with antibiotics, that the scalpel needed to do its job and the sooner the better. So that was what I did. I was a very proud father-to-be and wanted to be as fit as I could get. When it comes to your health, it is better to be safe than sorry.

Marisol had learned how to knit, embroider, and sew skillfully when she was a young girl. She was encouraged by her mother who did all those handicrafts herself with amazing dexterity. All by herself, she took charge of preparing the entire layette. In turn, in my father's carpenter's shop, I drew some cartoon characters on a piece of plywood and, assisted by the electric saws and the chain saw, I cut them out, sandpapered them to polish them, painted them with watercolors, and finally varnished them before fixing them on the legendary mahogany cradle in which all my siblings and I had slept. It was a family relic, and in spite of all the criticism by friends and relatives alike, who opposed my idea, I thought that my offspring should provide that tradition with continuity because, in addition, the cradle was in a perfect shape. The only thing it really needed was to get a new coat of oil paint, which I gave it right away. After that, it looked brand new. It was nice to think that my own children would sleep in the same old cradle I had slept in as a baby twenty-five years before.

Marisol endured thirty long hours during the labor process in her first pregnancy. My beard literally grew out waiting for so long in the lobby of the Luyanó Hijas de Galicia Maternity Hospital. The baby had changed its position at the very last minute, and in those conditions, it was next to impossible for him or her to go out through the birth canal in a physiological delivery. The medical team on call managed somehow to place the baby back in the right position when it seemed practically impossible. Finally, on January 25, 1987, at 4:20 in the afternoon, it was announced by speakers of the hospital sound system that Marisol Alvarez had given birth to a female baby and that both were doing fine. The baby girl's crying was also heard, amplified using a microphone.

Marisol and I with baby Wendy

After a time that seemed immensely long, relatives were authorized to go upstairs, two at a time, to meet the newly born baby. I do not have the right words to describe the emotion that took hold of me when I saw my little daughter through the glass panel of the nursery, the newborns section, for the first time ever. It was a wonderful sensation that shook up the deepest fibers of my whole being. There is not enough money in the whole world to pay for the value of that indescribable and priceless instant. It was like traveling towards another direction, unknown up until then, like discovering myself for the first time. My heart would not fit in my chest, and a couple of teardrops rolled down my cheeks, oblivious of both time and place. Oh my God, what a delicious moment that was! With my eyes still moist and blurred due to that deep emotion, I looked at her keenly – wrapped up in those green swaddling clothes – and told her mentally, "Be welcome Wendy! Daddy is right here very close to you, my dear, and he can't wait to kiss you for the first time, my little baby girl."

When Wendy was born, I was 26 years old. That day, in order to mark her birthday symbolically, and unable to avoid being the country boy that I was, I had the idea of planting the pit of a beautiful and tasty Catalina avocado in the bottom of our backyard. Thus, both would grow together: that fruit tree and my girl. The only thing missing was for me to write my own book so as to fulfill José Martí's proposal. At that time, I was teaching the eleventh grade students because my school had been transformed into a vocational high school specializing in the exact sciences. Twenty-two months later, on December 10, 1988, my second treasure, Betsy, arrived in this world. As a matter of fact, I was disappointed upon her arrival because, after two different ultrasound tests performed during Marisol's pregnancy, it had been forecast that there would be a baby boy this time. I had even been shown the emerging testicles on the monitor screen. What is more, we celebrated that happy piece of news with pizza and spaghetti right after the second confirmation of our baby's gender. We had even chosen his name already: Randy, and should there be a second boy, Rodney.

Out of one of those amazing chances that life has, Wendy and Betsy were delivered by the same obstetric team at the Hijas de Galicia Maternity Hospital. For me, it was as if time had not elapsed at all, and when I saw Betsy in the newborns section for the very first time, it was like seeing Wendy again two years later, for they were almost identical as newly born babies. I experienced again that sweet sensation that was already registered in my brain, and I enjoyed my twofold paternity thoroughly. When I saw her, it took me just a second to put an end to my stupid disappointment, and I felt guilty about the feeling I had lodged a few minutes earlier when witnessing that the baby was indeed a girl and not a boy as we had expected.

Alberto and Marisol with baby Betsy

I even took the precaution of making sure that the same pictures were taken with both of them. Intentionally, I even wore the same shirt both times so as to avoid future jealousies. It would also serve as a clear example that I loved them both the same way, despite that sudden change – that bait and switch at the very last minute. With all due sincerity, I keep on saying today that I would not change my two daughters for anything else in the world, for they are the greatest, most important, and most beautiful thing that life has presented me with. I would like to publicly apologize to both of them in the pages of this book if, at any time whatsoever as a father, I have failed to be at the level they have always deserved or expected me to be. As we country people used to say, "they have turned out to be golden."

Waiting for better times

Both girls had been born, yet I had not been able to build our new home for various reasons, including all the cumbersome red tape required to build a house, although I already had the two most important requirements: the blueprint and the lot. I went to see Manolito, a community architect and friend of our family. When I explained my problem, he told me that the only real possibility by means of which I could be granted the right authorization for such construction was if I could manage to get hold of a set of prefabricated pieces meant for the small houses of the ubiquitously known Sandino model that were swarming everywhere back then. Then the government would allow me to purchase the remaining construction materials to complete the rest of the house. It goes without saying that I saw my solution, knowing that if I managed somehow to acquire that prefabricated module, I could at long last begin the construction of our new house.

Overnight, I became an unbearable chatterbox, asking everyone who stood in front of me if they knew of anybody who was selling the pieces for a prefabricated house. After just a few days, bingo! I found it, and it was totally legal, with its purchase invoices properly in order, at a family's house in the town of Las Guásimas, a halfway point between my house and the Lenin School.

Sure enough, I was granted the corresponding construction license, but then I faced another problem I had not anticipated. As the blueprints I had were meant for a different house with another design, I would not be authorized to carry out the work if I did not submit new blueprints justifying the use of the prefabricated pieces I now had available. The architect Manuel Llerandi, the husband of one of my co-workers, was in charge of drawing the new blueprints, which he completed as soon as he could. To make a long story short, as it is said in English, I spent two whole vacations, working from sunrise to sunset, building that new house. My father taught me how to make the steel cage structures of the 12 cubes and the foundations for the base of the house with steel reinforcement bars and wire rods, and I even learned how to lay the cinder blocks. I could not afford to pay a mason to do that job after having invested all the money that I had been saving for years on end – since I graduated in fact – so I decided to learn how to do it myself. Thanks to God, I managed to do it with the constant and timely supervision of my father and my brother Armando.

Hoeing weeds while taking care of Wendy

I had to start that long-expected construction project by trimming the grass and cutting down a whole grove of fruit trees before beginning work on the actual foundation. Holding a heavy hatchet in my intellectual hands, starting before daybreak, I cut down coconut, orange, custard apple, soursop, banana, and guava trees. The pain in my bones and muscles and the burning of the huge blisters in both hands were unable to make me give up in my earnest determination to provide a more comfortable home for my precious little girls. Marisol brought cold lemonade and coffee to the construction site. Those treats, along with looking at our little girls running all around me and fetching me a glass of water every now and then, were huge spurs that made me squeeze strength from unexpected places at the toughest moments when I was about to falter.

When I managed to have the housing project structure almost complete, up to the level of the supports that would allow for the concrete deck to be cast, an unexpected frustration appeared. It was the year

1989, and the Union of Soviet Socialist Republics had collapsed, after 70 long years of a Leninist revolution. At the wrong time! What a debacle, what a disillusion, what a bucket of cold water was poured on top of my head just when I most needed the opposite. Thus the sadly celebrated Special Period started, bringing with it shortages and restrictions in the availability of construction materials. The new house, needless to say, was paralyzed, frozen, waiting for better times, though they were not foreseen at all, on any horizon, in the short or the long term. "Wow! There were too many of us and Catana gave birth," as my grandpa used to say at moments like that, when unbelievably the situation was turning even worse than what it was already. Could I someday be able to finish our house and enjoy it as I wanted? From then on, this became a another concern to add to the long string of anguishes in my already overstressed head. The construction of the house, far from being a solution, would now become one more problem instead.

Another challenge

With the changes implemented in the light of the latest transformations carried out by the Ministry of Education, one of the tasks we English teachers were charged with was precisely what I had already done in my previous experience at the technological institute, when I was fulfilling my social service. A syllabus for the twelfth grade students did not exist, but it needed to be created. We had to search for scientific texts that were consistent with the exact sciences and create exercises to guarantee the students' reading comprehension. It was a time consuming job that required patience, dedication, and research. That was indeed another challenge for my restless neurons, so I gave myself to the task right away by implementing a few basic actions that I had tested and confirmed by my empirical research.

If we wanted to succeed with the task requested, we needed to start out by examining the expectations of our students. It would have been way easier and less cumbersome just to look for a few texts, make some exercises about them, and take them to class. Those who were used to conformism would opt to do that as the easiest and fastest solution. I, however, could not tolerate the idea of entering the classroom with material that would cause the students to get bored and reject what I was presenting. They were in their last year of high school and were more concerned about their future major and entrance examinations to the university than about their English lessons. If we were to offer them reading materials randomly chosen and poorly prepared, it would not make any sense to go to the classroom to teach at all. I could not resign myself to such an alternative. I started out by applying a survey to find out what scientific topics were the most interesting to our students. That provided me with the necessary information for the selection of appealing texts that would ensure their attention and motivate them to try to understand them better. That was precisely the main goal of their grade in our subject. Eight texts with their corresponding sets of exercises were needed.

Information science, sex education, technological breakthroughs, and scientific discoveries, among others, occupied the first few ranks along that ladder of motivations and the professional vocations of our teenagers. The text on contraceptive methods and the one about bilingual children were, by far, the ones having the greatest acceptance. When going over the material carefully, I came to realize that both happened to be precisely the ones that had the best teaching aids available to complement written information with the visual support that is so greatly needed. It is no longer a secret that about 80 percent of knowledge is acquired by means of eyesight.

In the case of the bilingual children, the text was about research carried out by some French scientists with children who had been exposed to two languages since their birth. It presented their conclusions as well as related suggestions. My personal motivation with that linguistic research, also associated with my addiction to the English language, was so huge that I decided to use my firstborn, Wendy, as a guinea pig. She was newly born with a brand new brain, which would be able to show, in a rather short time, whether those scientists were right or wrong. I spoke to my baby girl, from the very beginning, only in English, including children's songs, tongue twisters, pieces of poetry, and everything else off the top of my head. I even composed a lullaby in English for her entitled "My Little Wendy," which I used to sing to her at bedtime in a rocking chair.

Those were months requiring a lot of patience. I took to documenting everything: each new word that she learned, every single advance she made showing certain progress in the acquisition of a second language. The French researchers were absolutely right, and I was demonstrating it in my own family setting. At the age of two, Wendy was already able to hold fluent conversations in English with me and could use simple sentences with basic vocabulary. It occurred to me that I should record a fifteen-minute conversation and start using it in class as a teaching aid to complement the text about bilingual children. It was a rousing success. My students were so motivated that they asked me to take the girl to school every now and then to see her speaking in English with me. They were flabbergasted, in awe, admiring both the little girl and her father, of course, who showed her off with great pride.

At the Pedagogical Meeting that school year, I managed to finish a booklet with scientific texts for twelfth-grade students of the Vocational High Schools of Exact Sciences. Due to the importance of such material, the board of directors of my school supported me thoroughly, and at the school printing press, in a very handicraft way, by typing, mimeographing, and book binding, we managed to make a whole stock of booklets for each of the six English departments of our school. I received an award during the scientific event at the Lenin School that year and, later on, at the municipal and provincial levels. I ended up at the national level with my scientific texts. During the Fifth National Pedagogical Meeting, held in Cojímar, at the headquarters of the Educational Improvement Institute in May 1989, I presented my paper, carrying a transcription on newsprint of my conversation with Wendy, an audio cassette with her tape recording, and an enlarged colored photo of her that was taken when she turned two years old.

The impact of my presentation before English professors from all over the country was amazingly gratifying. In that venue, experiences of all kinds had been shared, including those about teaching English to children at different educational levels, even in the first grades of elementary school. At about four o'clock in the afternoon, the turn for my paper was due, and the beehive was stirred up. Everyone wanted to take a copy of my little girl's recording. They made me feel like the most important professor – and father for that matter – in the world. My work was awarded at the national level; it was generalized to the rest of the Vocational High Schools of Exact Sciences of our country, and thanks to all that, I was later on bestowed with the Forgers of the Future Medal, which was granted by the Youth Technical Brigades of the Young Communist League. The solemn rally was held at the theater of the Ameijeiras Brothers clinical surgical hospital, and it included a money reward of $500.00 pesos, which was very welcome because, by that time, Wendy had her little sister Betsy, and obviously the needs of our family had increased. Thus, those unexpected extra pesos had arrived right on time.

My success with that experience became one more incentive for me to go on with my fondness for the English language. Some of my colleagues who worked in my department made fun of my obsession. Jokingly and as an endearment, they referred to me as either the "walking dictionary" or the "two-legged dictionary." Often, instead of looking up the meanings they needed in the bilingual dictionaries on their desks, they preferred to ask me. They could not understand how it was possible that, after staying in our school overnight in our weekly guard duty, instead of going back home to rest and catch up with my sleep, I would rather take my bike and go all the way through up to the Central Building in Ciudad Libertad, so many kilometers away from our school, to join an oral training post-graduate course. There was evidently something wrong with me, they commented. One had to be insane to do what I did, they claimed. They used to tell me, "You will keep on getting paid the same old salary. Your wage is not going to be raised." They were absolutely right. What they could never understand was that it was not a matter of money. That was not my motivation at all. That is why, in order to avoid getting involved in trivial arguments, I would just smile at them and reply, "Why do you suffer so much with what I enjoy?"

It was true, though, that steel willpower was needed to pedal so many kilometers at noon, right after lunch, particularly during the spring and the summer months, to bridge that huge distance between the Lenin School and Ciudad Libertad. It was especially difficult on the way back home in the late afternoon because my home was eight more kilometers beyond my school. I would leave Marianao in daylight and arrive home in Managua at night, sweaty, hungry, and completely bone-tired. I was exhausted, but I was happy because I had learned something new. I had grown in my English, and that was more than enough for me. That huge effort, according to the criterion of my colleagues, made a lot of sense the way I saw it, even if nobody else understood it. I could not care less if they didn't. For me, that upgrading was really a pleasure, an injection of intellectual and linguistic growth, and the satisfaction of a pressing need. As my grandmother used to put it, "If you are fond of scabies, it does not itch, and if it does, it doesn't bother you."

Fortunately, Marisol understood how important my ongoing upgrading in the English language was. She rejoiced with every single success that I attained throughout my journey towards the materialization of my dream. She happily sacrificed herself so that I could go to my post-graduate training courses in English every single school year. She was always cheerful and happy to see me so blissful, and I felt blessed to have her as my partner. She was undoubtedly the right woman to mother my daughters.

Once ,I arrived home late at night, exhausted after riding my bicycle for over twenty kilometers, to find that Wendy, just 8 months old, had fallen from the dining-room table. Marisol was so busy doing so many different things at the same time all by herself that she could not prevent it. Although Wendy was not badly hurt and was only frightened by her fall, she was crying uncontrollably. I felt guilty and selfish, and I told Marisol that I would quit my weekly post-graduate course.

Even in the middle of that stressful situation, she refused to allow that to happen. She encouraged me to move on, not to give up. That shows how altruistic and selfless she has always been. I have to admit that had it not been for her unconditional support, contribution, and encouragements, I would never have been able to have kept both our beautiful family and my career together. If my dream came true, I owe it to Marisol to a great extent, for she has always been there for me, every step of the way, through thick and thin, rain and shine.

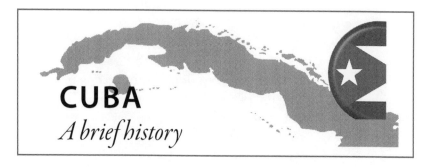

CUBA
A brief history

The Early 1990s: Collapse and Rebirth

In 1990, Fidel declared that Cuba was in a "Special Period in Time of Peace." The subsidies from the USSR had disappeared; our island would have to survive on its own. It was an austerity program to confront the nation's worst ever crisis; as Soviet oil imports dropped, Cuban industry and agriculture rapidly ground to a halt.

Previously, almost all our sugar went to the socialist countries. In return, we imported two-thirds of our food, nearly all of our oil, and 80 percent of our machinery and spare parts from them. When the Soviets pulled the plug, the Cuban economy went into free fall. From 1989 to 1993, our GDP fell by half. Imports fell by 75 percent. The impact on living standards was crippling. Without oil, the economy fizzled. Industrial production fell to just 15 percent of capacity.

The US saw the withdrawal of Soviet subsidies in 1989 as a great opportunity to administer a coup de grâce to our Revolution and implemented two pieces of legislation: the Cuban Democracy Act by Senator Robert Torricelli in 1992, which extended the trade ban to overseas subsidiaries of US companies, and the Cuba Liberty and Democratic Solidarity Act (Helms-Burton Law) in 1996, which aimed at hindering foreign investment in Cuba by threatening to prosecute US companies trafficking in property nationalized by Cuba and previously owned by US citizens.

Cuba moved dramatically to restructure the economy. The dollar was decriminalized in 1993, and the flow of migrants from the countryside into Havana jumped from 10,000 to over 26,000 a year. Worried by the inflow, the government restricted internal migration. Nonetheless, thousands of newcomers continued to be drawn to Havana and other tourist enclaves.

Several aspects of the Special Period worked to accelerate emigration. From 1993 to 1995, Cubans experienced a level of material scarcity unknown since the Revolution. The social safety network established by the Revolution was not only fraying, it was disintegrating. Basics such as food, medicine, and fuel were simply unavailable. The émigré community in the US continued to beckon, and more and more Cubans began to consider emigration an option. In the summer of 1994, some 35,000 Cubans fled to the US in fragile sea craft. The US and Cuba reached an agreement known as the "wet foot, dry foot" policy (welcoming those arriving on US soil and returning those picked up at sea) to end the uncontrolled exodus in favor of establishing a quota of 20,000 yearly visas for Cubans wanting to migrate to the US. The agreement did not, however, improve relations between the countries.

In 1990, Cuba spent 20.08 percent of its GDP on social benefits, including social security, health, and education. Despite the dislocations caused by the fall of the Soviet Union, Cuba's commitment to maintaining a social safety net was strengthened. Throughout the 1990s the share of Cuba's GDP spent on social programs increased by 34 percent.

Most critically, the 1990s brought complex social changes that challenged Cuba's commitment to equity. Rapid changes in income distribution brought new wealth to some and added to the number of economically vulnerable families, increasing social strains.

At the end of 1994, the Ministry of Tourism was created. Several capitalist corporations were founded with the goal of fully developing the tourist industry, destined to become the country's most important source of revenue. But tourism also has had a political impact. Cuban socialism was based on the concept of equality and equal access. The tourism industry challenged that ideology because it operated as a dollar-dependent enclave within the country. Cubans working in this industry could earn dollars to spend on basics like food and clothing.

The country decided to go full throttle on tourism development. Italian, Spanish, and Canadian tourists flocked to the island and investment in industry boomed. Joint ventures worth $600 million were underway in 1997, and dozens of new resorts were in the works. As the 20th century closed, Cuba walked a tightrope – adapting socialist values and principles to a new capitalist-tinged economic plan.

The Sadly Celebrated Special Period

Then Jesus said to his disciples, "Therefore I tell you,
do not worry about your life, what you will eat;
or about your body, what you will wear.
Life is more than food, and the body more than clothes."
Luke 12:22–23

One day, in my eagerness to find out the availability of courses in different institutions, I learned that at the Foreign Languages School of Havana University, there was a whole cycle of translation-interpretation post-graduate courses, which had just begun. They were just what I had been looking for. They were the theoretical tools I needed to be able to realize my dream – if the greatest chance of my life ever came my way. During our training as teachers, we were taught an assortment of subjects including psychology, pedagogy, philosophy, didactics, linguistics, literature, grammar, phonetics, and many others; but we did not learn anything about translation-interpretation at all because that was not our professional profile.

I was anguished when I learned that a translation course had already started. I doubted that I would be accepted. However, the worst action is the one that never gets done. My grandma used to say that it wouldn't hurt trying, so I went there on a Friday afternoon. I tried to arrive as early as possible to talk with the professor, Lourdes Llansó, who was starting the class by teaching the note-taking technique intended for consecutive interpretation, a sort of shorthand using interpretation symbols of all kinds, including those created on our own. I let her know that I was aware that enrollment had been closed, the deadline had already expired, and I was not entitled to join the class, but that I had just learned about it, and that was why I was beseeching her to please, please let me enroll in her class or at least to audit it. Fortunately, she gave in, smiling at my energetic plea because I almost knelt down in front of her to make sure she would accept me in her classroom. I did not miss any sessions from then on and eagerly learned everything she taught us, doing the assigned activities with a lot of enthusiasm and actively participating in class whenever she would allow me to do so.

On the last lesson before the final test, I approached her and asked her earnestly to let me take the exam, just for practice, to test what I had learned; although I was aware that I did not have the right to an evaluation because my name did not appear on the official enrollment. My intention was merely to demonstrate to myself that I had indeed learned that for which I had been looking so intently and at long last, late but sure, I had managed to find. She did not even let me finish speaking. She kindly smiled and told me, "You are going to do the test, not because you are asking me to let you do it, but rather because I am the one who wants you to do it. You have gained that right with your attitude and with your own knowledge."

That very day, she added my name to her attendance record: an act of kindness, good will, and basic justice. I treated her to my widest smile, which stretched from ear to ear. I studied as I had never done before while getting ready for that final exam. I implemented the best of all the studying methods: namely, the repetitive-continuous-systematic-progressive one. I could not let her down after she granted me such an unexpected and wonderful opportunity. The following week, I took the test and got the five points that I desired so much. In that unique way, I earned my first official credit on my path toward the remote possibility of working as a translator – if eventually such a job were to show up. That grade was my very first score in translation, my first step towards my dream of eventually becoming a translator-interpreter.

I would play translator for a while

Because the Lenin School was a center of national reference in the Ministry of Education, it was frequently visited by foreign delegations. Whenever there was an English-speaking group visiting, mainly from the United States, I felt envious when witnessing the professional interpreters doing their job. Usually the visitors would stop at the language laboratories, and that would give me the chance to talk with them. I used to fully enjoy those short dialogues with the North American visitors, and step-by-step, I began to be bolder. The time came when the guides who led the delegations asked me if I wanted to translate a little bit, so they could take a break for a while.

Even though I got pretty nervous and felt my heart beating rapidly under my humble shirt, I volunteered very willingly and played translator for a while. I felt something like a poor boy playing with a toy borrowed from a rich boy. When I was enjoying it the most, the translators returned, and I wished for more time. As my great friend Vladimir used to say, those happy moments tasted like more. My joy was so great when I had each of those experiences that I did not even need to tell my wife about it when I arrived home. She was able to easily guess it just by looking at me. Women have that sixth sense always on call. They cannot be easily fooled. She would immediately ask me, rather stating it as a fact: "A delegation came to school today, didn't it?" "How do you know?" was always my question. "Your eyes are sparkling, and I only see you beaming like that when you are very happy." She was never mistaken in her witty perception. The eyes are indeed the windows to the soul.

Some times, when very large delegations visited our school and it became necessary to split them up, our school English teachers who were not teaching at that point were asked to help with interpretation and to serve as guides. In our school there were about 50 English professors in six teaching units. Some of them would hide themselves to avoid the task, which they feared for various reasons or because they did not like to do it and it was not required.

I, on the contrary, would regret it a lot if I could not translate because I happened to be teaching. If I was available, I would immediately walk to the central block where visitors were gathered. I was always in a hurry, experiencing a mixture of nervousness and euphoria that would shoot my adrenaline to the very top. That routine became a habit, and I ended up believing very seriously all the praise I used to get from the visitors and from the people who were in charge of them. They would encourage me frequently by saying things such as, "Young man, what are you still doing here? You've got what it takes to be an interpreter. The only thing that you need is practice." My

God, how I liked and needed to hear those praises! Each time that I did those sporadic translations, I levitated increasingly higher. They made me soar and dream, both asleep and awake. Anyway, they just made me happy.

In the summer of 1991, Cuba was the site of the Physics International Olympiad, which was held at our school. Almost all the members of the English staff were asked to help because the event was conducted in English. Each foreign delegation was made up of five high school youth. I was charged with the one from Italy. One of the activities scheduled within the framework of that Olympiad was a visit to the pavilions of Expocuba.

When all the delegations had gathered in the lobby of that huge fair facility's central hall, a local official asked who the translator was so as to start with welcoming remarks and an introduction to his facility. I was not given time to think about it. A hand pushed me forward very strongly, and a male voice shouted over my head, "This one over here!" It had been Jaime, one of my colleagues, who immediately pushed the hot potato away by passing it over to me. I did not have time to refuse because the official was already speaking, addressing the attentive, young international crowd. I began to interpret for him, trying to the best of my abilities to conceal both my insecurity and my nervousness. Luckily, I did a good job, and in the end, I was even glad that Jaime had pushed me forward. *Everything happens for a reason.*

The straw that broke the camel's back

The following year, 1992, Marta María Gómez (Martica) – a friend and colleague who worked in my department, the wife of Luís Marrón, an official of the Cuban Institute of Friendship with the Peoples – trying to help me with what I liked the most – told Marrón about my passion for the English language and particularly for translation. That was how, in April of that year, I managed to get involved as a volunteer, rendering my services at the Julio Antonio Mella International Camp in Caimito, for the 23rd contingent of the Venceremos Brigade. It would be my first experience facilitating communications between North Americans and Cubans in solidarity activities.

That unforgettable experience was the straw that broke the camel's back. All remaining doubts about my true professional vocation disappeared. I demonstrated to myself that all those who had encouraged me so many times to make up my mind and take a step to change my profession were right. I drew the conclusion that so many people could not be wrong.

When I saw the professional interpreters doing their job in the presentations, I was increasingly sure that I both wanted to do and was able to do what they did with relative ease. The only thing I needed was practice. Instead of hours on my buttocks, as it is said vulgarly about time spent in front of a computer, what I really needed were tongue hours and nothing else.

Upon returning home after those 15 days, I was never the same again. The little bug had entered my body and was threatening to stay there forever. From then on, I began to reject teaching. Even my wife realized it and occasionally asked, "What is wrong with you? You no longer go to school with the same enthusiasm you did before." She was absolutely right. I felt as if I did not have enough strength to pedal my bicycle to school. I was bored and indifferent and began to feel very bad. This also overlapped with the worst stage of the so-called Special Period. In fact, there was nothing special about it but its name.

In the Venceremos Brigade, I had met John Murcko, a lawyer from Oakland, California, with whom I struck up a friendship and kept up correspondance. In one of his letters, he told me that he was coming to Cuba as a member of the first US-Cuba Friendshipment Caravan organized by IFCO-Pastors for Peace. They would be arriving in November 1992 and would be lodged at the Tritón Hotel in Miramar. In his letter, he urged me to go to the hotel one evening because he was bringing me some books for teaching English as a second language using the Spectrum method, and he wanted to hand them to me personally.

At that time, with the shortages generated by the pressing economic crisis and the skyrocketing rise of prices everywhere, I felt compelled to start teaching privately, beginning in October, 1992. Even though in those hard times, doing so was illegal, I was neither stealing nor begging for money from anyone, so I never hesitated nor did I have the slightest scruple when doing it. It was a survival strategy. The money I earned in those private classes was not even enough to pay for the sacks of charcoal that I had to buy at the inflated price of 100 pesos a bag. It was used as fuel for cooking because kerosene was unavailable most of the time. The charcoal was made out of very bad quality wood, so it did not burn long and soiled everything with soot. So much grime and no detergent or soap with which to wash the dishes!

Now I am really insane

At last, the long expected day came in November when the visitors arrived in Cuba. I decided to travel all the way to the Tritón Hotel in Miramar to pick up the promised books despite the critical conditions of our public transportation system back then. The books would be very useful for the private classes that provided me with extra income.

That day, something happened that left me very worried, to such an extent that I even thought that after so much stress I was losing my mind. After waiting for a very long time in La Víbora, I managed to get on board a bus of the 100 route.

Upon arriving at the Tritón Hotel, the Caravan buses were ready to depart for a reception that the Caravan members were to have with Fidel. I recognized several people who had come a few months before with the Venceremos Brigade, but when I asked them about Murcko, they told me that he had to take care of a very important litigation at the last minute, and that was why he had been unable to come.

It was like having a bucket of cold water suddenly poured over my head. I had tried so hard to get to that place only to get such a disappointing piece of news. I had been so excited, looking forward to getting those wonderful books on which I was already counting, but I had miserably wasted my time. How frustrated I was!

Then I remembered that the route 100 bus on which I had come would be back in a few minutes because its final destination was the nearby El Náutico beach. I could not afford to miss it for the world. I was lucky and managed to get on it once again at the 3rd Avenue and 70th Street bus stop. My state of mind could not have been worse. When the bus crossed 5th Avenue, a woman getting off at the next stop stood up and gave me her seat. I was so tired and downcast that I did not have words to thank her. I just dropped down on that hard plastic seat, leaning my head against the dirty glass pane of the window. It was right then and there that the unheard-of happened to me. I heard a voice, and even though it was deep down in my being, it was not my own. It was telling me lovingly, "Don't worry. You are going to work with the pastors and will even be on TV."

I heard that prediction very clearly despite all the noise of the bus engine and the muttering of the people on the bus. I shook my head several times, kind of scared, and even laughed at myself. I thought, "Now I am really insane. This is just what I needed." That voice repeated the same thing three or four times with the same intonation and at the same pace. Then it let me alone. All the way back home, I tried to find logic, a cause, or a reason for such a revelation. Or was I by any chance losing my sanity? I will never know, but I am as sure that I heard that voice as I am sure about the fact that I am writing this book. I had many other experiences of that nature.

After the trip, I went on as usual, working at school, which in the light of new shortages of all sorts associated with the Special Period, had restructured the timetable of its professors to make sure we did not have to go to work every day, but only when we had to teach or to carry out specific activities. This situation made it possible for me to open a new group for private classes in the morning on those free days, and that was exactly what I did.

As I described previously, the decade of the 1980s was the best of all for me. Many important things happened to me that I will never forget. Little did I know that the following decade would be just the opposite, the appalling onset of what would later be known as the Special Period, which was already powerful and was felt not only in our household kitchen, but in the family economy and our daily social life.

It was not special at all

Just as the '80s were undoubtedly the golden decade within the revolutionary period, the '90s became the hardest years of the so-called Special Period. Usually, one has the tendency to associate the adjective "special" with good, pleasant, unique things; for the semantic load of this word reminds us of positive aspects.

That was the name given, however, to the 1989 economic crisis in our country. It followed the collapse of the former Soviet Union and the other Socialist Eastern European countries with which our island used to have 85% of its foreign trade. At the same time, the US economic, commercial, and financial blockade against Cuba was intentionally tightened even further, precisely aimed at suffocating a whole people out of starvation and despair.

I was never able to understand why this period was called "special." The way I saw it, it was not special at all. I could not see the common sense anywhere, no matter how hard I tried to find it. But, anyway, it is said that common sense is the least common of all senses. There are some unique little words that really give us a hard time. It is better not to dig too deeply into them lest one ends up with a headache.

Many times I have heard that true recovery from a crisis of that nature is witnessed in the kitchens of regular citizens. As long as what to cook tomorrow is a constant concern for the great majority of poor families, we cannot speak in terms of an economic recovery.

Even though it currently can be difficult to solve many problems, nothing compares to what we lived through at the beginning of the '90s, particularly during 1993 and 1994, which were, by far, the two worst years within that awful decade. The true creativity of Cubans was displayed during those hard years as we strove for the survival of our whole people.

In our family, as in so many others, we had to use our ingenuity the best we could in order to cope with daily life challenges. One could never lean one's head against the pillow and really rest, as God commands. If we managed to solve one problem, others soon appeared, and many times, they would combine so as not to give us any respite.

Our daughters, Wendy and Betsy, were born in early 1987 and late 1988, respectively. When the impact of the crisis began to be felt with the beginning of the last decade of the 20th century, they were still very young, for they had not even reached school age yet.

Personal hygiene items were among the pressing shortages. Riding a bicycle over a distance of eight kilometers in the full summer was incompatible with the most elementary requirements in that regard. Lacking deodorant, we resorted to sodium bicarbonate to neutralize body odor from armpits that became unpleasant at the slightest neglect.

Since we did not have toothpaste, there was no other choice but to use sodium chloride, regular table salt. As there was no shampoo or detergent at all, rainwater would smooth the hair better than regular water out of the tap, and it would make more foam when doing the laundry.

We used to boil the green peels of plantains and bananas and grind them in the meat mincer to produce some sort of vegetable "mince" to replace ground beef, thus trying to fool our depressed palates. When we ran out of rice, we broke up spaghetti or noodles and pretended they were rice grains.

Once, when we were missing animal protein so badly, we ate a wild cat that we had stuffed with rice and roasted on a stick over charcoal embers. Our neighbor Elier Machado found the cat somewhere in the woods. That timely feline tasted delicious, with a flavor somewhere between chicken and rabbit that would whet anyone's appetite.

Marisol was the exception to the rule. She refused to taste it, claiming that she was nauseated. Our girls, on the contrary, ate it willingly and the following morning asked me if there were any cat leftovers.

As to the financial part, we implemented many initiatives that proved to be highly successful, even though they took a high toll in terms of the time employed in them plus the energy that was required to be able to carry them out successfully.

Gradually, I became an unusual hybrid, an interesting combination of state-run/private English teacher, street vendor, small agricultural producer, craftsman, carpenter, painter, and peddler – all in one person. I was something like an orchestra man, musician, poet, and crazy man. Days needed to have more than 24 hours in order for me to do everything I came up with, which was aimed at earning enough money to make ends meet and ensure a minimum of comfort for my family. It was very frustrating.

On the small parcel of land at the back of our house, I planted string beans and kitchen tomatoes that were perfect to cook with in our Cuban cuisine. Both crops required a short cycle, which provided me with an almost constant flow of harvested products, although on a rather small scale. My colleagues who lived in the city and did not have the opportunity to garden were my most grateful clients.

I still recall how embarrassed I was when, one afternoon, a Spanish professor approached me to ask if it was true that I was selling string beans. I was glad to think that she might be a new client, so I enthusiastically affirmed, "Yes, I am. How many handfuls do you want?" She had not come to buy anything from me. As a matter of fact, she had heard the rumor and was there to keep me from doing that illegal activity within the school setting. She had been assigned that task in her cell of the Communist Party of Cuba. Despite my discretion in selling the produce, as it is so rightly stated even in our pop songs: There is always an eye looking at you.

I went to the woods and returned with sacks full of leucaena and acacia seedpods. We then boiled them to soften them and while they were still moist and tender, threaded them with a needle and string before hanging them to dry in the sun and wind. Later we varnished them.

Then we made necklaces, bracelets, and earrings, which we wrapped in cellophane paper and sold to our trade union leaders who were always looking for inexpensive little gifts to pass out on occasions such as Teacher's Day, the International Women's Day, Mother's Day, and so forth.

Availing myself of the great blessing of having my father's carpenter's shop quite handy and resorting to my very basic skills in drawing and painting, I designed little cartoon characters for children's cribs and decorative figures of cooks with pegs to hang washrags and matching pot holders. I was in charge of everything that was done using wood, paint, and varnish.

I had become an expert with my father's borer and circular saw, outlining the contours of those figures in small pieces of plywood. Marisol, in turn, was in charge of the handicrafts that utilized her old Singer sewing machine as well as her skills in cutting, sewing, knitting, and embroidering. Long before Mother's Day, we would get all our products ready. When at long last the selling date arrived, we both went to work: me, to the Lenin School, she, to the radio assembling factory. Each of us carried a backpack chock-full of items that lasted what a cake at a school gate would.

At the end of the day, we returned home extremely tired after working so many days in a row in that grueling job, staying up until very late at night, but satisfied after having raised the additional funds that our housekeeping economy demanded. Anything would do but stealing, as my grandpa used to say.

I was aware that what we were doing was beyond the framework of the law, but I was managing to do it at the expense of a lot of sweat and personal effort. It was a survival strategy. Besides that, the one who was not sinning should throw the first stone. On second thought, all those who were buying those crafts and agricultural produce from me would fit right in as perfect criminal candidates when committing the crime of purchasing illegal items.

I did all those things without neglecting the preparation and the teaching of my private lessons in the evenings, three times a week, in two different classes. No wonder I was skinny and haggard with huge dark circles under my eyes. As a matter of fact, I tried by all means not to get undressed in front of the mirror of the dressing table, so as not to feel pity for myself when witnessing all my ribs sticking out under my skin.

My collarbones sank so deeply that they looked like soap-dishes. I was so scrawny and malnourished that it was painful to see myself naked. But I hoped that better times would eventually arrive. My little girls would certainly deserve all that sacrifice and much more. Thinking about them, I managed to find the strength that I needed to move on, no matter what.

As we Cubans rightly state, it was not easy at all. That would have to change some day, somehow, although I did not have the slightest idea about how, let alone when. In the meantime, we had to fight tooth and nail, comforting ourselves with our well known proverb: *There is no evil lasting one hundred years or body enduring it.*

Those 16 kilometers of daily biking were taking a toll. I was becoming increasingly skinnier. My spine hurt whenever I fell into a pothole or hit a bump on the road. It goes without saying that I was very poorly fed, with only one small cup of black coffee for breakfast, a lousy lunch at school, and no snacks or refreshments between meals.

I was so starved, particularly at mid-afternoon, that I resorted to chewing mouthfuls of brown cane sugar that we kept in our department to placate the dragon that was consuming us all slowly but relentlessly. The only thing available on the cafeteria menu of the central building of Ciudad Libertad, where I used to go every week for the post-graduate course – which I never quit, not even in the hardest times of that appalling stage – was a hot infusion made out of orange tree leaves. I drank it upon arriving there, drenched in sweat and totally exhausted, so as to recover a little bit from exhaustion after riding my bicycle over 20 kilometers, many times pedaling against the wind.

Many basic items, such as soap, detergent, shampoo, deodorant, cooking oil, fuel with which to cook, and electricity were unavailable to our family. Our girls were increasingly losing body weight, and their collarbones protruded more every day. There were days when the only things available on the table were black bean soup and cabbage salad without dressing.

I still carry deeply engraved an imperishable image of my girls' disappointed and sad little faces whenever they looked at the contents of their small plates. They pushed them slowly towards the center of the table, shaking their small blond heads in a determined and unequivocal rejection of eating the same thing for the umpteenth time.

I wore myself out every day, trying to get more money by illegally teaching private classes. I arrived home very late every night, exhausted from the extra effort I was making to ensure us a minimum of resources. Sometimes, I was so tired that I would lie on my back on the floor to stretch my muscles and rest my whole body, which was complaining about so much daily biking. Often I did not have enough energy to get up, take a bath, have dinner, and go to bed, for each cell in my body was asking me to remain in that cadaver position, eternally quiet, and to rest until I was satiated, if that was even possible.

Only God knows how I felt during those difficult times and everything that crossed my worried mind. I tried long and hard, but I did not manage to see the light at the end of the tunnel. Oh my God! How much longer would such an unpleasant situation last? How much worse could it get? Would I be in condition to undertake the challenges?

I spent the little additional money that I managed to bring home to buy vegetable charcoal, which we used as fuel so we could cook. It was the only alternative left after the kerosene shortages. That is what we previously used to cook at home. I had to ride four kilometers to get those sacks of charcoal, and I had to bring them back bound to the rack of my bicycle.

Our girls did not have dress shoes, and it was both hurtful and humiliating for us when they were invited to a birthday party and had to wear tennis shoes along with the same old dresses they always wore. Other children, some of them with relatives abroad, would boast about their patent leather shoes, which were in fashion back then. Everything was very hard to deal with for us as parents.

I even felt guilty for having brought my two little girls into this world. They did not deserve to go through so many shortages. I certainly did not want them to endure what I had already endured myself. I had studied a lot and sacrificed myself to be sure that they would have a better future that was more humane and promising.

Being the head of my family, I was aware that I was both the provider and the protector of this new and beautiful family, which I had created with so much love.

My God how much longer could I hold on and stand such an unbearable situation!

Be careful with what you say

One morning when Wendy was about three years old and her little sister, Betsy, was not even two, before leaving for my school, extremely worried due to the dream I had the night before, I asked Marisol beseechingly to please take good care of our little girls. It was Monday, so

THE SADLY CELEBRATED SPECIAL PERIOD

it was my turn to stay overnight in the school on my guard duty team. I would be up until noon the next day, and then – as every Tuesday right after lunch – I would go straight to the Ciudad Libertad school complex in Marianao for the post-graduate course that I wouldn't miss for the world.

I explained to Marisol that in my dream, rather my nightmare, I saw a small child drowning in a bathtub. She, knowing me so well, as if she had given birth to me, said, "Go in peace. Today I will stay with the girls overnight at my mum's house, so they will be better taken care of with their grandma, who loves them so much." That made me feel much better. I tried not to worry so much with each and every dream I had because, if I did, I would not be able to live in peace at all. It would be unbearable and inhumane.

By the time I returned home from the post-graduate course the following day, it was night already. I was falling apart from hunger and fatigue after pedaling so many kilometers on that heavy Chinese bicycle, but my weariness disappeared the moment I entered the house and looked at Marisol's face.

She did not have to say anything for me to know right away that something bad had happened. She kissed me very seriously and told me, "Don't freak out. Everything is under control. We were frightened, but it is over now. You need to be careful with what you say." She led me to our bedroom, turned on the light, and showed me Wendy. She was already asleep in her crib, but one of her eyes was totally covered with a piece of gauze bound with adhesive tape.

My soul froze when she told me that when the girl was peacefully playing in her grandmother's garden, she stumbled against a cactus tree while she was running and had one of those terrible thorns stuck in her right eyeball.

She had to be rushed to the polyclinic first, and from there, she was immediately transferred in an ambulance to the Dr. Ángel Arturo Aballí Hospital where, in an emergency ophthalmology microsurgery, they successfully removed all the fragments of the thorn that nearly left my little girl one-eyed. Thank God, it did not damage her pupil or iris. Miraculously it only penetrated the white part of the eyeball, near the inner eye corner, just a few millimeters from her cornea. It could easily have detached her retina as well, heaven forbid!

I was flabbergasted when hearing the details of that hair-raising account, for I had had the gut feeling that something bad was going to happen. I was still trying to picture the event and digest all that painful information when Marisol added, "That is not the end of the story. There is more. Do you still remember what you dreamed about? Chito almost got himself drowned. He was scooped out of the old bathtub that is full of rainwater over there, behind Marlene's backyard. What a scary experience they went through with him!" She meant Eliercito, my father's wife, Natalia's, grandson, who lived in the house next door. No wonder then that I had to respect my animal instincts. With such thundering, who was going to sleep?

The most sincere and desperate prayer

In early December 1992, I set out riding my bike to see my grandfather, looking for a piece of wise advice, an oasis, something to hold on to, so as to walk out of the hole I had fallen into. He was sitting on the church square when I approached him. He was very concerned when he looked at my face because he was able to read very clearly on it all the anguish that was consuming me in silence.

He told me that I had to have a lot of faith in Saint Lazarus, that I had to be very strong, that I should not freak out in front of anything, that I should take advantage of the upcoming pilgrimage and join it, that I should walk all the way to the shrine of El Rincón on the eve of December 17th and that once over there, I should ask Saint Lazarus to help me get out of my depression.

That was exactly what I did, down to the letter. My grandfather loved me very much, and I enjoyed knowing deep down that I was his favorite grandchild. He had said so himself many times. I was sure that whatever he advised me to do was for my own sake and that even if it didn't work, it would not hurt me at all. In order to feel better, even if slightly, I would not withhold any effort or sacrifice.

It was up to me, so on December 16, 1992, when I arrived home from school, without sharing my plan with anybody but my wife, I put on two pairs of socks to avoid foot blisters during a very long walk of approximately 22 kilometers and a long-sleeved wool shirt because it was cold. I dropped a water bottle into a little handbag and set out on my pilgrimage with all the faith of the world along with a good share of concealed prejudices.

I did not want to be seen participating in this pilgrimage, because it would not be well construed by many people, and I was quite aware of the fact that it was not expected from me. That was why, in order to disguise myself a little bit, I put on a dark baseball cap. Nobody had to know what I had decided to do. I did not have dark sunglasses; otherwise, I would very likely have put them on, as well.

This was a very private problem, which I had to solve on my own, trying by all means to recover my emotional balance and desire to live and striving for the sake of my family and my own well being. When you come to think about it, I was not committing a crime. Hundreds of people took pilgrimages every year, and so many people could not be wrong. If they did it in such large numbers, it was very likely because it had worked out for them. I was totally determined to do it, no matter what, for the sake of my two daughters. For them, I was willing to make any sacrifice whatsoever to improve a situation that was turning increasingly worse day by day.

I began to walk slowly, for hours on end, eventually joining dozens of other pilgrims. All of us were heading to the same destination, united only in one faith, a common purpose: asking help from Saint Lazarus on the occasion of his day and at his national sanctuary.

I witnessed human scenes that were truly heartrending and amazing. It is incredible everything that a human being is able to do for his own sake and out of faith. I saw people who were bleeding profusely, dragging themselves along the street, almost naked, dirty, grimy, dressed in jute sackcloth, pulling thick chains bound to heavy rocks of unimaginable dimensions. They were all paying their vows, eternally grateful before the granted petitions. It was something like being inside the live taping of a film – a horror movie or a thriller. Without a doubt, I may say that it was one of the strongest experiences that I have ever had in my whole life.

It was still about half an hour short of midnight when at long last, I managed to reach the main gate of the shrine. It was next to impossible to get closer to the chapel before the midnight bell tolled, which would indicate the arrival of the long expected and traditional December 17th, Saint Lazarus's Day.

That uncontrollable human crowd started to push me, an inch at a time, like the flow of a huge flooded river, overflowing, drifting, out of control. I was fearful for my own physical safety because it was really dangerous to be inside that human sea, euphoric, overwhelmed with faith and hope, gratitude and confidence, carrying flowers and candles, dogs, crutches, wearing jute sack clothes and violet pieces of fabric, and covered with skin sores.

What a deep emotion that was! I will never forget it! It was scary to be part of that unique, unrepeatable experience, to be aware that this would be both debut and farewell at the same time. There are no words capable of expressing thoroughly what I felt and lived through during those minutes before, during, and after the midnight bell tolled.

The people were hysterical. They were crying, laughing, shouting, asking, hugging one another without having met before, kneeling down, jumping, singing, and dancing. Not even in the most charismatic worship services have I seen anything like it. I still remember that while I was in the middle of that frenzied and wild crowd – hardly breathing, paralyzed with so many people around me – I asked Saint Lazarus to help me get out of that crisis in which I found myself.

When I managed to disengage myself from that entangled human heap – inching myself away from it, a step at a time, advancing a meter per minute at best – when relaxing all the tension I had built up until that point and having my body cooled down, I felt that all my bones and muscles were suddenly hurting. I could hardly walk. I was personified subhuman tiredness in the flesh itself. I had accomplished the mission my grandfather had commanded me to do.

Originally, I had planned that pilgrimage to be one way only, just like most people do it; however, once there, in spite of the superlative exhaustion and strain that I was feeling in every single piece of my whole body, I suddenly felt the pressing need of scourging myself, a self-imposed punishment so to speak, like an irrational masochist or a cloistered monk. I needed to experience physical pain, extreme exhaustion, hunger, fatigue, and cold in my own flesh.

I do not know how to explain why I made the decision that I did, but truthfully, it was an unfathomably spiritual need that I felt compelled to meet at that moment. It was a very cold, full moon night, which undoubtedly made that unique experience a whole lot more bearable. I could have taken some kind of transportation on the way back, but I preferred to walk all that long way back home, even if it took the whole night for me to do it. It had been decided already.

With the passing of every single minute that ticked away, my feet hurt even more along with my hip joints and my life itself. I had to, as it is colloquially said, ask permission from one of my feet to be able to lift the other, so as to advance. When I was approaching the Sierra Maestra neighborhood – just a few kilometers in the outskirts of Santiago de Las Vegas, towards Managua – I suddenly felt as if I was going to faint.

I was afraid because I was walking all by myself along the shoulder of that road really late into the wee hours of the night. I had to stop for a few minutes in order to recover the scarce energies left in my body reserves. The physical exhaustion mingled with the spiritual emotion and my deep desire to improve my life and that of my family. I could not afford to fly off the handle when my wife and my little daughters needed me the most. I could not let them down in that unfair way. I could not afford to lose my sanity when I needed it the most as a human survival strategy.

That cold night under the moonlight, the silence of the very early morning hours witnessed the most sincere and desperate prayer in my whole life. A few days before, during a very bad moment of a brief nervous breakdown, I lost control and, for the first and only time, I hit Wendy's little face when, while running inside the house, she bumped into her little sister and knocked her down to the floor.

It was an apparently harmless slap, but it made her nose bleed. That hurt me in the core of my soul. I felt extremely guilty and knew then and there that I would never ever forgive myself for having done that.

I will take that thorn to my grave nailed to my heart. Nothing at all that I could ever do – no matter how good it may be – will ever be able to compensate for that huge injustice that I committed with my little girl. I know too well that she forgives me, but the point is that I cannot forgive myself. The fact is that I gave an undeserved blow to her, who I should have been protecting the most, particularly during those difficult times. There is nothing in the whole world capable of justifying such a violent attitude from a parent towards his child. I will forever ask God to forgive me for that reproachable action.

Even though at that point in time I did not know the right way to pray (if there is one), I looked up at the sky – completely cloudless in the peace and tranquility of the night – and asked Jesus Christ in a very humble way that if his existence was true, he should please then help me recover my sanity so as to able to cope with that unbearable situation.

I did not want more money or luxurious things or preferences: the only thing I was begging Him for was not to let me be held by violence under any circumstance whatsoever. I asked that He should allow me to ensure, at any price necessary, the stability of my family and the happiness of my daughters. I confessed to him, with tear drops falling down my cheeks, that I was no longer enjoying my job as I used to, and that I needed to find another job in which I could feel encouraged to give the very best of myself, as I had always done up until that date, even if it were not economically advantageous.

My request was quite sincere for, the way I see it, money is not everything in life. Sometimes the wealthiest are the unhappiest people on earth. I was not asking for money, but simply for happiness, peace and harmony. I needed to have irrefutable evidence of the divine existence, which would encourage me to move on, to strive without fainting, and to succeed in life. When I managed to calm down, shortly after that plea of sheer catharsis that shook me from head to toes, I resumed my slow walking, aching even more, but determined to get home even if I had to drag myself along just like all those pilgrims I had witnessed with my own eyes a few hours earlier.

Finally, almost fainting, I managed to get home at about five o'clock in the morning, when the roosters were already crowing, announcing that daybreak was coming soon. Marisol was already very worried because she did not expect me to take that long to return. In the midst of that country where we lived, there were no phones within a diameter of several kilometers around us; therefore, communication possibilities were absolutely non-existent.

I was feeling so bad that she had to undress me and help me get on the bed, for I could not do it all by myself. I could not even raise my feet on my own. A few hours later, I was unable to walk due to the excruciating pain that I had in my hipbone. I could not go to work that day. It was impossible to ride my bicycle in that state even if I had the willpower to do it, which was not the case. I had pleased both my grandpa and my conscience. The only thing left for me to hope now was that either Saint Lazarus or Jesus Christ or God, Himself, or the three of them at the same time, could grant me what I had petitioned from them so faithfully.

There was something wrong with me

When I got upset that day and slapped my little Wendy's face, I realized that I was losing control, that the feelings and emotions with so much accumulated frustration and helplessness were sprinting ahead of me, and I could hardly handle them any more.

I got upset quite easily for any reason and sometimes, for no apparent reason at all, I started quarrelling, which had never characterized me before. Even in school, I had some intense arguments with colleagues in my department over trivials, things that were not really worth the while at all.

Obviously, there was something wrong with me. One day, I almost got into a fistfight with Agustín García, our nearest neighbor. Another time, I held an empty liter of milk, planning to smash it against the head of Rey Alvarez (Papito), my brother-in-law, during a huge outburst of unjustified wrath.

From his carpenter's shop, which was very close to our little house, my father heard every now and then my unjustifiable outbursts, which were making him worry a lot, particularly because he had always seen me as an example of good behavior with family and interpersonal relations. One morning, knowing for sure that I was home alone, and feeling the pressing need to talk to me and let me know about his concern and desire to help, he approached me.

Holding a hoe in my hands, I was painstakingly cleaning a small drainage ditch in my backyard. It was that dialogue with my father that really sensitized me to my nervous breakdown. He advised me that I should go to see either a doctor or a medium who could take care of me because, if I continued like that, I could end up in very bad shape. He reminded me to think of my little girls and pointed to what it would be like for them if I lost my mind. I promised him that I was willing to go anywhere and to do whatever it took to make sure that I could be normal and feel all right again.

After one of those unbearable fights, Marisol was fed up – "her pipe filled up with smoke," as we country people claim – and in order to avoid further complications, she decided to leave with our two daughters to live at her mother's house.

When I was left all alone, not even knowing how to fry myself an egg, the whole world came tumbling down for me. It was like losing water and air at the same time. I felt like the most despicable person on earth, and an acute depressive crisis got hold of me as well as some unfathomable guilt feelings. I felt so under the weather during those days that I decided not only to go and see a psychiatrist, but a spiritualist as well. I had to get out of that pit somehow.

What I was concerned about the most was my mental health. I was terrified by the thought that I could go crazy if I did not act immediately to avoid it. If I did not do something right away, I could easily end up hospitalized at a psychiatric facility, as so many other people had. Would, by any chance, the prediction of my junior high classmates materialize, "Mazorra is asking for crazy people, and Alberto is almost there?" No way, I could not allow that to happen.

This was the second time that I had to be absent from my job, giving my health priority; but this time, it was not a physical problem but an emotional one. Sure enough, I was diagnosed with a temporary neurosis, and I began to go every day to the Santa Amalia Day Hospital in Arroyo Naranjo, where I was taken care of holistically by a team

THE SADLY CELEBRATED SPECIAL PERIOD

of psychologists and psychiatrists, using individual, marriage, group, and occupational therapy, as well as electro-dream, physical exercises, recreational activities, and medicines prescribed by the physicians, of course.

All those things helped me to some extent, but I looked like a zombie under the strong effect of the antidepressant and anxiolytic pharmaceuticals prescribed for me. This comprehensive multi-therapy was supposed to last for at least three months.

After a few days elapsed, however, Natalia, my father's wife, volunteered to take me to see a very good female medium whom she knew.

As I was not really feeling better, but rather very weird, confused and disoriented from taking all those pills and listening daily to the problems of so many patients around me, I decided that it would not hurt to see a medium, for I would not lose anything at all by trying.

Natalia came to the clinic to pick me up at noon one day and took me to Santos Suarez to see Berta Zumeta, a renowned medium with a widespread reputation. She was a stocky, heavy-set, mulatto woman, very sweet and talkative, with a deep voice, rather husky, extremely caring, which inspired confidence right away.

This was the first time that I would be checked by a medium, and I approached it with a mixture of curiosity, incredulity, skepticism, and nervousness. I had references from my grandfather Pedro, who used to consult Iluminada, in La Palma, whom he trusted a lot.

The sheer fact of meeting Berta Zuma was impressive. When we were introduced and she made eye contact with me, her hair visibly stood on end, and she told Natalia, "Oh my God. This young man has a very strong mediumship!" I did not know what she was talking about, but I guessed that it had to do with my extra-sensory perceptions.

That first remark stressed me out a little bit. She soon realized the impact her words had had on me, and she began to chitchat excitedly to relax me. Natalia let her know that I did not want anybody to know about my consultation with her, so as to avoid what people might say. She laughed while making that comment and widely smiling, spreading her thick lips all over her kind face, she told me, "Don't you worry, sonny. Nobody will know about it from me. But if this makes you feel any better, I want you to know that there was this official from the Ministry of the Interior who came to see me very stealthily, sneaking about, asking me to please keep absolute discretion, for nobody in his job could get to know about what he was up to. His surprise was really big when walking back into the waiting room he ran into – out of those weird coincidences that life has – none other than his own boss."

I had to resort to my linguistic skills during that consultation, for the spirit that took hold of her was from an old African slave man who spoke in the ñáñigo dialect. She smoked a thick cigar and was amazingly transformed, taking on a voice and some facial and body gestures that were really noteworthy.

She told me many things that impressed me a lot and many others that I doubted and questioned for a while because they seemed to be out of the question back then. She categorically affirmed that I was protected by the spirit of a very educated woman who, surrounded by many books, dressed in white, and seemingly a medical doctor, was my guardian angel.

She also told me that I would travel to other countries many times, that my daughters would travel even before I did, that I would work with foreigners, and that despite the fact that I was the youngest of all my siblings, I would become the head of them all. Before finishing, she asked me if I wanted to know anything else about my future. Even though I could not wait to get that whole thing that was scaring me over with, I took advantage of the chance to unload one of my greatest concerns, "When will I be able to finish my new house?"

After pondering my question for a while and rolling her eyes up, she earnestly asserted that I should not worry about that issue. She said I would never complete that house, for there was a better choice in store for me, and that my old dream of leaving the countryside and living in the city would come true.

Although I did not want to be disrespectful and was really longing in the bottom of my heart for that lady to be right, I refused to believe a forecast that was so tailor-made, fitting right in, matching exactly what I had desired all along.

When I said good-bye to her that afternoon, I thanked her most sincerely, but I doubted deep down the extent to which all those things would be true. She even advised me that I should attend their séances, special training sessions on Thursday evenings for people like me with the gift of the mediumistic capacity. She said that if I wanted, I could develop it by fully combining both theory and practice. She also said that by doing so, I could be useful too, helping other people who might need those services in the future. I told her I would think about it, although deep down I was quite sure that I would not do it because it was scary just to think about it.

Had she spoken to me about either the past or the present, I could have easily ignored what she said, for there were human ways to know about them. Besides that, I was aware that Natalia, my father's wife, knew her, so through Natalia, it was relatively easy to get to know about my personal problems.

However, to honor the strictest truth, almost everything she predicted was to be found in the future, and that could not have been fully known by anybody who was not gifted with supernatural powers. Would that be her case by any chance? I wondered. It was just a matter of time. Only the passage of time would either confirm or deny what she said.

I did not wait to finish the three scheduled months at the clinic. Pondering over the issue slowly, for now I had all the time in the world to do so, I drew the conclusion that the very best physician, the best medium, and the best of medicines – if I decided it firmly – were none other than myself.

I did not even complete the first month. On my own, I quit taking my medication, deliberately stopped going to the clinic, went back to school, and returned to my regular life.

I felt a very deep spiritual freedom when doing that and perceived that I was taking a burden from my mind. I could not go on in that state, so dependent on somebody else's will, fulfilling to the very letter every piece of advice given to me, and reacting as a weather vane at the mercy of the wind, even if it was out of good faith.

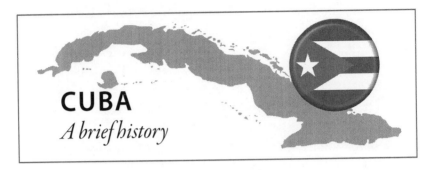

CUBA
A brief history

The Mid-1990s: Back From the Abyss

Starting in 1994, economic reforms began to gradually ease the crisis – but at the price of encroaching capitalism and consumerism. By the late 1990s, Cuba was inundated with material goods, but these goods were available only with dollars, and dollars were available only through income from exports, the tourist sector, or relatives abroad.

Cubans have lived with food rationing since 1962. Rice is a staple, but we don't grow enough, so we must import it from Asia. After supplies of fuel, fertilizer, and pesticides from the Soviet Bloc were cut off in the early 1990s, rice harvests at state farms fell by as much as 75 percent. The same situation was true for coffee, which to Cubans is almost a sacrament.

Food from the bodega is not enough to live on. It may take you halfway through the month, but no more. But despite the shortages, most people don't seem to hold the government accountable. Rationing has been around for so long, it's an accepted part of our daily life. And for the most part, Cubans sympathize with our state's efforts to distribute available food as fairly as possible.

During the 90s, our government implemented a number of reforms that fundamentally changed the face of our economy. It eased restrictions on the domestic economy and began to open up to foreign investment. It did so by developing the tourism industry and authorizing self-employment for 150 occupations.

The government's opening to small business was reluctant, and there were lots of complaints. For example, the state allowed small private restaurants called *paladares*, but no *paladar* was allowed more than 12 chairs; employees had to be family members; and license fees were stiff. Inspectors made surprise visits, and receipts had to be kept for proof of purchases.

The consequences of the "dollarization" of the Cuban economy were contradictory. More Cubans were able to purchase a wider variety of products, yet rising social and racial inequalities, increasing crime rates, and the expansion of the black market indirectly resulted from the proliferation of dollars.

Access to dollars could dramatically alter any Cuban's quality of life, creating rifts between those with access to dollars and those without. The lure of dollars created a strong pull towards the service and tourism industries, where pay and tips in dollars were much more common. Also, access to dollars reawakened racial tensions within the Cuban society.

Cubans of European ancestry had more access to dollars through what seemed to be their disproportional presence in the tourism industry. They also were more likely to have relatives abroad who could send remittances than did Cubans of predominantly African ancestry. This racialized "dollarization" further deepened the divide between Afro-Cubans and European-Cubans, which was, ironically, an inequality the Revolution had sought to erase.

The government also "rationalized" the sugar industry, shutting down inefficient mills and stabilizing production at four to five million tons. In a desperate attempt to garner hard currency to pay for imports of food, medicine, clothing, and spare parts, the government pursued foreign investors. Tourism and nickel production replaced sugar as the major dollar earners.

In January 1998, Pope John Paul II paid a historic visit to Cuba. He censured the US for its trade embargo while urging the Cuban government to cede political space to opposition voices. The Revolution then faced its biggest challenge: to build a pluralistic, participatory democracy based on social justice while finding a place in the emerging global economy.

The programs and subsidies that make up Cuba's safety net cover its citizens from cradle to grave. The 1999 Human Development Index ranked Cuba 58th out of 174 countries. Primary indicators for Cuba were: life expectancy at birth (75.7 years), adult literacy rate (95.9 percent), combined enrollment in school (72 percent), and increasing per capita income. In 1996, over 20 percent of the country's budget was devoted to health care and education. Enrollment in Cuban universities was then and now remains highly competitive. Fourteen percent of Cuban workers have a university degree.

The other major accomplishment of the Revolution had been health care, which remains free to every citizen. In all of the Third World, no country has achieved such remarkable success in such a short period of time. There was an impressive layered system of health care delivery from *consultorios* (small family clinics) to polyclinics, to hospitals and national research institutes. Basic health institutions are head and shoulders above Third World norms and, in some cases, ahead of Western countries. According to UNICEF, the infant mortality rate in Cuba fell from 60 deaths per thousand in 1958 to only 7.9 in 1996. This rate is roughly half that of Washington DC.

Free, high-quality health care and free education were the foundation of the Castro government's legitimacy. Yet, despite Havana's best efforts to maintain health and education budgets, cracks were beginning to show. The country's health-care facilities were also badly run-down and getting worse with the impact of the US economic blockade.

Yes, I Can Do It

*Have I not commanded you? Be strong and courageous.
Do not be terrified; do not be discouraged,
for the LORD your God will be with you wherever you go.*
Joshua 1:9

On Saturday, January 30, 1993, only a month after my breakdown and during one of the harshest years of the economic crisis, I arrived home from school early after riding my bike, and, being hungry and tired, I lay on the bed for a while to recover a little bit before going to the day-care center to pick up my girls.

There I was, lying on my back, thinking about a thousand problems and my situation, which was becoming increasingly unsustainable, when, suddenly, I heard a bicycle bell ring and shortly afterwards somebody knocking on my front door. A friend of mine, Juan Carlos, had come to let me know that officials from the Cuban Institute of Friendship with the Peoples (ICAP) were trying to locate me urgently. He said they needed to talk with me before 4 o'clock that afternoon; otherwise, they would have to find somebody else.

The sheer mention of ICAP filled me with such energy that I didn't really know where it came from. I was wearing shorts and flip-flops, but just like that, without combing my hair, I pulled a T-shirt over my head and rode my bike to town.

When, after many failed attempts, I managed, almost at 4 o'clock, to get through to the ICAP, Luis Marrón asked me flat out, "Albert, do you think you have the guts that it takes to be the translator for a Pastors for Peace delegation?" My knees were shaking. I was both startled and encouraged by the question. I was temporarily speechless, pondering what to say.

He, in turn, realizing my hesitation, insisted, "Listen up. This time is not what you did with the Venceremos Brigade. If you make up your mind, you will be the official interpreter for the group, and that entails radio and television interviews, press conferences, whatever it takes."

That timely clarification intimidated me even more instead of relaxing me. I was afraid to say yes, but I was even more fearful to lose that unique opportunity for which I had long been waiting. Nothing has been written about cowards, and besides that, he who doesn't take risks does not break even.

I told him, "I cannot promise you that everything is going to be perfect, but YES, I can do it! Just tell me where to go and whom to see." He started to laugh while saying, "I did not expect less from you. Tomorrow at 8 o'clock in the morning, you must be at the Martin Luther King Center in Marianao. See either Daisy Rojas or Joel Suárez. Pack a small case with everything you might need because you will be lodged there for ten days." He gave me the address and the telephone numbers of the center, explained how to get there coming from La Víbora on bus route number 100, and before hanging up, he added, "Do not let me down. Good luck my brother!"

That "yes" over the phone gave my life a 180-degree turn, literally. I was bold enough to accept that proposal without requesting authorization from my school executives. I had never before done anything like this, nothing as daring as this in my whole life up to that point, but in the state of mind I found myself back then, there was no room for hesitation or doubt at all. This was something that might mean my future, the materialization of my old dream.

As there were only ten days, including a weekend, I did not have to be absent from work for a long time. I did not want to lie, however, by claiming that I had been sick or anything like that. I preferred to accept all the responsibility, telling the truth and facing the consequences.

The first thing I had to do was look for a small case that I could borrow to hold my belongings because I had none of my own. Félix Delgado, one of my brothers-in-law, offered me his. I have to admit without shame that, on the eve of my first experience as an official interpreter, I hardly slept.

I was afraid I might not wake up early enough or that I might be late, not succeed, or let down the ICAP. I had every single fear associated with what is new, unknown, and challenging. If I were to fail, at least I would have the satisfaction that I had tried and that despite everything, I had mustered enough courage to face that monster that was attracting me with an irresistible magnetic force. I felt every inch a David ready to fight against a Goliath, but I did not really know if my sling would be effective enough to knock him down. The only thing needed was time.

I premiere as a translator

I left my house before 6 o'clock in the morning, but I still managed to arrive at the Martin Luther King, Jr. Memorial Center in Marianao a few minutes late due to public transportation problems. To be able to get on board a bus first thing on Monday morning at La Víbora was next to impossible. If there is something in life that I hate, it is tardiness. I can't stand being late anywhere, let alone know that somebody is waiting for me.

I arrived late and introduced myself. Luckily for me, Daimy Penichet, the translator of the Center was already there and about to start her job in the first meeting, which was led by Rev. Lucius Walker, Jr., director of the Interreligious Foundation for Community Organization (IFCO) – Pastors for Peace.

Not interested at all in stealing the protagonist's role, with all due humility and transparency, I confessed to both Daimy, the translator, and Daisy, the guide and program coordinator, that I was just an English teacher, who very much liked to translate, but that I was very nervous although ready and willing to do it when needed.

I guess I must have had a very frightened face, because Daisy calmed me down right on the spot by telling me that Daimy, who was already experienced, would start out in that first meeting, and that I should not worry too much. Later on, at about 10 o'clock in the morning, there would be a presentation by a writer; if by that time, I decided to break the ice and begin, it would be perfect; otherwise, Daimy would undertake it, as well.

When Daimy translated the initial meeting, my fears were slightly calmed. I was able to understand the North Americans very well when they were speaking, and that was precisely what I was most concerned about. If I managed to understand them, then I would find a way to provide what was left. Somehow, for better or for worse, I would come up with something.

As soon as Daimy finished her interpretation, I approached her, mustering all the courage that was still in me, and asked her to let me do the next presentation. She accepted very gladly.

The speaker was the outstanding journalist and writer Nicanor León Cotallo. His presentation was about the consequences of the US blockade from a historic perspective that started with slavery in Cuba. His lecture took place in the conference hall that would eventually become the Center's library.

Then and there, I began to work as a translator, experiencing my first embarrassment at the very beginning of my performance. The speaker introduced himself with his full name and when translating it, seemingly due to my nervousness when breaking the ice, instead of Cotallo I ended up saying Tocayo, which means namesake in Spanish. Luckily for me, he smiled and, with a fingertip, he pointed out his family name on the cover of one of his books to help me correct my first boner.

He began his dissertation, and I – holding a ballpoint pen in one hand and a blank notepad in the other, intending to jot down the figures, if any, for they were my greatest concern – pricked up my ears to the best of my abilities. Little by little, as I began to settle down and do my job much better than what I had honestly expected, I started to relax and feel much more confident.

The ICAP officials attending that meeting looked at me inconspicuously and slowly nodded their heads while witnessing my performance. Then they looked at one another and made subtle gestures of approval. They will never know how much support they gave me with those gestures, whether unintentional or deliberate.

I knew that all the eyes and all the minds were focused on me, the rookie, the daring country boy who had come all the way from Managua with his plaid shirt and his borrowed small case. In fact, they were assessing my job, checking how I was performing to see if I was fit. I did not know anybody there but Luís Marrón from the ICAP, who smiled every time he looked at me so as to cheer me up and encourage me. He was fully aware of the meaning that unique opportunity had for me.

To a great extent, I owe to him and to his wife, Martica, my entrance into the fascinating world of translation and interpretation and, in fact, my very entrance to the Martin Luther King, Jr. Memorial Center. In Cuba we say, "He who has friends has a sugar mill."

Right after the lecture, the journalist Zenaida Costales interviewed Rev. Lucius Walker for Radio Rebelde. Daimy, the translator, approached me to ask, "Do you dare do the interview as well?" I told her that I would do it but that I would like her to stay handy, close by, just in case I might need her as a prompter. Fortunately, that never happened.

Interpreting at a radio station

I had been emboldened with my first performance in spite of the initial tiny mishap. How deceived this country boy was! After the presentation and the radio interview, I thought I was already capable of translating at the United Nations. How naïve of me to think that way! Of course, in that initial euphoria, I never imagined that everything would not be rose-colored and that I would go through very distressing moments of all sorts from then on.

I had been sent for because Lucius had invited a TV crew from Channel 4 in Minneapolis to escort his first delegation to Cuba shortly after having brought his first US-Cuba friendshipment caravan. Two full-time interpreters would be needed because one was required to be at the disposal of the TV crew to cover all their movements and interviews because they were taking footage for a documentary.

That is why the Martin Luther King Center, even though it had an interpreter of its own, upon learning about the needs of this upcoming group, asked the ICAP to provide a second interpreter. Luckily for me, they did not have one available at that point and remembered me. Thus my history as an interpreter began.

Those were ten wonderful days during which I was totally convinced that I had found myself at long last. This was just what I had been seeking for the longest time and which, fortunately, I had found. There was a pastor in that faith community, Rev. Moisés Abella Díaz, who approached me on the front porch of their church wearing a wide smile on his face and predicted something that I will never forget and that filled me up with new hope. He placed his arm over my shoulders and told me pastorally, "Let nobody ever confuse you sonny. It is crystal clear that you are cut out to be a translator."

His timely words hit the spot. They were exactly what I needed to hear then and there. The only thing missing was to be given other opportunities like that one – and often. I was bothered to think that after those ten days were over, I would have to go back to school again, back to my 16 kilometers of daily bicycling, and back to the routine of the classes. Even though I used to enjoy teaching them, they did not have the same flavor any longer.

That first experience marked me indelibly. I even had to translate before Cuban TV cameras during a visit to a hospital and a sugar cane mill in San Cristóbal, Pinar del Río. Amy Marsalis, an anchorwoman journalist from North American TV, along with her cameraman, Joe Berglove, interviewed me by the Malecón seawall. Later on, with Lucius, she sent me a video tape cassette containing the news report about their visit to Cuba. I could not believe that such thing had really happened to me. As I looked at myself on the TV screen, I saw myself translating those exchanges and being interviewed for American TV – and in English on top of that!

I remembered the predictions of my beloved friend, Professor José Casanova, when he told me that I would get very far, that he could see it coming. The mere fact that a country boy like me was aired translating on national television was already way farther than what I had ever imagined. He was a true prophet, and he was totally right in his well-aimed forecasts. May God always keep him in His glory!

How short-lived happiness is in the poor man's house! But something is better than nothing. When we were inside the VIP section at the airport, bidding farewell to the first group I worked with at the Center, Rev. Suárez, its director and founder, approached me and asked, "If we were to need you again in the future, could we count on you?"

Those words were like music to my ears. It was just what I wanted to hear without having to ask him. Although I knew that they already had a translator, another chance like this might very likely be repeated. It had to be repeated! It did not matter what it would cost me. I was willing to do anything at all to make it possible.

When I returned from that job, I showed up at the head office in my school. Once there, I simply said that the ICAP had called me to render my services, and I had volunteered right away due to the rush with which they had sent for me. Given the urgency and importance of that delegation, I had accepted the challenge without thinking too much about it.

Fortunately, my excuses were verified just a few days later, when the director of the North America Division of the ICAP, Sergio López, saw fit to send an acknowledgment letter to the Lenin School as a token of their appreciation for the services I had provided. How right I was when I decided not to use a white lie.

To tell the truth, accepting that job did not bring about any negative consequences for me. On the contrary, the school was rather honored and took pride in the fact that one of its teachers had been called to grant his services as an interpreter for a Pastors for Peace delegation, which had already brought a whole humanitarian aid caravan in solidarity with Cuba and had even met with Fidel Castro himself. It was a top priority that was not supposed to be set aside.

The letter issued by the ICAP, dated February 16, 1993, bore witness to my good performance, in spite of the fact that it was the first time I had interpreted officially. That undoubtedly inspired me even further to achieve my dream, for it was predicting a promising future for me as a translator-interpreter.

Maybe what happened next was not very worthy of me, but truthfully, I would feel very bad by distorting the facts to spare myself from shame. This is supposed to be my memoir – at least, that is how I have conceived it – so I have to be faithful to the events that took place. It is said that every person is the sum total of their past. I am who I am at present, to a great extent, thanks to the outcome of decisions that I made and risks that I took. I do not hold any regrets at all for the things that I did because I managed to fulfill my objective by so doing. I had to be very pragmatic in order to make my dream come true.

I returned to my daily life with my head overflowing with wistful thought – as we country people say, "full of colored birdies," My thoughts were soaring over the clouds, hoping that what Suárez had asked me would materialize.

On the other hand, I was fully aware that my school would not be willing to "lend" me if other opportunities emerged. Those were very hard times, not only for me, but also for all my colleagues in our department. It was not fair that each time I was away to realize myself professionally, they would have to teach my classes and be even more overburdened than they already were.

I could not allow myself to commit such an injustice in order to feed my self-esteem. It was in order then that I should make an immediate and radical decision, and so I did. From then on, everything began to change for the better, even in the midst of the most brutal stage of the economic crisis.

Backwards, not even to gain momentum

The last two months that I worked in my school seemed never-ending to me. I went, but reluctantly. Everybody asked me if I was feeling all right. The eyes are certainly the expression of the soul, and they turned me in at all times, even when my lips would claim otherwise. One night I could not sleep at all, suffering with unbearable insomnia.

When I got to school the following morning, I heard that inner voice – the inner self, my alter ego, my own conscience, an incarnated spirit, or whatever it was – once again. It was urging me energetically to quit, to risk everything flat-out. It was asking me to make one of the most difficult and riskiest decisions of my whole life because, if

I failed, I would lose everything at the awful moment of the Special Period. My students did not deserve that sudden lack of interest that was overwhelming me now in a very strange way. I have to admit and I swear that it was not easy at all for me to do it, but we need to face the consequences of our own acts. *Nothing has been written about cowards as of yet.*

Instead of going to the Teaching Unit 4 where I worked, I went straight to the office of the general heads of the different departments. Right there, just as expected, I saw Matía Legrá sitting at his desk. I was afraid that if I did not find him in his habitual site, I would give up if I thought too much about it and change my mind if I did not take advantage of my momentum.

However, I was determined and ready to deal with the consequences. I greeted him and told him that I had something very serious to talk to him about. He offered me a seat. I begged him to please not interrupt me. I asked that he should let me speak through and, afterwards, he should honestly tell me what he thought.

I confessed to him that even though teaching was very rewarding for me and he knew this better than anybody else did, that although I had devoted myself thoroughly to my profession and had dedicated the best years of my youth to teaching, being a translator-interpreter was indeed the great goal of my life, and an opportunity had been granted to me that I could not overlook because, maybe, I would never have another one again.

He took a lot from my mind when he spoke, for he told me just the opposite of what I was expecting to hear. I thought he would come up with obstacles and red tape to retain me, advocating for his interests and those of our school. "Can you wait until the school year is over?" he asked. I did not have the courage to lie, so I limited myself to shaking my head.

He then told me that even though he was sorry to lose me, he could not be selfish by depriving me of a possibility for future professional development. He said he knew very well that the school was already too small for me, that I had outgrown it, taking into account my great interest in advancement. He said the only real concern he had was that, if by any chance I did not succeed and had to return, he might not have a job to give me.

I thanked him from the bottom of my heart for his understanding, his concern, and his sincere words, and I promised him that whatever happened after that, either good or bad, I would not return. That feeling had stuck itself between my eyebrows; therefore, going backwards was no longer possible. I evidently inherited that stubborn and uncompromising attitude from my father. As he himself used to say very frequently, "Backwards, not even to gain momentum."

Job transfers were frozen at that time. I drafted a lengthy letter to the general director's office of the school explaining that I needed to be immediately liberated from my teaching job because I was needed to interpret for foreign delegations at the Martin Luther King, Jr. Memorial Center. I could not wait until the end of the school year.

Thanks to the great prestige that I enjoyed at my school, the Ministry of Education gave me the green light that I so badly needed. In less than 24 hours, I was discharged, and I was paid the 15 days of vacation time I had accumulated. I was a free man; however, I committed myself to work one more week in order to leave everything in an orderly fashion and be able to bid farewell properly to everyone.

The hardest part of all was giving my students the news and saying good-bye. At that point, I was in charge of four classes of tenth graders. I went to each of those groups and explained to them my decision and the reasons I had to do it that way. What they did in the very last class period shook up my conscience and made me feel guilty. They organized a farewell activity in which they read beautiful things, presented me with gifts, cried, and almost made me cry.

I had to be strong because everything they prepared for me was very emotional. They encouraged me by saying that even though they would miss me a lot, they were all there trying to achieve their dreams. The students said they would come and go and would stay in school only three years. It was not fair for me to go on being stagnant there, sacrificing my true vocation so as not to damage their interests. I should definitely take advantage of that great opportunity. They taught me a unique lesson of empathy and human solidarity.

The last trip home by bicycle was the saddest of them all. The whole time, I was thinking about the sudden avalanche of loving care and understanding that I had received from the students that I was now forsaking, and I was wondering with concern, "My God, and now what will I do?" I knew, of course, that I could go on teaching privately, but that was illegal, and I did not want to be an offender forever.

I could not throw down everything that I had achieved with so much sacrifice for so long. It was not fair to either me or my family. Having two little girls to rear in the middle of a serious economic crisis, that action could easily be the greatest craziness of my life. I was fully aware that I did not have anything secured yet and that my dream might be an illusion or wishful thinking about a remote possibility that would never arrive.

But I had done it, and now I had to undertake my full share of accountability. I was taking for granted an extremely subjective desire as if it were a tangible reality, but thus far, it was nothing but a dream.

Those first few weeks away from school, far from being a relief, were psychological torture. I went through some very difficult days. I focused all my attention on the preparation of private lessons and on looking for the proper teaching aids to increase their quality.

That was exactly what I did, and that is also why I had decided to leave the school for good. What happened to me next, however, was incredible. My extra-sensory perception was sharpened even further and showed me that one must respect oneself a lot. Whenever you have a premonition, a gut feeling, a strong hunch, a drive to do or to refuse doing something, whatever that may be, you should heed yourself, not ignore yourself. Nobody is able to understand you better than your own self.

What I had dreamed about so much

I was worried about the fact that I was already running out of those few remunerated vacation days I had accumulated. Soon, before the law, I would be one of the voluntarily unemployed persons of my country. Never before had I found myself at such a crossroads, but I did not have any other choice, at least as far as my will was concerned.

To make a long story short, the very day I was enjoying the completion of my "vacation" time, I was at the home of a family to whom I used to teach English privately twice a week. A few minutes after I started that day's lesson, the devil took hold of me. My students realized that there was something unusual in my behavior, and visibly worried, they asked me, "Teacher, is something wrong with you? Are you all right?"

My inner voice was urging me to call the Martin Luther King Center, but it would not tell me why or what for, only that I should call. That urge was getting on my nerves and making me increasingly restless. I apologized to my students, for I could not focus on what I was doing.

I canceled the class and asked to use the school's phone. After several failed attempts to get through to the Center, I decided to call Daisy, the guide-program coordinator for the delegations, who worked at the National Institute of Sports, Physical Education and Recreation – just to say hello – because I did not really know what else I was going to say.

The person who picked up the phone at the office was not Daisy, but Marcelo, her husband, who, when recognizing my voice told me, "Albert, I am not the right person to do it, but I advise you to call the Center because they have a piece of news to give you over there." Right after that he said good-bye, hung up, and gave me no time at all to react. "Oh, oh! A piece of news for me? I cannot believe it."

I thought it likely that this was about another delegation that would arrive in the near future, and I hoped they might need me again. How I wished to be right about it! But I would not know it if I did not call or go over there. I was afraid that if they tried to locate me and failed to do so, they would call someone else. I could not allow that to happen. There were many others with enough capacity, training, and willingness to replace me.

I thanked my students and apologized again for the inconvenience I had created out of the blue. I took myself to the street, looked both ways, pondering what to do next, euphoric as a dog recently unleashed from his chain. The voice was whispering to me now, "Just go to the Center!"

At that moment, a white Russian LADA squealed its tires against the pavement right in front of me. Behind the steering wheel was the mother of two of my private students. "Professor, do you have any problem?" she asked. Instead of answering her question, I asked her "Where are you going?"

Following suit, she did not reply but asked again, "Where are YOU going?" When she learned that my destination was Marianao, she volunteered to give me a free ride up to El Capri overpass on Calzada de Bejucal over 100th Street. When I got out of her car at the bus stop, I saw a frenzied crowd trying to get on board the 113 route bus that had just arrived from El Cotorro. I did not have to struggle to get on the bus; I was pushed in. In 22 minutes I made the incredible trip from Managua to Marianao during the most critical period of our public transportation system.

When I got to the Center, Adalys Vázquez, Suárez's secretary, was surprised to see me. While laughing mischievously, she told me, "Sonny, the Lord brought you! Did you know that we were trying to locate you? I was close to developing a callus on this fingertip dialing the number of that country where you live. The whole morning ring, ring, ring, and nobody would pick up." Then Daisy came walking down the stairs holding a glass of water which she handed to me while saying, "Sit down and drink it! You will need it to get some good news."

At that second, I became a gigantic ear, ready to listen up and understand what they needed to tell me, anticipating already that it would be good. Smiling ever so slowly, she told me, "Suárez asked me to call you. Do you remember Jeffrey McCrary, the one who came on the delegation you worked with? The point is that he fell in love with Daimy, the interpreter – love at first sight you know."

"Suárez is going to officiate at their wedding here in our church next week, and as she is planning to live in Houston, Texas, he sent to ask if you are interested in being the official interpreter for the Center." BINGO! At long last, what I had been dreaming about all along had come true and right on time. Exactly the day that my paid vacation was over. Thank you Lord!

How thoughtful of Daisy to have brought me that glass of water! I do not have the slightest doubt that it was blessed water. But even better was what Jeffrey did when having a crush on Daimy because by so doing, he left the path open for me. That was the news of the century. It was hard for me to assimilate, believe, and digest it. It was just too good to be true.

But it was true. Daisy knew quite well how important her news would be for me, and she would not dare play with my feelings. It was not a dream because I was quite awake; but on second thought, yes, it was a dream indeed, but one that came true at long last! I still remember that I left the Center that afternoon relaxed and carefree. I could not have cared less if I was hungry, if it rained and I got wet, if transportation was lousy, or if I would get home late.

I was feeling so emotionally relaxed and blissful that none of the things that under other circumstances would have disturbed me were bothering me now at all. It was like walking in mid-air, oblivious to everything and everybody – like an astronaut walking on the moon. In those moments, I was floating in Nirvana, and I did not want to land on any daily life triviality.

My dream had materialized, and that was the only thing that mattered to me. Everything else could wait. I was happy, very happy, and when one is that happy, even bad and ugly things take on other hues. I was 32 years old then, with 16 years in school, four years as a student teacher and 12 years as a graduate. Up until that moment, I had dedicated half of my life, 16 of my 32 years, to teaching English.

From that moment on on, I felt that I was entitled to develop myself as a full-fledged translator-interpreter because ever since I heard the English language for the very first time, that was my dream, my goal, my good old chimera. *It is never too late if fortune comes.* That proverb is correct, because fortune is always good. It may arrive or not, but if it is fortune, it follows that it is good. Mine arrived, and was very good, thanks be given to God.

Looking now in hindsight, I have to admit that I was very lucky despite all the hardships I was going through. While the "special period" was so desperate, and I had fallen apart and could not hold it together any longer, the point is that within three short months, I had been invited to interpret, had quit teaching, and had been hired by the MLK Center. Everything happened very quickly, just in a few months, I was transitioning from despair to elation and finally to my new calling! My prayer was indeed answered at a fast pace. The way things started to unfold was a real miracle for me, and it happened just when I was most desperate.

When I arrived at the Center in 1993, I did not know anything about the Bible at all; I had never read it. I did not even know that there were clear differences in terminology between Catholics and Protestants, such as: mass and service, priest and pastor, chapel and sanctuary, Eucharist and Holy Supper, to mention just a few of the most evident ones.

I can still recall the day when I was working with the first delegation at the Marianao Ebenezer Baptist Church. Pastor Clarita Rodés asked one of the North American guests to lead us all in prayer. When translating her request, I used the word "sentence," for it was the only word in English that I knew was translated as *oración* in Spanish.

They all laughed, and sweetly smiling, she corrected me right on the spot: Prayer! Thus, I began to learn, little by little, a step at a time, committing mistakes, being embarrassed, reading a lot, watching more experienced colleagues keenly, and learning along the way; for in doing, we learn empirically.

Receiving my first bilingual Bible, delivered by Ellen Bernstein of Pastors for Peace

On February 6, 1993, Rev. Raúl Suárez presented me with a Bible in Spanish when I finished my first experience with them at the Martin Luther King Center. I devoured it from beginning to end, although I later learned that such was not the best way to read the

Bible. I read it through again afterwards, but that time in English and honoring the order suggested by theologians.

It was cumbersome for me to carry two Bibles along, one in Spanish and the other in English, when translating during religious worship services. Julie, a Lutheran pastor from Columbus, Ohio, while visiting our Center, promised me that she would solve that problem for me once and for all. With the following delegation, she sent me the most useful and timely gift I have ever received: a bilingual Bible. I no longer needed to carry a couple of Bibles everywhere; now I had both in one volume, with parallel texts side by side in both languages.

That, my favorite Bible by far, was and continues to be a great blessing today. There is no better gift than the one meeting a pressing need. She had undoubtedly hit right on the target because that Bible was to me what a ripe banana is to a mockingbird.

I met Rev. Suárez and Rev. Walker on the same day, at the same time, and in the same place: the conference hall of the Dr. Martin Luther King, Jr. Memorial Center, at 8:15 AM on Sunday, January 31, 1993. Both deeply impacted me from the onset. With them, I started to understand and appreciate many things, and it was quite clear to me after meeting them that one could be Christian and revolutionary at the same time without contradictions.

They opened my eyes and my conscience, and with them, I started to gradually get rid of many deeply rooted prejudices and began to do away with a large number of mental cobwebs. Up until that time, at least for me, having faith in God would bring about underestimation and mockery. The faith I always had, inculcated by my grandfather Pedro and further inspired by that of my own mother, was kept deep down inside me as a sacred treasure, a secret, something very private in a safe box inside my being.

It was not convenient to reveal it, at least within my workplace setting, because I knew too well that I would be looked down upon if I did. I was very much acquainted with the way of thinking of my people and what they used to say about the students who identified themselves as Christians.

Translating for Rev. Suarez

Upon getting to the King Center, meeting Suárez and Lucius, and listening to them preach and address the economic, social and political realities in their reflections, I realized that there was something wrong with me that needed to be corrected right away. In their company, I stopped being ashamed of my faith, and that feeling was transformed into a healthy pride that set me free.

That new insight took a weight off my mind, and I experienced a sense of relief like never before. It was something like being born again, spiritually, just as a butterfly must feel when at long last it manages to painstakingly get rid of the chrysalis in which it has been isolated in order to start flying away in absolute freedom. From then on, it will never again return to the chrysalis. I was able to scream at the top of my lungs, as Martin Luther King, Jr., said in one of his most celebrated speeches, "Free, free, free at last!"

Debut and farewell?

In July 1993, just a few months after I had premiered as an interpreter, the second Pastors for Peace Caravan arrived in Cuba, and with it, I went through one of my most embarrassing experiences. Of course, I was still green as a translator, and I therefore lacked the resources and the tactics to walk out of difficult situations elegantly. Even though I had willpower to spare in terms of undertaking the task, my sheer desire to do it was not enough. I endured a bitter experience, which made me feel so bad that I was close to quitting.

On the day the Caravan arrived, a press conference had been scheduled at the International Press Center in El Vedado. It was held at about 11 o'clock in the evening due to the Caravan's delayed arrival and a few other logistical issues. Major activities requiring extreme formality within the official schedule were usually undertaken by professional interpreters of the government agency providing interpretation services by the name of ESTI, which operated under the Council of Ministries.

That made me relax a lot because this translation was stressful, particularly for an inexperienced rookie like me. When we got to the CPI, the ESTI interpreter who was supposed to be there was nowhere to be seen, so Luís Marrón, the ICAP official, asked me if I was bold enough to do it.

I regretted having undertaken that interpretation job a thousand times afterwards, but I naïvely thought that, since it was so late, there would be four cats over there at most, so to speak, to listen to the details of the Caravan, and they might ask one or two of their usual questions.

Nothing was further from the truth. When we entered the small theater of that facility, there was lengthy and noisy welcoming applause, and the place was totally packed with journalists from all over the world. There were more cameras, lights, and mics than at a television station. My legs wobbled, but I had committed myself and could not back down. It would have been unworthy for me to do it.

I was asked to be seated on the right end of the platform, too far away for my taste from Lucius, the key speaker, who was sitting a few meters away from me, almost on the other end of the dais. With the glare shed by the spotlights over me, I could hardly see his profile, and that bothered me a lot.

One of the gigantic speakers was placed almost by my side, and the amplification of the sound was causing a very strong feedback effect that made it even more difficult for me to listen properly and to understand clearly. Seemingly everything was in a plot to make me go through a very distressing moment and to teach me a lesson about the unpleasant aspects of my new profession. Much as I would like it, not everything would always turn out right, and certainly there would be other demanding tests like the one I was facing now.

To top it off, I learned that, due to its relevance, the press conference was being televised live by Cuban TV. Thousands of TV viewers all over the country would be witnessing my performance. Wrong time! There were journalists from different news agencies who, being bilingual, when asking their questions would start speaking in one language and finish in the other.

To make a long story short, and so as not to overwhelm anybody with too many details, that was by far the worst interpretation job of my life. Sometimes I was unable to understand what Lucius was saying. Several people in the audience and a few caravanistas who were sitting right behind me on the podium, in an attempt to help me out as very polite teleprompters, told me the words that I needed in unison, and the cacophony of their sympathetic voices triggered the opposite effect, for they blocked me even more than I was already, and my nervousness grew with each passing minute.

Afterwards, I was told that there was a point in which Lucius turned around and very discreetly asked Peggy Hopson, a Mexican American, if I was doing a very lousy job. She told him that I was just freaking out. As a matter of fact, there were whole sentences that were left untranslated. When the meeting finally came to an end and everyone started to exit the hall, I remained seated, consumed by shame, my self-esteem shattered into a million pieces.

Some people who were honestly worried approached me and asked, "What happened to you?" There was a little bit of everything, including very callous comments such as, "What you did sucked!" Tell me about it! I knew it far too well. I did not really need anybody reminding me about it, because it was like rubbing a wound, poking a sore with a finger.

Nobody knew better than myself everything that had gone wrong. I didn't need to hear about it. Unfortunately, however, we humans are too often characterized by our lack of tact and sympathy right at the moments when we need them most.

There was only one person, may God keep her forever in his glory, who had enough sensitivity to wisely realize the bad moment I had just gone through and the one I was still enduring as its outcome. She approached me ever so slowly, kissed me softly and motherly on my forehead and said "My son, it shows that you are really exhausted!"

That was by far the best compliment I have heard in my whole life, coming from an angel's soul who was trying to show her timely empathy. It was Clarita Rodés, Suárez's wife, who was characterized by gestures of the most authentic human solidarity and love to her neighbors, simple but profound acts that would get right to your bone marrow, just like the one she had just made for my sake, right at the very time in which I wanted to be invisible. I simply wanted to be swallowed up by the earth.

That night, I could not sleep, thinking of the possible consequences of that fateful event. Would that by any chance be my debut and farewell? The journalist Maribel Puerto of Cuban TV had called the Center first thing in the morning the following day to find out who the "little bearded guy" was that had been asked to interpret for Lucius. I had overlapped so much, it had made their television editing work next to impossible.

That was the very last drop that overflowed the cup. I had to save face. I was in no mood to hear any other complaint. I was so overwhelmed by shame that I thought I had let everybody down, all those who had trusted me both at the MLK Center and at the ICAP. The caravanistas were transferred to Varadero beach for a couple of days, but I was feeling under the weather. My state of mind was down and out, so I refused to tag along.

I took my Chinese bike and rode it all the way to my humble little wooden house in the countryside, a victim of a visceral disappointment that was eating me away slowly, thinking very seriously about speaking with Suárez to apologize to him and give everything up.

Being unable to avoid the perfectionist in who I am – a Virgo no less – I was exaggerating the issue, making a storm in a glass of water. It was really hard for my family and friends to talk me into accepting that it had not been as catastrophic as I claimed and that such a thing could have happened to anyone, even more so in the case of an inexperienced interpreter like myself.

Deep down in my heart of hearts, I knew that they were absolutely right, but that did not spare me the shame I was feeling, particularly because it had been aired on national TV, and all those mistakes had been quite evident and exposed publicly. They had already been recorded, forever registered there as part of the history of the US Caravans to Cuba.

Fortunately, they managed to convince me, and by the time the caravanistas returned from Varadero, I was waiting for them at the King Center. Suárez was every inch a pastor. When he learned what I planned to do, he spoke with me immediately and took a load off my mind. Better times would eventually come. All interpreters had to go through experiences like that, he assured me. Only the fire is able to polish the clay. Fire is needed for the real enamel to be able to shine and to show its own gloss. How nice to hear those words! The sky was not going to collapse. To err is human.

I decided that I should no longer make firewood of the fallen tree. Instead, I would prepare myself even further in my self-taught fashion to improve my professional performance in the future. Why should I give up of my own free will what I had attained at long last after striving so much? Why would I give up what I was enjoying so thoroughly? I did not deserve anything like it.

I needed to strive in order to improve from all perspectives, no matter what. Men are not measured by all the times they fall down but rather by all the ones when they get up and move on. I was willing, like the phoenix bird, to rise up from the ashes with new stamina.

Repetitive-Continuous-Systematic-Progressive

From that moment on, I designed a strategy aimed at acquiring new vocabulary and consolidating other linguistic skills. In the free time between delegations I worked with, I began to listen to radio programs in English as ear training. I recorded them and later on transcribed them and read them aloud. I was implementing and applying to myself what I have always advised to all the people who ask me about the best method to learn English.

There are, of course, many methods, and new ones appear all the time in ever increasing number, variety, and sophistication. However, none will pay off if not undertaken with soul, heart and life. Thus, my favorite method, which I will always promote, is the one I have whimsically called "Repetitive-Continuous Systematic-Progressive," which means to take it very seriously, be totally devoted to it, and not forgive ourselves if one day goes by without having fed our brains with the foreign language we are trying to master.

The ways to achieve mastery are plentiful: reading, listening, writing, reciting, speaking, singing, translating, interpreting, repeating, memorizing, dictating, telling stories – whatever it takes – but doing something with it. That is all food for the brain. Planting is needed so as to be able to harvest something eventually, for nobody can really give what he or she does not have. You must not expect the impossible.

I used to take advantage of opportunities delegations gave me to engage in informal conversations with as many people as possible. I would strike up new friendships, practice the language, and if they allowed me, I would interview them, recording them with a journalist's mini-cassette recorder that I had been given as a gift. Those conversations become raw material for my self-taught training course – a never-ending comprehensive, linguistic upgrading.

Initially, my goal had been to learn English and later on to become an interpreter. Now that I was taking my first steps, sometimes doing a better job than others, my ambition was to be able to do simultaneous interpretation fluently, in real time, as the interpreters at the United Nations do, inside a booth wearing a headset. That was my long-term goal.

I knew, however, that achieving it would not be fast or easy, but not be impossible either. Many colleagues in different parts of the world did it on a daily basis. Why couldn't I make it? What did they have that I did not? Whatever it was that was still missing in me was really up to me, as usual, so if I made an effort, by force of perseverance...

I started out by repeating, in real time, what was said by the speakers on TV and radio shows until I got tired or could no longer follow their line of speech. I used to do that mainly in English – particularly because it was more difficult for me – in order to strengthen my concentration and memorization tools, which are of paramount importance for a translator-interpreter.

On March 31, 1994, we were able at long last to leave the countryside and move to a small apartment in the city. That was indeed a turning point in our family life. Later, when I managed to acquire more vocabulary and fluency, I began working on simultaneous interpretation, carrying out my first humble attempts in the Sunday worship services at church.

Every Sunday, I tried to sit in one of the pews closest to the pulpit, so I could clearly hear the preacher's sermon. Very discreetly, I bowed my head when the homily was due. I placed one of my hands over my mouth to conceal the movements of my lips and to go unnoticed. Thus I started to interpret what the speaker was saying simultaneously. Eventually, when I was ready, I volunteered to do it for real. I was no longer just pretending to play simultaneous interpreter.

This became quite a habit, a true mania, a sweet addiction, which I enjoyed thoroughly. Another habit I had fallen into since I started to develop my fondness for reading in English was that of reading out loud, not necessarily in a loud voice, but pronouncing and intoning properly while not totally in silence.

It is true that one gets tired faster when doing that, and the vocal cords complain about their work overload. It is nonetheless worth the while, particularly when it comes to learning a foreign language.

In English, there are some sounds that are non-existent in our language. If we do not train and adapt our speech organs all the time to articulate them properly, it would be very difficult for us to eventually master them. Reading in this way, as if we were reading for somebody, facilitates fluency. When listening to ourselves verbalizing what we perceive with our eyes, we further reinforce the understanding of what is read.

When articulating the sounds, we are actively engaging a larger number of our brain cells, which undoubtedly favors our own mental health. Of course, we do not need to overdo it, and it is indeed advisable to keep the throat moist. It would be pointless to be able to read efficiently but have chronic hoarseness or nodules on the vocal cords.

I have learned something from each of them

I could easily write a whole chapter about the most unfortunate moments during my interpretation jobs over nearly 20 years; they are rather plentiful. Years later, they seem funny, and telling them serves as a catharsis. I have learned something from each of them; therefore, deep down, I appreciate them all.

Besides, I am comforted to be aware that we have all made mistakes of one kind or another. The point is that not everyone is bold, honest, and modest enough to share them, reveal them, and even laugh at them. Whether we like it or not, they undeniably happened, and nothing is solved by pretending otherwise and trying to forget that they make up an important part of our own pasts.

We each have our own share of vanity, our professional self-consciousness, our tiny jealousies, and a self-esteem needing to be taken care of with well-deserved praises. That is not a sin at all; it is rather something that is intrinsically human. As it is said, everybody likes their job to be acknowledged.

One experience that could easily qualify as my most embarrassing mistake happened at the beginning of my professional work as a translator-interpreter in, of all places, the Office for the Care of the Religious Affairs at the Central Committee of the Communist Party of Cuba.

It was one afternoon in 1993, with one of the first delegations with which I worked. It was made up of North American Catholic nuns from San Francisco, California. They had a meeting with Silvio Platero, who was serving as an interim after the passing of Dr. José Felipe Carneado. I felt extremely nervous, for it was the first time that I visited the offices of the Central Committee, and both my insecurity and my fear of failing at my job had taken hold of me in an amazing way.

The nuns were seated in a conference room around a large Formica oval table, while I very timidly settled next to Platero. He started out by introducing himself and welcoming those Catholic sisters most warmly as they solemnly looked at him with undivided attention.

He addressed them all as follows, "You are visiting the office for the care of religious affairs of the Central Committee of the Communist Party of Cuba, which centers its attention on channeling the problems of the churches within our Socialist society." All my neurons at that point were getting ready to understand the speaker and to convey his message as faithfully as possible into English. The golden rule of interpretation claims very rightly that ideas and not words are what should be translated.

When listening to the verb he had used in Spanish, *centrar*, I automatically thought of an option I had never used before, but which would fit right in according to the essence of his first idea. Maybe the fact of having watched so many North American films on Saturday nights for so long could be held accountable for my unforgettable and gross mistake. The word that suddenly came off the top of my head as an equivalent or synonym for "centering the attention" was no other than "focus," relatively difficult to pronounce properly if one is not duly and fully aware of it.

Unfortunately, my tongue got twisted just as I uttered it, and what I said was "FUCK YOU!" No comments, nothing but a gross offense, and on top of that, as if it were not bad enough just the way it was, one that was sex related.

For a split second, I thought that they had not realized my unforgivable mistake, with nobody but an audience of celibate nuns and at the Central Committee of all places; however, the youngest of them could not help cracking a boisterous peal of laughter that triggered a whole wave of noisy giggling around the table.

I wished the Earth would have swallowed me up right at that instant. Platero, puzzled by that sudden highly contagious laughter, demanded that I explain to him what was going on. He could not understand why they were laughing so hard because he had not said anything funny. I told him that he hadn't, but I had. He got even more worried.

"You are here to say whatever I say and not what you want," he asserted. I apologized to him, thinking that was going to be my debut and farewell in that place. He insisted that I should let him know what I had said, so he would be able to understand the laughter that seemed to be never-ending.

"Do you really want to know? I warn you it is not good at all," I told him. After much insistence from him, I finally dared whisper that barbarity in his ear, fearing his reaction upon learning about it. Luckily for me, he had a laughing outburst that caused a second round of hysterical laughter around the table.

We had to wait for a few minutes to placate the spirits that had been aroused so much. How embarrassing that was! What I caused by uttering only one worwas just amazing.

From then on, whenever he saw me arrive with a new delegation, he would greet me smiling and warn me jokingly that I should be very careful with what I was going to say, asking me if I had brushed my teeth. It was absolutely impossible for him to see me coming without recalling that shameful moment the first time we met. It was evidently very funny for everyone but me.

CUBA
A brief history

The Late 1990s: Getting Underway in a New Direction

The end of socialism in Eastern Europe endangered Cuban security. Our economy was devastated practically overnight as a result of that unexpected situation. Industrial production dropped to 15 percent of capacity, but even then, workers were sent home with only 60 percent of their salaries for at least one year.

Public transportation came to a halt; one million bikes sent as gifts from China took to the roads to counter the effect of petroleum shortages, which also caused long blackouts as well as a flourishing of black markets. The sudden devaluation of the Cuban peso and the appearance of US dollars in our economy changed society very quickly.

While Cuba began reaching out to capitalism in the 1990s, the continued US embargo dragged down economic progress. However, reforms to the Cuban economy during the early 1990s opened new markets. Foreign investors and exporters responded, taking modest but real steps to engage economically with Cuba. Official Cuban reports indicate that there were at that point 658 foreign companies registered in Cuba and that Cuba had commercial offices in 28 different countries.

According to the US-Cuba Trade and Economic Council, 345 joint ventures were approved by the Cuban government. Seventy-five percent of them were concentrated in mining, tourism, construction, agriculture, energy, finances, real estate, and the food industry.

In order to stimulate economic development, three trade zones were opened. The main food exporters to Cuba since the economic reforms of the 1990s have been France, Canada, Spain, Argentina, China, Mexico, and Thailand.

Like it or not, Cuba joined the capitalist world, and social inequalities started to reappear. The constitution adopted in 1976 was deeply reformed in 1992. In addition to economic changes, atheism was no longer the state religion. Communist Party membership was opened to religious believers. Since then, all religions have been on an upswing. Afro-Cuban religions are widespread and practiced by all races.

In 1995, the GDP increased 2.5 percent from the previous year. New industries developed with nickel, oil, tourism, root vegetables, green vegetables, and tobacco leading the way. The exchange rate was reduced from 130 to 25 Cuban pesos to the US dollar. The fiscal deficit was considerably reduced, and the excess of circulating money was cut down to 25 percent.

Transportation was slightly improved. Food sales and self-employment grew. However, sugar cane production was very low for three consecutive years. Meanwhile, tourism kept growing despite its social price. The peso was recovering its value, but retail prices were still very high. Dollars supplemented the income of many families, but the major state services continued to be funded. The hardest times of the struggle for survival were fortunately over, and an economic struggle toward a viable recovery was underway.

In a huge effort to identify the most pressing needs of the population, social workers played a paramount role. Funds were made available to alleviate the worst situations, and families were linked to highly needed services. In one year, more than 1,000 young people began training as social workers.

There has been a growing public debate about US policy toward Cuba over the past several years. The visit of Pope John Paul II to the island, the Elian Gonzalez saga, the growing number of Americans who have traveled here, and the post-Hurricane Michelle sales of US agricultural products to Cuba have all focused public attention on this issue.

This debate will continue over the next several years. There will be efforts to further ease restrictions on food and medical sales, efforts to end the travel ban, and calls to lift all sanctions on Cuba. The US embargo on Cuba is hurting both nations.

Farmers, agricultural exporters, the transportation industry, and others are losing trade and investment opportunities. US citizens who could benefit from medical advances in Cuba are being denied access to new drugs and technology here.

Social justice and a powerful conviction keep the majority of Cubans united. The defense of national sovereignty is a priority. Cuba has been a valuable laboratory for alternative possibilities for many peoples. At the very least, Cuba has provided an alternative to capitalist societies that claim that they are the only possible choice.

Nothing Like Personal Experience

*God is our refuge and strength, an ever-present help in trouble.
Therefore we will not fear, though the earth give way
and the mountains fall into the heart of the sea.*
Psalms 46:1–2

When I was doing my social service in the technological institute, I applied through the trade union movement to go on a self-financed trip to Czechoslovakia, but due to the neglectful attitude of the person in charge of my paperwork, that never became a reality. Czechoslovakia was a very good choice for me, taking into account that several of my old pen pals lived there, with whom I kept in touch for years on end and who were looking forward to meeting me personally. That was my first travel disappointment. My second frustration took place some time later, when I was already working at the Lenin Vocational School. I had been chosen to go to Guyana, in South America, to take part in an intensive English language training for three months in a row; however, when the paperwork was about to start, the officials of the Ministry of Education decided at the very last minute to send another colleague who was much more experienced as a teacher than I was.

Two trips abroad had been spoiled for reasons other than my will, almost when they both were about to materialize. I still recall that I was so eager to finally travel that one day, without paying much attention to what I was saying, I expressed, "I can't wait to board a plane to go to any other country even if doing so may cost my own life." I needed to see for myself if the saying "the third time is the charm" was really true. Would I ever get a third opportunity by any chance? Only God knew, but he was not telling me. It did not matter because I was fully aware that the last thing lost is hope. Anyway, I did not have any other choice but to wait for better times.

More than ten years elapsed before that proverb came true, but it was indeed a reality, and the first country I had the opportunity to visit was the United States, where I stayed for six consecutive weeks, absorbing every single detail of its society and its people. It was a great occasion to train my ears and my brain in terms of the systematic practice of the English language.

Boasting a very black beard

When I was a professor, I could not grow a beard because it was prohibited unless one had a skin disease and a medical certificate issued by a dermatologist justifying it. As that was never the case for me and although I always longed to have a thick beard, I had to shave all the time. Once, in the Lenin School, I got upset during an argument and asked why we could not have a beard, protesting that I did not understand the reason. There is nothing more natural to a man than a beard because, whether you like it or not, unless he is hairless, a beard is going to emerge and grow. If you come to think about it, what is not natural is shaving. In films from many countries, I saw how distinguished professors from prestigious institutions had beards without posing any problems at all. Having a beard does not give or take morality away from anybody. I said that even Fidel, himself, had a beard, which was a symbol identifying him the world over. Why. then, could I not grow mine? They tried to convince me, claiming that Fidel's had grown under the rattle of the bullets during guerrilla warfare in the Sierra Maestra mountain range. I, in turn, neither slow nor lazy, held that mine could easily grow under the chalk dust in the classrooms of the Lenin School, each within its own historical moment and role. My arguments were to no avail. *There is no worse blind man than the one who refuses to see or deaf man than the one who refuses to hear.*

Much as I tried, I never managed to understand this policy. That was a disappointment because I hated shaving. That was why, when I started working at the Martin Luther King Center, without that old prohibition that repressed my desires for so long and still young enough to boast a very black beard – at the age of 32, no gray hairs appeared on my face – I decided to stop shaving for a whole year to see how long my beard could get and thus to enjoy without restraints at all that unheard of hair-growing freedom.

On July 24, 1996, I was summoned to go to the US Interests Section in Havana for the first time to apply for my visa. Afraid of providing a wrong image of my person bearing that huge mega-beard, it occurred to me to ask my wife to roll it all up under my chin and stitch it by using a length of black polyester sewing thread. I went by bike all the way from Marianao to the parking lot of the Funeral House of Calzada and K streets in El Vedado because the public transportation system was unbearable in the midst of that harsh Special Period. The interview was way too long, and I was asked the same questions several times, formulated in different ways, in an attempt to catch me red-handed with any inconsistencies that would give them the pretext to deny me the required permit. In order to double-check that I was not lying when claiming that I was travelling in the capacity of an interpreter for the religious delegation, the consular official held the conversation completely in English.

My mega-beard

While the North American agent was interviewing me through the glass window with his cold metallic voice, my stitched-up beard was itching terribly due to the sweat that had accumulated in mid-July after having pedaled several kilometers to get there. I could not scratch it out of fear that it might be unstitched and cascade apart in front of that inhospitable window. Finally, when I had lost all my hopes of having a visa granted, he asked me a question that left me stupefied, "You have a daughter who traveled to the US recently. Has she returned already?" Fortunately, I had been alert, and just in case, I had taken with me the passport of my older daughter, Wendy, who had recently returned from the United States. I handed it over to him. He took his time looking at it, checking the rubber-stamped information in it and the already-used visa. It was only then that he realized I would not be a possible immigrant. Happily, he decided to grant me a visa.

Half of my beard was unstitched and came apart on my way back home as a result of my scratching it so much, for I could not stand the itching it was causing me. I did not care any longer whether it was totally exposed in its full length because at that point, I was already carrying my passport with the granted visa in one of the pockets of my *guayabera* shirt. I was sure of one thing, though. That was definitely the last time I would experience such a distressing moment. I promised myself that I would never again have my beard stitched up that way, and I was true to my word down to the letter.

August 1996 was the first time I traveled away from Cuba. I had been officially invited as the interpreter for a clergy delegation of the Fraternity of Baptist Churches of Cuba, which would join the annual assembly of the Progressive National Baptist Convention to be held in Kansas City, Missouri. It was the same old Baptist African-American convention to which Martin Luther King, Jr., belonged. Upon arriving at the Miami International Airport in Florida, the customs agent who took care of me, when seeing my huge beard and my Cuban passport, exclaimed with certain sarcasm, "Just like Castro!" Those were the first welcoming words I got upon arriving in the United States of America.

Six weeks later, however, on my return trip to Havana, when I got to Cancún from Chicago and the two Mexicans who were in charge of me at the immigration check point saw my beard – even longer after six additional weeks of growth – they asked me with certain mischief, "Cuban, right?" I smiled and nodded. They looked at each other, and the younger of the two, making a well-known gesture to imply the beard, concluded categorically, "It shows!" The references to my beard in the United States and Mexico were obviously about Fidel; however, there was in both an underlying intention and a huge gap between them.

The aforementioned Mexicans taught me an unforgettable lesson of solidarity that day. I had to wait for eight long hours inside the airport in Cancún before taking the CUBANA return flight to Havana. As I did not have a Mexican visa, I could not leave the air terminal. My traveling documents were taken away, and I was placed in a completely isolated section, surrounded by huge glass walls, like a gigantic fish tank. I had been charged $31.00 USD for my overweight luggage. Being a Cuban living in Cuba right in the middle of the Special Period and coming back to Havana after a month and a half in the most developed country in the whole world, it seemed to me that it would have been an unforgivable crime not to be overweight not only in terms of luggage but in body weight as well. Back then, the prevailing money exchange rate was 1.00 US dollars = 130.00 Cuban pesos. That is to say, in a basic arithmetic calculation, I was made to pay the equivalent of 4,030.00 pesos. With a deep pain in my soul, I was compelled to part with that money and everything that it was expected to buy. But I did it very gladly. My only other choice was to reduce the weight of my luggage by discarding items I had been given as gifts for my family. Obviously, I was not going to do that.

I received a wonderful surprise eight hours later when, full of emotions, I was waiting my turn in the line to get my boarding pass and passport back at the threshold of the walkway providing access to the CUBANA airplane. Sure enough, the two Mexicans were there again, in a great mood, doing their job. When they handed me my traveling documents, they shook my hand in an unforgettable gesture of a friendly farewell and told me, "Here you are, your $31 back. You Cubans have always been our brothers, and right now you are going through a very difficult situation. Please take that money to your family. Have a nice trip!" I was so happy that I asked them to let me have a picture taken with the two of them. I did not want to forget their kind faces after that extraordinary gesture of altruism and solidarity. I boarded the plane with my heart hardly fitting into my chest. It was the first time that I was returning to Cuba from abroad. On top of the characteristic joy of returning to one's homeland, now there was also deep gratitude for the sympathetic manner in which those Mexicans – who did not even know me – had acted for my sake, expecting nothing in return.

A panic attack

When I returned from the United States, the culture shock I had submitted myself to during the previous six consecutive weeks was so huge that I had a frightening panic attack, something that I did not even know existed until I endured it in my own flesh. Truthfully, it was something I do not wish on anybody. The convention in the US I had been invited to join as an interpreter lasted only one week, and I had been granted a visa for 45 days. Of course, I took advantage of each and every day to the fullest and stayed until the very last day. I hardly slept, accepting every single invitation I was extended to go to places and do a million different interesting and exotic things that were totally new to me. I stayed in many different places and was put up by a number of people who had come to Cuba and who, upon learning about my trip to their country, organized my free time with a packed itinerary, making reservations for my flights and taking charge of all the logistics. The point is that with so many and varied stimuli for my brain, which was not used to all those new and exciting experiences, my central nervous system was so overloaded that, upon my return, it got even and took its toll on me.

The first night, I collapsed on my bed, totally exhausted, but on the second one, very late at night, something terrifying happened to me. I woke up all of a sudden with a shortness of breath that was suffocating me, as if I were a chronic asthma patient. I sat up on the edge of our bed completely oblivious of my whereabouts. I could not identify whether that room was an airplane, a ship, a train, or a hotel. It was the most unpleasant sensation in the world. The worst part was that I lost the sense of my own identity. I did not know who I was or what I was doing. Marisol, extremely worried, thought I was having a nightmare and tapped my back over and over trying to alleviate my labored breathing. In her anguish, she asked me what was wrong, but she was unable to understand what I was telling her because I spoke only in English. My brain's cables had been crisscrossed in a deeply entangled way. Everything seemed to indicate that my Spanish language wanted to go on enjoying its well-deserved vacation after six weeks out of use.

I cannot say accurately how long that awful experience lasted. I just know that the doctor who checked me the following day, after learning about the details of my recent trip, concluded that I had been the victim of a panic attack, that my brain had been flooded with too many activities during a long time, nonstop, and was now getting rid of all the stress in that abrupt way. Other people claimed from their own perspectives that as I had taken so many planes in such a short period of time, my body had already arrived in Cuba but my soul was still traveling around very confused, trying to return to Havana. I don't know when my soul came back, but for a long time I kept putting off my bedtime till the very last minute lest I go through a second chapter of that creepy episode.

Fortunately, it did not happen again. Everything seems to indicate that my soul had indeed returned to my body and was in charge of stabilizing it properly. Maybe that was the price I had to pay for playing with the bewildering, consumerist, capitalist society and the impact of readapting myself upon my return. After six weeks of spinning like a top around the United States, visiting and learning about so many places, my return to Cuba in the midst of a terrible economic crisis, with so many shortages and blackouts, was really traumatizing. It was only then that I learned in my own flesh what the famous cultural shock I had heard so much about really meant. That trip was the first of many I made to the United States because, from then on, I started to go there twice a year, escorting Cuban clergy delegations from churches of the Fraternity of Baptist Churches of Cuba and the East Cuba Baptist Convention from all over our country to the assemblies of the Progressive National Baptist Convention.

Interpreting for Rev. Lucius Walker

During my first trip, I had the opportunity to visit the Salvation Baptist Church in Brooklyn, New York, ministered to by Rev. Lucius Walker, director of Pastors for Peace. He volunteered to baptize me then and there with his congregation, but with all due diplomacy, I turned down his offer. I thanked him from the bottom of my heart and explained to him that I would rather have him do that while in Cuba – in my church, in my faith community, and with my pastor, Rev. Raúl Suárez – even if I had to wait whatever time was needed. Fortunately, I did not have to wait long. On Sunday, September 15, 1996, as part of the program of activities scheduled for the 6th US-Cuba Pastors for

Peace Friendshipment Caravan, I had the honor, just as I had requested, to be baptized by both Rev. Suárez and Rev. Walker at the same time in the baptism pool of our beloved Marianao Ebenezer Baptist Church as part of the liturgy of the Sunday worship service corresponding to that day. It was a unique ceremony, for I had to translate my own baptism, and right after it, I had to dry myself a bit and change clothes in a matter of seconds because Lucius preached that day, and I had to interpret his sermon. I did it virtually trickling water, but blissfully, because my request had been granted and gone way beyond my expectations. To make that moment even more memorable, as part of the worship service that day, my daughters performed in their liturgy choir, Generation with a Purpose, both before and right after my baptism ceremony. Without a doubt, it was the greatest spiritual experience in my lifetime.

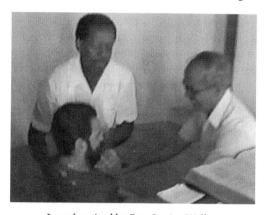

I was baptized by Rev. Lucius Walker and Rev. Raúl Suárez

Generation with a Purpose

Being baptized by the founder and leader of the Pastors for Peace project was a great honor. Rev. Lucius Walker and his solidarity project meant a lot for the Cuban people. They brought dozens of buses, all packed with needed goods and food, that had been donated and driven from the US into Mexico before being shipped across to Cuba – all against US law.

Rev. Walker and the people who gathered from all parts of the US and even from other countries were too powerful a humanitarian statement to be stopped by the US government; however, it was never easy for them to cross the border. They were often given a hard time, and different things were confiscated every now and then. When the first yellow school bus was detained in Laredo, Texas, in 1993, Rev. Walker and a few other members of the Caravan went on a hunger strike that lasted 23 days until the bus was finally released and sent to Cuba, to our local church.

That is why Rev. Walker was so important and is still so admired in Cuba. His Pastors for Peace missions provided amazing relief and support at a very critical time, showing us all very clearly that the people of the US are not all in support of their government's hostile strategy against our dear country. Even though Pastors for Peace collected and brought tons of highly needed material aid, what we appreciated most was the injection of moral support and human solidarity they provided when we needed it most. They showed great courage, and we are most grateful for their sympathy.

Visiting the country of my favorite singers!

In September of 1996, I was chosen out of 14 Cuban candidates to take a course on human rights and the equality of women sponsored by the Swedish International Development Agency, an organization granting scholarships to people from third world countries to train them in issues related to human development. The Swedish Embassy in Havana urged Cuban prestigious personalities to nominate candidates with all the established requirements for this international course. Rev. Raúl Suárcz thought it fit to appoint me for such an event because he thought that I had all the required conditions. The demand they prioritized above all was a good command of English because the training would be taught in that language. When the Swedish consul summoned me to his embassy so as to interview me and learn about the status of my language mastery, he admitted that my English was obviously better than his own, which pleased me a great deal.

When I received the official news that I had been chosen to represent Cuba, I could not believe it. It was "too good to be true," as it is said in English. Sweden was ABBA's country, and they were undoubtedly my favorite music group during my prime years. The possibility of visiting the country of my favorite singers was one more blessing, another dream that now would come true, thanks be given to God. I was in the United States when my wife gave me the happy piece of news over the phone.

After our meeting was over, I took advantage of the remaining time granted by my six-week visa to visit several North American friends whom I had previously met when they visited Cuba through the Martin Luther King Center. The night I was at Scott R. Littler's house in Urbana, Ohio, his telephone rang. To my surprise it was a collect call from Cuba for me. This was the first time ever that I was abroad, away from my family, and our girls were still quite young, seven and eight years old at that time.

That telephone call made me hold my breath because, unavoidably, one always thinks about bad things first; at least that is my experience. My heart stopped beating because I was aware that only an urgent reason would compel my wife to make a collect call to the United States. Knowing me well, and in order to keep me from having a heart attack, the first thing she did was laugh to encourage me to anticipate good news. Right after that, she told me, "Don't freak out. Everything is OK! Nothing bad has happened, just the opposite. I am calling you because Suárez asked me to do it. Congratulations, country boy, you were chosen to go to Sweden!" I could not help but jump with joy right there in Scott's kitchen. He immediately opened a couple of beers to celebrate such good news.

I returned from the United States and stayed at home for just a few weeks because all the paperwork was almost completed for my new experience. All my life, I had been longing to travel overseas, and now, when I least expected it, I was coming back from North America after six weeks, and I was already heading towards Europe to stay for a whole month in Scandinavia. The training course would be held at the Raoul Wallenberg Institute of the Law School at Lund University in the south of Sweden. Lund is a beautiful medieval city from the ninth century. Part of the training would include several visits to Copenhagen, the capital of Denmark, as well as a four-day trip to Oslo, the capital of Norway.

One of the first things I did upon arriving in Sweden, at the Concordia Hotel, where I was lodged, was to request a city map and learn the addresses of the local Baptist churches, so I could visit them and join their Sunday worship services. When I arrived at the hotel for the first time, very late at night, along with the money I was given as a *per diem*, I was handed a dark blue umbrella to welcome me to Sweden and to Lund. When witnessing the expression of awe upon my face, the receptionist at the desk told me, "You will need it very soon." She was absolutely right because the following morning it was raining, so I had to premiere my brand new umbrella right away in order to walk the five blocks between the hotel and the university.

Sweden was an abrupt change from Cuba. Along with the seven hours of time difference, the climate was completely different from ours. What surprised me most was that as early as four o'clock in the afternoon, it was almost dark. No wonder so many Swedes suffer from depression. Many public services provide phototherapy, where people go to be exposed for hours on end to an intense spotlight inside a room with walls painted all in white. They do this to keep themselves from falling into depression and other emotional disorders.

One evening during the first week, equipped with a city map in one hand and several previously identified addresses in the other, I headed towards the Baptist church that was closest to my hotel, just a few blocks away from it. I did not like at all the recently sprayed graffiti on the church's red brick facade: "Fundamentalists!" Being so liberal and progressive myself, I thought I may have arrived at the wrong place and consequently would not be welcomed. Slightly worried, I knocked on the closed door because I thought I heard some music playing inside the building.

I repeated my careful knocking at the door several times. When I was about to leave in frustration, the huge door was suddenly opened, and a bearded young man with long hair looked at me in amazement. He was not expecting anybody at that time, let alone a foreigner. With my thick black beard and Latino complexion, I was obviously an exotic visitor in the midst of so many blond, blue-eyed, and pink-cheeked people. I was taken by many people for somebody from the Middle East, particularly from Iran. I introduced myself right away and let him know about my intentions. His name was Martin, and he was from Yugoslavia. He told me that he was a sound technician and was fixing some musical instruments as the pastor had requested. Nevertheless, he asserted, "Don't you worry, because I have a friend who is doing his practices in this church, and I am sure that he would like to meet you and invite you to come to worship on Sunday." He gave me the telephone number of the seminary student he was talking about, Christoffer Antlab, who lived in one of the suburbs of the city. I should clarify, in order to avoid misunderstandings, that the word suburb does not have the pejorative semantic implication of our country. On the contrary, a suburb is a residential neighborhood, usually located in the outskirts of the city.

As soon as I got back to the hotel, I called him. I was curious about the impact my call would have on that stranger whose name I hardly knew. He was, however, anxiously waiting for my call because the sound technician had shared with him what had taken place just a few minutes before. In spite of the fact that it was drizzling, which is quite common in Sweden during the fall, he asked if I was free that evening and could walk to the railway station near the hotel, where he would be waiting for me. I gladly accepted his kind invitation, for I was the only Cuban among the group made up of 23 students from all over the world. I wanted to be known and strike up friendships with the locals as soon as possible in order to really get to know Sweden, its culture, and its people. That is undoubtedly the best way to do it according to my modest experience.

With the inseparable company of my timely umbrella, I walked under the unceasing rain along those old cobblestone streets up to the railway station, where we met personally. He invited me to his apartment, which he shared with other young people. This is customary in the developed countries to reduce rent bills. We walked all the way there under the ever-falling rain.

Another cultural impact that I experienced was the fact that I was expected to take off my shoes upon entering his apartment so as not to damage the polished wood floor. I could not help worrying about the impact that such an action might have, particularly since I had been walking a lot, and with so much rain, my shoes were wet. With the ominous combination of rainwater and smelly feet (knowing only too well that my feet smell really bad), I had to think twice before abiding by the local cultural expectations. My host appeared to read my mind and immediately brought me some paddy slippers. What a thoughtful man. Slightly more relieved, I thought, "You better put them on." Your first image is quite important, and so are your first smells, aren't they?

He effusively introduced me to his roommates, who were eager to know about Cuba. They had not met any Cubans before so this was a unique opportunity they could not miss. I had to represent and speak on behalf of my eleven million fellow citizens and not let down the image that, through me, they would shape about Cuba. That social gathering was extended until two o'clock in the morning. They grilled me with all sorts of questions. They filled up a whole table with fruits, cheese, chips, sweets, nuts, wines, tea, chocolates, and other snacks. It was an amazing experience.

It was only my third day in that faraway and exotic country, and I already had a circle of friends with whom to share my free time. They kindly offered me their house, made their bicycles available to me – the means of transportation par excellence in Lund – provided me with free-of-charge access to their e-mail services, invited me to go to the movie theater, play computer games, and eat out in restaurants. To sum it up, they made my stay in Sweden very pleasant. I really enjoyed every single minute in that wonderful country where I witnessed an almost perfect combination of the best achievements of both socialism and capitalism, a society worthy to be respected and emulated in the best senses of the words.

As a good Cuban, since the day I arrived in Sweden, I implemented several strategies to save money, so I could go shopping during the last few days and ensure the expected *pacotilla* (gifts) that every single Cuban who travels abroad strives to bring along upon returning home.

I was not the exception to this rule, of course, so I tried to save every last penny possible, so I could afford to purchase a few things for my large family. It goes without saying that the economic crisis was still worsening in our country halfway through the 1990s, so anything I could bring home, no matter what, would be both welcome and highly appreciated.

Breakfast was included in the arrangements with the hotel, but we had to pay for everything else, including transportation and other meals. The living standards in Sweden are very high, and everything is excessively expensive. How did I solve my problem, then? Well, quite easily because where there is a Cuban, there is creativity to spare. Each morning, I climbed downstairs to the hotel basement restaurant with my fanny pack fastened to my waist, but completely empty. Breakfasts were buffet style – a Swedish table *(smorgasbord)*. It was a real waste of food that overwhelmed me. There were no restrictions on how much food a diner could take, and everything was flawlessly packed, designed, conceived of and presented in an exquisite and impeccable way – just what I needed to get away with it very discreetly.

It was a timely blessing that the assortment of cheeses and hams of different kinds were packed in air-tight, transparent plastic bags. To make it possible for me to procure food for lunch, I always tried to sit by myself during breakfast – in a corner and behind a pillar or a flower pot holding any plant with thick foliage. That was the method that I implemented from the very beginning and which always worked out as expected. When I climbed the staircase to my room right after breakfast, there was always a big lush apple, cheese and ham slices, cookies, soda crackers, and a few other snacks in my fanny pack. I stored all that valuable content for my food security in the small refrigerator in my room, which I fortunately did not have to share with anybody else. Then I put my camera back into my multi-pocketed fanny pack where it belonged.

Upon returning from the university at noon, I enjoyed the prerogatives I had as a hotel guest, which entitled me to have free access to sweet cookies, chips, tea, and hot chocolate from the dispensaries that were located in the lobby area – a complimentary service of our hotel that was located right across from my room. I fixed myself a mug of hot chocolate, grabbed a handful of cookies, and went to my room, where I placed them on top of my desk next to everything I had saved from breakfast. There, while watching TV on any English channel of my choice, I had lunch happily. For a Swede, that was a snack at best, but for a Cuban like me, coming from such a poor social background and in the midst of the economic crisis, that was a hearty lunch, which sometimes made me feel guilty while enjoying it and thinking about what my little girls were eating in Cuba.

Those feelings are difficult to reconcile. On the one hand, I had in front of me so much food, so many tasty things to eat, and I was hungry enough to eat them; on the other hand, I was aware that far away, at that same moment, my small children and my wife were eating whatever was available, what was left over, what was reheated, what they managed to get, what somebody saw fit to exchange or to hand out. How I would have loved to share this tangible joy, this evident pleasure with them; how disappointed and helpless I felt that no matter how much I loved them and however hard I tried, it was not humanly possible. It is honestly very strongly bittersweet. As we Cubans claim, "It is not easy!"

Another strategy to save money that I implemented since the first week was going to dinner at a pizza place owned by some Armenian immigrants. I would order only one item that was plentiful and more than enough to be split up by two people. I used to share it with César Guillermo Castillo Reyes, the Guatemalan lawyer who was my classmate in the course. One day, I would pay the bill, and he would do it the following day. We took turns and thus saved money that we both needed. In this austere fashion, by stretching my breakfast to turn it into lunch and by sharing dinner expenses every other day, I managed to save a good amount of Swedish crowns, which I kept for the very last Saturday because it was the day when the flea market (the popular second-hand street fair so coveted by us Cubans abroad) was open. There many good quality things could be bought at very reasonable prices. Bargaining was allowed as well.

Eight unforgettable minutes

The last Friday in Sweden, I dreamed about my family and woke up with a deep homesickness. I felt a strong mixture of longing, sadness, and an urgent desire to communicate with them. I would have given anything to listen to the sweet voices of my little girls, whom I missed so much. The phone was right there by my side. The fact that just a few hours were separating me from them did not placate my feelings – just the opposite – it exacerbated them even more. I did not think about it twice and thus made, inadvertently, one of the biggest mistakes in my life by being incautious, by letting my feelings totally loose, and by pleasing my emotions at all costs.

From the comfort of my hotel room, I requested an international call to Havana, Cuba. I knew I would have to pay for it, of course, but I never ever thought that just a few minutes of telecommunication would be so extremely expensive. I managed to talk with my wife and kids for hardly eight minutes, disregarding the time that elapsed while Cora, our dear neighbor, picked up the phone and told my family about my call. The three of them ran across the street to get to her house. Back then, we did not have a telephone of our own.

That was, undoubtedly, the telephone conversation I enjoyed the most in my whole life. Listening to the voices of my little daughters from so far away, yet feeling them so close to me – sensing their emotions, their joy, their nervous giggling, even their agitated breathing after running because of their joyous excitement about talking with their daddy – was a most divine experience.

Almost immediately after I hung up the receiver in my room, with my heart swollen from so much emotion, I got a telephone call. It was the hotel operator asking me, "Mister González, are you aware of what you have just done?" My reply did not take long, "Of course, I have just called Cuba and spoken with my family." "Yes, I know that, but do you happen to know what that means in terms of payment by any chance?" I admitted, "No, I don't, but now you are making me nervous. Can you please tell me?"

When she told me the cost of that unforgettable call, I could not believe my ears. I thought it very likely she was just teasing me, but she was not. Nothing was further from the truth, for she really meant it. On that call, I spent all the money I had saved during the whole month that I was in Sweden so I could buy a few things for my house and family. I was dumbfounded for a little while. It was as if I had received a hard blow on my head. I was speechless and did not know what to say or do. The operator, suddenly concerned about my telltale silence, wondered, "Do you have enough money to pay for that telephone call?" I responded, "Yes, yes, I do, of course. Please don't worry." Right after that, I thanked her and hung up.

What happened to me next was one of the greatest faith experiences that I have ever had. Just a few minutes before, I had been the happiest man on earth; now, however, a deep sadness and even feelings of guilt were overwhelming my soul. Fortunately, that was very short-lived because all of a sudden, a thanksgiving sense the size of the sun took hold of me. I knelt down on the carpeted floor of my room, right there in front of the telephone that had made me feel so happy a few minutes before, bowed down my head, and with tears of gratitude in my eyes, I thanked God for allowing me that unique gift of speaking with my wife and daughters. That gift was priceless because the way I saw it, there was not enough money in the whole world capable of buying what I felt during those eight unforgettable minutes.

Thank you, Lord, I told Him, because that money was not mine, and You gave it to me; because if I am here, I owe it to You, too, and it has been a blessing. After my most sincere amen, I recovered my joy and left my room euphorically towards the reception desk so as to pay for the most expensive call of my life. When I was getting ready to carry out such operation, however, I was told that it was not necessary to do it right away, that it was done customarily at the very end, when guests were expected to service all their debts with the hotel at the check-out time. In my case, that would be at six o'clock Sunday morning, when I would be picked up by a taxicab and taken to the city of Malmö so as to start my happy journey back to Cuba.

Life surprises you, and when prayers are truly sincere, they are rewarded. I have not a single doubt about it. That day was Friday, and we had already finished all the activities of our training course, including the graduation ceremony, in which I had been chosen as the spokesperson of the class and had to speak on behalf of the whole group. The only thing that still hurt me was that I would not be able to buy anything I had planned. All the money that I had, I owed now to the hotel to pay for that call. Gee whizz! To be in Sweden for a whole month saving money day in and day out and now to be able to take home not even an *alpist* (a tiny canary grass seed). Even if it were for the fairest cause in the world, it was not an easy feeling to live with and to carry in the deepest core of my conscience. I thought my family would never forgive me for that sentimental weakness, that sudden breach in my resilience. I thought I would be blamed for the lack of gifts upon my return home.

So, instead of going shopping and packing the long expected *pacotilla*, I began to wander down the streets for the very last time, taking pictures around all the places I used to pass by riding the bicycle I borrowed from Christoffer, so as to immortalize that experience of my stay in Europe, in that beautiful city with the largest churches I had ever seen. I wanted to trap with my lens all those fantastic cobblestoned streets and the multicolored dead leaves in their unceasing falling down all throughout the autumn. I went to bed that night thinking about the fact that the following day would be the very last one for me in that gorgeous Scandinavian country, where I had such a wonderful time in spite of the telephone call at the very end that had taken me to bankruptcy in just eight minutes.

At seven o'clock in the morning, I was awakened by the telephone. I was startled because it was still quite early. It was Christoffer, my good Swedish friend, who immediately apologized for calling me at such an inappropriate hour, "Alberto, I learned about what happened to you yesterday. The hotel reception desk clerk is a friend of mine, and she told me that you committed the unpardonable mistake of calling your house from your room. I, both as a Christian and as a Swede, feel ashamed that an international call to talk to your family was so ridiculously expensive. I cannot allow such an abuse. But you don't need to worry about it, for I have already taken care of that issue. You don't have to pay for that call at all. I did it for you already, and I won't take no for an answer. You already know the city very well. Take your money and go shopping to get everything your family may need. Remember that today is Saturday, and the flea market is open. Don't miss it!"

I could not believe this was really happening to me. Was I dreaming by any chance? I was so deeply moved by that amazing gesture from him that I said, "Hey, my brother. You are going to make me cry." He laughed when replying, "So cry baby as much as you want, but do not forget to go shopping." So I did, and I did a great job indeed! I managed to buy much more than expected, to such an extent that everything did not fit in my two pieces of luggage. A hotel staff member gave me a cardboard grocery box that was empty in their warehouse in which to pack everything that was left. As if that were not enough, Christoffer showed up at the hotel at mid-afternoon and asked me if I had finally bought what I wanted. I thanked him once again and showed him my whole luggage. He looked at me and smiled when he saw the cardboard box wrapped up with duct tape. Smacking his lips noisily and shaking his head sideways, he exclaimed, "How come a professional like you is going to fly over the Atlantic travelling with a grocery box?" I was slightly embarrassed with his remark but did not have any better choice. Right after that, he flung his arm over my shoulder and told me, "Come along because we need to correct that."

He took me to a department store just a few blocks away from the hotel, where he bought me a huge blue canvas duffle bag, one of those famous "worms" in which we easily accommodated the contents of the humble grocery box. He bade me farewell in the hotel lobby with a bear hug and an unforgettable, "May God bless you!" The emotion and gratitude that I felt my last night in Sweden were so strong that I could not manage to sleep all night long. That day, I learned that God acts in many different ways and that we should never lose our faith in Him, because He can do anything at all. For Him, nothing is impossible.

Marisol made it possible

When I was away from home for days, weeks and even months in a row to fulfill my dream and to accomplish myself professionally, Marisol carried a two-fold load. She undertook full parenthood, became mother and father, and tackled whatever came her way with pride and dignity. She has always been every inch a woman. And she has always smiled and laughed even during the direst situations we have gone through. That marvelous good humor, she inherited from her mother. That is why she has so many friends. It is not a small wonder that people love her everywhere she goes, and everyone who meets her falls in love with her right away. I am very proud of that most characteristic feature of her personality.

As an interpreter, I started to travel every year after 1996 to the United States for the most part and I usually stayed there between four and six weeks at a time. During each trip, Marisol became the super-mom in charge of everything that was needed, even taking good care of my pets. When we were still in the countryside, she fed and cared for our livestock: a few chickens, some rabbits, and a pig.

There is nothing more educational

Fortunately, those meetings to which I went to translate in the USA were intentionally held in different cities each year to ensure that they would bring about a good financial boost in each and every one of them. The gigantic convention would gather over ten thousand people, and that obviously had a favorable impact on the local economy for a whole week. In the month of January, the sites were found in the South of the country; whereas, in August, they were chosen in the North, so as to flee from the cold and the heat respectively. Thanks to that planning strategy, I was able to visit almost all the most important cities of that country, as well as a good number of its fifty states. The more I visited the States, the better I was able to understand the questions asked all the time by the North Americans I worked with here, and I could do so in an increasingly tolerant and unprejudiced way. A whole lot may be learned by reading, looking at pictures, watching films and documentaries, or listening to other people's experiences when they are shared; but undoubtedly, there is nothing more educational than to travel and witness things first hand. Thus the wise proverb *seeing is believing*.

I had the privilege of following the footprints of Martin Luther King, Jr., through the southern states of the United States and of personally meeting and speaking with his widow, Mrs. Coretta Scott King. I was in his church, on his grave, and at the center that bears his name in Atlanta, Georgia: Martin Luther King, Jr. Center for Non-Violent

Speaking with Coretta Scott King

Social Change. I also met Rosa Parks, the courageous lady who, in 1955, marked a turning point in the history of the struggle for civil rights in Montgomery, Alabama.

Likewise, I had the opportunity to follow the steps of our beloved José Martí in Ybor City, Tampa, and I was able to visit the cigar factories where he did so much for the sake of the unity of the whole Cuban people.

Being at the spectacular Niagara Falls, in the city of Buffalo, New York, and reading the plaque immortalizing the work of our dearly-loved poet José María Heredia in that majestic place was, among many other experiences, an unforgettable moment, which I will treasure and appreciate forever. I documented it and other special occasions with pictures and journal entries. Writing a diary, always in English, on each of my trips abroad has been part of my insatiable addiction to this beautiful language. In fact, that has been one more initiative that I have seen fit to implement, so as to apply to myself the infallible teaching method that I call repetitive-continuous-systematic-progressive.

My beard did not grow under the chalk dust in school, but it did in many other places both inside and outside Cuba while I was doing my job as translator-interpreter for many delegations. After a year had elapsed, it became part of my official identity in photos on my ID card, my passport, my business cards, and my driving license. I showed it with pride during many years until the gray strands of hair that began to pop out on my chin ended up convincing me that it was about time for me to say good-bye to it. Anyway, it had already accomplished its mission. Besides, instead of satisfaction, as had been the case, my beard was bringing about problems. I resembled an Arab with it, I always ended up being a target for hand searches, body frisks, cross examinations, fingerprinting, face picture taking, and luggage inspections in every single airport I arrived in, even more so in the

United States – particularly after September 11, 2001.

In the summer of 2000, I was in the United States, in the city of Nashville, Tennessee, where I was translating at the Glendale Baptist Church in that beautiful southern city. As a matter of chance, my two daughters were, at the same time, participating in the Children's Crusade that was held in Philadelphia, Pennsylvania, which had been organized by the Bruderhof Community of Rifton, New York. Boys and girls from all over the world gathered to protest against the death penalty in a gigantic pacifist activity right across from the jail where Mumia Abu-Jamal was behind bars on death row. They would return to Cuba via Jamaica from New York a couple of weeks earlier than I would, for our objectives were different. They were traveling through the auspices of the Martin Luther King Center; whereas I was doing it through the Fraternity of Baptist Churches of Cuba.

On the day prior to their return trip, I received a telephone call from Glen Kilgore, a North American friend from Savannah, Georgia, who was acquainted with the details of our itineraries. After greeting me, he asked, "Alberto, would you like to go to see your daughters off tomorrow in New York?" I thought he was kidding, so I replied, "It is too far away, and the air ticket with such a short notice is too expensive." Laughing, he asserted, "I know that it is indeed far away and expensive, too, but that is not what I am asking you. Would you like to go to bid them farewell at the airport or not?" I told him that, of course, I would love to do it if I could, but that it would be out of the question because they were leaving the following day, first thing in the morning. "That is not a problem," he assured me. "Take your passport and go to the airport because you have an e-ticket in your name departing to New York late this afternoon and returning to Nashville tomorrow at ten o'clock in the morning. How do you like it?" I could not believe what was happening to me. *He who has a friend has a sugar mill.*

That night I stayed overnight in the Bronx at the home of friends who very kindly took me to the airport at five o'clock in the morning. My presence would be a total surprise that my daughters, of course, did not expect at all. They knew that I was in the United States but thought I was far away from New York with a very tight work agenda. When I got to that humongous airport, the Cuban children were already there checking their luggage at the counter of Air Jamaica. Just by chance, Betsy, my little one, was at that precise minute lifting her bundles to place them on the scale and have them weighed. When she saw me face-to-face, barely a meter way, she abruptly popped out her eyes and could not help but drop her package. What cheerful joy! That instant was worth a million dollars. I helped them both to check their luggage and even managed to have breakfast with them right there at the airport before seeing them off on their way back to Cuba.

Some neighbors in Cuba bet money claiming, "This time around, he stays there for sure. He's got to be too stupid to miss the great opportunity of being with his two daughters over there in the *Yuma* and not to stay, particularly when the three of them speak English." I let them down big time. I am really sorry, but truthfully, that idea has never crossed my mind, and it has not been due to the lack of opportunities. Thanks to God, I have traveled quite a lot, actually much more that I could have ever expected. I have visited the United States many times. I have also been to Canada, the Bahamas, Jamaica, Mexico, the Dominican Republic, Guadeloupe, Venezuela, France, Sweden, Denmark, and Norway, but I will not leave my Cuba for anything in the world, regardless of everything I would like to change in my country for the sake and well-being of all my fellow citizens.

I belong here

I neither applaud nor criticize anyone who decides to try for better luck in other lands. Everyone knows why they do it, and they have all the right in the world to do so if determined. Like Ecuadorians, I firmly believe in the universality of citizenship, for all of us are in fact citizens of our planet, the Earth, of our sacred *Pachamama*. Ever since immemorial times, there have been human migrations all over the world seeking for better living and working conditions, which are a human necessity. It has been scientifically demonstrated with DNA research of the current populations dwelling on our planet that, if the whole world is populated today, it is precisely due to the plentiful and massive human migrations that started in Africa thousands of years ago at the onset of our civilization.

I love to travel, of course. What Cuban would not like to do it? I have had the privilege of that wonderful opportunity, which I have exploited to the maximum and enjoyed thoroughly. I wish everybody could say the same thing because traveling is by far the most educational experience ever. You may read a book, watch a film, or listen to an account, but nothing compares to the first-hand personal experience of getting inside another culture and witnessing through your five senses whatever is going on daily in it. In addition, I appreciate the fact of having gone not only to the touristy developed places, to the most industrialized capitalist countries, but to others as well, which, by the way, have made me feel very, very proud to be Cuban. Even in the United States, in its own capital, Washington D.C., I witnessed things that I have never seen in my own country despite our alleged backwardness and underdevelopment.

I know of many who would be willing to give anything away so as to have one of the many opportunities I have had to travel, particularly to the United States. As far as I am concerned, however, I belong here. Everything that is important for my life is here in Cuba: the sacred graves where the remains of my parents, my uncles and aunts, and my grandparents rest in peace. Here I also have my daughters, my wife, my best friends, and a job in which I am thoroughly accomplished from the professional perspective.

To sum it up, what I love and need to give and to receive is found here, among my roots, my culture, my identity, my coffee, my music, my food, my neighbors, my coworkers, and last, but not least, my dearest pet, Doggy, whom I love and take care of as he were a child. My family setting would be incomplete without a dog, for I will never get tired of repeating over and over again that I am fully convinced of the fact that I either was or will be a dog in another life.

Of course, I love to travel, particularly by plane, to go to places, and to know about things, but unavoidably, there comes the time, sooner rather than later, when I can't wait to go back home. Nothing compares to your own pillow or toilet, even though there are others of a much better quality in many other sites. My family knows it too well, so they would not let me lie about it were I to say otherwise. Upon getting home from any trip abroad, there is nothing I crave for more than a simple plate of plain rice with a fried egg on top and fried ripe plantains. The first thing I ask for upon arriving home from the airport is a good cup of Cuban coffee, with the works, regardless of how blended it might be with peas – not the cloudy, hot, watered-down liquid that is wrongly called coffee in other countries.

I have met fellow Cubans in all the countries I have visited. It is amazing. It seems that there is not a single corner in the whole planet where a Cuban has not arrived yet. We are something like a ubiquitous, contagious epidemic. I would not be surprised at all if, in a frozen igloo at the North Pole, there was one of my compatriots teaching the Eskimos how to dance salsa. My experience has always been the same, repeated over and over, with amazing similarity, in terms of the nature of the dialogues held during those special occasions.

Before beginning each animated conversation, I already positively know how our enlivened talk is going to end. When a couple of Cubans meet for the first time in any corner whatsoever of the globe, they befriend each other in a matter of seconds and feel as if they have always known one another, setting up an improvised family bond right on the spot. After the habitual questions that are always asked, such as "How are things at home?" the pressing need immediately springs up – especially if there are drinks around, which slacken our tongue, our soul, our feelings, and even our human conscience – of sharing our homesickness and nostalgia.

I have heard many of them say, visibly touched – with tearful eyes, a tightened chest, a lump in their throats, and a broken voice – that deep down in their hearts of hearts, they wish they could return to Cuba with me, even if for just a few days, to recharge their batteries, so to speak. They have confessed to me from the bottom of their hearts that they have everything that in Cuba they never managed to own but that they cannot help but feel a big vacuum in the deepest part of their being. They are unable to convey that with words, and they don't succeed in covering it with any material stuff either. The point is that the most valuable things in life are not purchased with money. One may buy the most comfortable bed in the world but not a good night's sleep. You may buy sex, but not authentic love; services of all sorts and a whole bunch of entertainment, but never a true and sincere friendship. The bottom line is that nobody really knows the value of what is owned until it is lost. Likewise, by the same token, we are all along criticizing and underestimating the real value of what we do have, thinking that, as a proverb claims in English *the grass is always greener on the other side of the fence*. Maybe it really is, but it does not taste like our own.

Either out of their own free will or not, they have been uprooted from the indispensable nutrients that would allow them to attain true harmony and spiritual balance. They do not realize that real happiness is not found in having what you lack; it is, rather, the other way around. Happiness is found in wanting what you own, regardless of how humble or scant it may be. It has been well demonstrated that the more we have, the more enslaved we are to what we own and, consequently, the more we suffer when for whatever reason, we lose it. The more we have, the longer the list is of new concerns that are added on top of the already existing ones in our everyday life experience. Contrary to the most basic logic, after a natural catastrophe, the victims who suffer the most and are most traumatized are precisely those who owned and thus lost the largest amount of resources. The moral of the story is that wealth is not necessarily tantamount to joy. You may be very happy with very little. Happiness is not to be found in the tangible material world outside us but quite the opposite. It is to be found in the abstract spiritual world we all carry inside. The one and only thing that is truly yours is what you still keep after a shipwreck: your own self.

CUBA
A brief history

The Early 2000s: The Envy of Other Nations

If US relations with Cuba were normalized, American citizens could freely visit the island nation for educational, cultural, economic, diplomatic, and tourist purposes. The international community has repeatedly denounced US policy towards Cuba. The UN General Assembly has voted to condemn the US embargo against Cuba. The US has also failed to compel Latin American nations to maintain sanctions on Cuba.

Commercial and diplomatic relations between Cuba and Latin America have been restored and continue to grow. Latin American countries have engaged in hundreds of millions of dollars of trade with Cuba.

"Cuba's achievements in social development are impressive, given the size of its gross domestic product per capita. As the human development index of the United Nations makes clear year after year, Cuba should be the envy of many other nations that are ostensibly far richer. Cuba demonstrates how much nations can do with the resources they have if they focus on the right priorities – health, education, and literacy," said Kofi Annan, Secretary General of the United Nations on April 11, 2000.

As new and complex problems challenge our social system, solutions are being developed with more collaborative and integrated approaches, especially at the level of service delivery. The experience of the local community development movement of the last decades offers an emerging model of small-scale, place-based, participatory planning and monitoring of services, which could greatly complement the reach and effectiveness of current models of service delivery. The experiences at the community level have developed useful methods.

Many of the reforms implemented in the early 1990s were aimed at market opening; however, after 2003 the Cuban government tried to restrict and turn back a few of these reforms.

In 2003, the "convertible peso" was introduced. Cubans could still have dollars legally, but it was pointless because we could not spend them anywhere unless they were changed into the new convertible pesos or CUCs, which from then on, were the only hard currency accepted at Cuba's hard currency businesses.

In May 2004, prices in the convertible pesos were raised between 10 and 35 percent, while in June 2004 peso salaries were raised. All of these measures served as a kind of levy on dollar-holders, compelling them to subsidize the peso economy. They were at the same time both an unjustified punishment for those who were better off in the new Cuban economy and an attempt to restore a certain amount of equity that had been lost.

Another group of regulations tried to undo the prerogatives that workers in the tourism industry enjoyed. In January, 2005, tourist workers were banned from taking gifts or benefits from foreigners they worked with. Corruption in the state-run companies operating in hard currencies seemed to be out of control. Accepting commissions from foreign businessmen, nepotism, selling jobs, and misuse of official cars, expense accounts and travel were some of the corrupt practices that started to appear.

At the same time, the new measures included new penalties on the self-employed sector, with a heavy taxation on the private restaurants *(paladares)* and further restrictions on foreign direct investments. The number of self-employed people declined in 2004 and continued to shrink as restrictions and taxation on them increased.

The impact of the economic blockade was exacerbated by a series of natural disasters. Our island was hit hard by five hurricanes during the first five years of the new millennium. The last two, Charlie and Ivan, both in 2004, caused $2.15 billion in damage. Prior to the hurricanes, in 2003, the country had been hit by the worst drought in over a century.

The year 2006 was declared the Year of the Energy Revolution. It was dedicated to improving the energy infrastructure, solving shortages and blackouts that afflicted the nation since the collapse of the USSR, and addressing sustainability by improving efficiency and reducing energy use overall. In a massive campaign of large-scale popular participation, energy-efficient appliances were distributed by the government (light bulbs, pressure cookers, stoves and refrigerators).

Cuba faced new challenges armed with a considerable accumulation of strengths. In a relatively short period of time, we drastically improved and maintained the health status of the nation, virtually eradicated illiteracy, and developed one of the most educated workforces in the hemisphere. With this extraordinarily high level of education, we have proven to have a high capacity for innovation and transformation. This has been demonstrated over the past 50 years, but certainly never more than since the beginning of the Special Period. The values of equity and responsibility that framed the development of social policy in the past and the practice of constructing a humane and equitable society will continue as we face the challenges of our future.

I Do Not Believe in Chances

*If any of you lacks wisdom, he should ask God,
who gives generously to all without finding fault,
and it will be given to him.
But when he asks, he must believe and not doubt,
because he who doubts is like a wave of the sea,
blown and tossed by the wind.*
James 1:5-6

During one of the many delegations I worked with as a translator-interpreter, I met a young Japanese woman based in the United States who practiced chiromancy or palmistry. One evening, in the lobby of the Martin Luther King Center, a delegation of young people from Pacific Lutheran University, in Cuba for ten days of study, had gathered before leaving for a scheduled activity. While they waited for transportation, the palmist was satisfying the curiosity of those who asked for readings. I was passing in front of her when she dismissed her last "patient" and without my asking extended an invitation, "Would you like me to read your palm?" I had never had that done before, but I thought it would not hurt to try, for there is nothing like personal experience.

A car accident

In the next few minutes, she told me things that strengthened my incredulity about her expertise reading and construing the anatomy of human palms. Back then, I was hardly 35 years old, did not know how to drive, and did not think I would ever learn to do so. Owning a car was so far out of my reach that I never planned to purchase one. When she held my hand in one of hers, she lingered for a while, thinking deeply, pondering what my palm was suggesting to her. I did not like the expression I witnessed when she frowned. She made a face, pursed her lips and twisted her mouth sideways.

She stared at my eyes in an uncomfortable and awkward silence that seemed to have no end. Then she asserted that, at about the age of 40, my life would be threatened by a car accident, but I should not worry about it because I would walk out of it unhurt and then would have a long life. She said that she pictured me behind the steering wheel. She told me a few other things that made much more sense the way I saw it, but that stuff about the accident rather tickled me. I felt like laughing at it, so I did not heed her predictions at all.

But in late 2000, I had an incredible opportunity to acquire a car. Even though I knew how to drive and had been granted my driving license in 1999, I decided to go to driving school for formal training and so I did, completing the course.

In the afternoon of July 17, 2001, I was returning in my car from Puerto Esperanza, driving on the six-lane highway connecting Havana and Pinar del Río. I was in a cheerful mood, singing along with an English song that we were listening to on the car CD player in the pleasant company of my friends Vladimir González, Eva Rodríguez, (the wife of Rev. Humberto Argudín, pastor of The Manger Pentecostal Church of Puerto Esperanza), her son, David Saúl D'Loyola, and his wife, Maité Fernández. These last three were traveling with luggage because they were going to the Central Railway Station in Old Havana in order to travel to the eastern part of our country.

We were driving along in the fast lane – the one closer to the grassy median strip – with plenty of hedges spread out, one right after another. They decorate the way during the daytime and diffuse the unbearable headlights of on-coming vehicles at night, thus reducing the awful dazzling that was blamed for so many night car wrecks.

I was driving right at 100 km/h, the top speed allowed on the highway, as we approached the main gateway to the ecological community of Las Terrazas in the Sierra del Rosario mountain range. At that moment, two people were walking across the road, one of them pushing a motorcycle. Recognizing the imminent danger, I slowed slightly and pricked up my senses and paid attention also to the many hitchhikers by the roadside flashing money, hoping someone would do the favor of picking them up.

In the twinkling of an eye, all the peace, joy, and well-being we were enjoying turned into one of the most terrifying moments I have ever experienced. The men who, just a few seconds before, had crossed the road with a motorcycle, without looking back, suddenly made a U-turn and started to cross the road in the opposite direction, giving me only a split second to react before my car hit them. If I had gone on straight, I would surely have killed them both. If I had turned to the right to avoid running over them, I would have struck the cluster of hitchhikers who were waiting there. By the grace and miracle of God, I decided to turn to the left, putting on the brakes at the same time, which made us literally fly in midair, after hitting one of the central divider hedges. We were projected upwards and began to spin around like a top at an amazing speed, hitting each other as we bumped against the inner parts of the car.

Although I totally lost control of the vehicle, I clung to the steering wheel and experienced what I had seen so many times in films. As a helpless victim of that extremely stressful situation, my brain activated its natural protection system. I started to perceive my situation as if I were looking at it in slow motion. I saw the people on the roadside raise their hands to their heads and open their eyes and mouths as wide as they could. With the terror of being eye witnesses to that accident right under their noses, some were screaming, while others were paralyzed in front of that metallic tornado, which would not stop spinning around like a carrousel – a flying saucer at full speed about a meter above the ground. I also saw how the dust, the stones, the leaves from the bushes, the grass, and the pieces of broken plastic and glass danced in the air in an amazing mixture, a reddish smoke in which all those objects were floating away from the force of gravity as if in a makeshift galaxy.

Eva, the pastor's wife, a woman with faith the size of the sky, did not panic in spite of that extreme situation but began to pray at the top of her lungs, asking Jesus Christ to save our lives. In each of our turns in midair, she said something different, with a shocking certainty, as if she were sitting in one of the pews of her church during a regular worship service. It was something really impressive and noteworthy. Eventually, when the inertia was broken and the momentum was lost, the force of gravity pulled our "flying saucer" towards the ground. The car leaned forward and fell down by its own weight upon its right front tire but kept on spinning over it as a real top.

It drilled a hole on the ground with the friction of that ferocious movement and its evident weight, uprooting weeds and branches from hedges that offered resistance. Little by little, it started to slow down in that dynamic turning that seemed to last an eternity. When we finally lost the impulse that was nourishing that voracious energy, the car collapsed and fell back down with a big thud over its other three wheels, jumping and rebounding several times, making a boisterous noise in the midst of that cloud of rarefied dust with the entire whirlwind created there just in a matter of seconds.

When we got to the neutral point of the movement and peace finally arrived, Eva shouted, "Thank you Lord!" We all crept out of the car step by step, dizzy, bewildered, frightened, confused, and disoriented. It was like living in another dimension where we were feeling things never experienced before. All the onlookers came over immediately to help us, expecting the worst. In the middle of that evident anxiety, it occurred to me to turn on the radio CD player. When the music started to play, I said, "What do we complain about if we still have music available?" We all cuddled up and hugged each other and were glad to be alive and not to have killed or injured anybody. However, we were in shock. Vladimir even threw up when he exited the car. Evidently, my blood pressure went up, for a blinding headache took hold of me in such a way that I could hardly see, so I had to squint.

As I sat on top of a big rock, right at the scene of our accident, the image of that Japanese palmist who had read my hand five years earlier came to me. She had forecast an automobile accident in which I would save my life at the age of approximately 40 years. It was July 2001; in September, just a couple of months later, I would turn 41 years old. I was indeed still 40! Would that be a matter of random chance? I refuse to think that such was the case. I do not believe in chances. There are many things that we human beings will never understand thoroughly. The Japanese palmist will never know how much I remembered her that day – or maybe she does.

Human solidarity wore its Sunday best that day. The local neighbors showed up immediately and volunteered to help in whatever way was needed. They brought us water, coffee, and pain killers. A farmer rode back to his house on his horse and returned shortly thereafter carrying a machete with which to cut enough grass to stuff the affected tire. That allowed us, after a couple of hours and all the painstaking and cumbersome process with the police, to resume our trip to our destination: Havana. The car suffered a lot but much less than what we expected with that impact. All of its right-hand side was displaced; the doors were dislocated; the floodlights were broken; the windshield cracked; and the right wheel steering rod was partially twisted, but in spite of all that, it was still running!

As for me, in the middle of all that fuss, I did not realize that my lips had been cut and that I had almost broken my left upper leg at the height of the thigh with the blows I had gotten from the steering wheel. It was not until I parked the car in the garage that I started limping out of pain. When I took off my pants, I saw the huge swelling that had already formed there – a gigantic hematoma that accompanied me for many days. But, fortunately, I did not suffer any bone fractures at all. The car would eventually be fixed. The most important thing was that we had managed to preserve the most valuable thing of all: our lives. Otherwise, we would have been only photos and memories, as the late singer Selena used to say in her popular song.

My small contribution to the church

After having worked systematically and intensively in the ecclesial world, translating and interpreting for pastors from many different religious denominations, both in Cuba and overseas, without seeking glory at all, I may assert that I know these professionals of the Holy Scriptures pretty well. Some of them, such as the well-known Baptist ministers Rev. Raúl Suárez and Rev. Lucius Walker, Jr., have inspired me so much that they have strengthened my faith. I might even attribute to them the merit of my conversion to Christianity. For me, Reverends Suárez and Walker have been two authentic contemporary prophets, denouncing injustice energetically and courageously. I have always felt that I was a communication bridge between them. And the whole thing turns out to be quite symbolic in its own right, full of meanings, for one of them is white, the other black; one is Cuban, the other North American; one speaks in Spanish, the other in English. And both have been stigmatized as heretics, apostates, and communists.

It was the pressing professional need of getting acquainted with the Bible that motivated me to enroll in the Higher Institute of Biblical and Theological Studies in Havana back in September 2004. A few months before that date, I had gone to this institute with a religious delegation from the United States as part of their scheduled activities while in Cuba. When I interpreted for Professor Midiam Lobaina Gámez, teaching vice-rector of the Institute, I learned about opportunities available there that would meet my academic needs. I was sorry that I had not joined them before.

To earn a degree, starting a second university major at the age of 44, I would have to sacrifice every Saturday during four consecutive years of my life. That important decision would also entail long hours of study, reading, consultations, research, library visits, drafting of papers and presentations, and evaluation. It would require a good share of dedication considering my already tight agenda and the loss of what little free time that I had, but I intuited that it would be worth the work and believed it was a step I should take without further delay. I promised Midiam that I would be their student that school year, and I was true to my word. I will never regret having done it. It was one of the most important decisions I have ever made in my life.

In order for me to be able to graduate as a bachelor when completing my third year in 2007, according to the academic requirements, I had to submit a small thesis called *tesina* in Spanish. It was a great opportunity to write about the "Reasons for the Emergence of the Fraternity of Baptist Churches of Cuba," the convention our local church has belonged to since 1989 as one of its three founding churches. Even though this modest contribution was undoubtedly worth it because the history of the FIBAC had not been written prior to that date, what really deserved all my time, my energies, my wakefulness, my undivided attention and my most committed research dedication, was the subject of my next thesis, with which I was applying to be granted the degree of *Licenciado* in Biblical and Theological Studies and which, thanks be given to God, was granted to me in July 2008.

I could have continued working on the original *tesina* on the Fraternity, submitting it the following year as a thesis proper. This unquestionably would have been much easier than the choice I made. But the point was not just to abide by the demands and requirements set by the ISEBIT in order for me to claim another university degree and to boast about it, framing and hanging it on the wall like a trophy. I rather wanted to come up with something that would solve an existing problem, that might meet a pressing need, and that could provide a practical and tangible solution to a real lack within my church setting. I started to brainstorm and ponder about the issue one Saturday afternoon upon returning home from my classes and – bingo! A light went on in my head with a happy idea.

In keeping with the history of the Baptist Church in our country, up until the late 1980s, there were only three conventions of this Protestant denomination. Each emerged from different sources and at different historical moments; namely: the West Cuba Baptist Convention, derived from the Southern Baptist Convention of the United States, the East Cuba Baptist Convention, derived from the American Baptist Convention from the north of the United States, and the so-called Free Baptists, which originated from the Free Will Baptists. Due to theological conflicts in terms of the way to live their faith and to undertake their social commitments, three of the churches that were former members of the West Cuba Baptist Convention up until 1987, were expelled from this organization. These dissident churches did not stay idle but decided to create their own association. Thus, the Fraternity of Baptist Churches of Cuba (FIBAC) emerged as the fourth Baptist group formed in our country.

This new denomination has had a rich trajectory in achievements and challenges, which have distinguished it in its theological and pastoral doings as an official denomination that belongs to the Council of Churches of Cuba. Out of only three founding churches – known as simply "The Fraternity" – have grown 35 congregations with more than 60 preaching points, or missions, scattered all over our national territory. This fact, in its own right, was worth deep study, for it shows the undeniable impact of its rather short denominational history.

One of the churches promoting The Fraternity was the Marianao "Ebenezer." It had over half a century of existence already and a rich testimony to contribute to the work of the Church, not only in Cuba, but also abroad. Unfortunately, the history of this outstanding Cuban church had never been documented, despite the important role it had played, the interesting theological and pastoral evolution it had experienced over the course of years, and the constant advent of new challenges in each of its different stages. Preventing such an important history from being lost or forgotten with the passing of the years and the unceasing maelstrom of everyday life was my goal.

I aimed all my research endeavors at that objective, working for many months in a row. It was very gratifying for me to be able to give to my dear church its written history in July 2008. My dissertation engraved an indelible imprint deep down in my heart because I was greatly blessed to be tutored by my beloved pastor, the Rev. Raúl Suárez. Present also on that day were the three new pastors of our Ebenezer: Raquel Suárez Rodés, Yhanco Monet Rodríguez, and Amós López Rubio, along with my wife, my daughters, my best friends, and a wide representation of the membership from our church, who filled a whole yellow school bus – donated by Pastors for Peace – so as to attend my presentation about the history of our church.

Nevertheless, the most exciting moment of all was when the oldest and most committed deacon of our faith community, our dear Ramiro Arias, presented me with a beautiful bouquet of flowers on behalf of the grateful congregation as an acknowledgment of my research endeavor, which brought about the history, in writing, of our beloved Ebenezer. For that reason alone, it was certainly worth working to graduate from the Institute. That was my small contribution to the church, my tiny grain of sand. I thank God for having given me the idea and the willpower that was required to carry out such a research project.

Everything happens for a reason

Interpreting for Rev. Lucius Walker

On May Day 2003, Rev. Lucius Walker was invited to be one of the foreign speakers who addressed the Cuban people at the central rally on the occasion of the International Workers' Day, which was held, as customary, at the historical José Martí Revolution Square in Havana. There were about a million people gathered there. I was asked, as was also customary, to interpret his speech. This was, by far, one of the most distressing moments I have ever had at public rallies. Among other things, he energetically criticized Cuba for the recent implementation of the death penalty, referring to the summary trial carried out for those who had hijacked the Regla ferryboat in the Bay of Havana and who, in a failed attempt to detour the boat towards the United States, had endangered the lives of all its passengers and crew members, including women, elders, and children. Being a pastor, he could not help but preach when he asserted with mixed feelings of pain and loving care, "Cuba, the death penalty demeans you."

When the rally was over, Fidel approached Rev. Walker to greet him, and they held a small, informal dialogue, which I had to interpret. On that day, I had to interpret before the largest number of people in my whole life. Standing in front of a gigantic sea of human beings at such a historic place and date, among so many important people, including Fidel himself, surrounded by TV cameras, microphones, and journalists from all over the world, and having to interpret such daring words, even though they were well-intended, was undoubtedly a very difficult moment for me. Important things are never easy. That is precisely what makes them important.

In spite of all the stress I had to submit myself to, it was fortunate that

I had this opportunity. Everything happens for a reason. Elina Morris, a French interpreter and one of the deputy directors of the Team for Services of Translators and Interpreters (ESTI), which belongs to the Council of Ministers, was in the midst of the huge crowd that day. When she heard my voice amplified by the humongous speakers and did not recognize it as that of one of her professional interpreters, she immediately asked who the interpreter was. When she was told that he was in charge of the Pastors for Peace Caravans, Lucius Walker's interpreter, as many people identify me, she sent for me to ask if I was interested in working for the ESTI, at least as a part-time collaborator.

There is always an eye watching you – to which I would rightly add – and an ear listening to you. I could not believe that I would be so lucky. The ESTI would provide me with the real possibility of developing my supreme goal, the simultaneous interpretation that I had so painstakingly striven to achieve, the most demanding and difficult step to attain by an interpreter. It was like a climber reaching the summit of a mountain after overcoming all the obstacles and challenges along the difficult and tortuous path. Simultaneous translation was the summit I wanted to reach eventually, but with what was happening now, it could become a tangible truth in the near future. For me, being able to work at the ESTI was like joining the Big Leagues for a baseball player. Better late than never.

The very first simultaneous interpretation I did through the ESTI was in room number eight of the Havana International Conference Center (also known as Palacio de Convenciones). When the ESTI's English Department called me at home by phone to coordinate my pickup and told me that I would work in Room Eight, I could not help but remember the famous film with that title, and I was kind of worried about such a coincidence, thinking that it might be a bad omen. In fact, it was one of the most exciting days of my professional life. Being inside a simultaneous interpretation booth at the Palacio, listening to the presenters through the headsets and interpreting for them in real time using a microphone, thrilled me like a child playing with his new toy. I was experiencing it, and yet I swear that I could not believe it. I wanted to pinch myself to realize, once again, that it was not a dream but rather its blessed materialization.

How far this country boy had gone! It was too bad that my parents had both passed away, so I could not share this achievement that was so meaningful to me with them. Deep down in my soul, however, I had the gut feeling that, wherever they might be at that point, they would be very proud of me, and that awareness encouraged me to go on honoring their memory. I was, as many people say in the countryside where my siblings still live, sticking out my face for my family members who never got a higher education.

Once, after several years had elapsed and I had developed certain skills in simultaneous interpretation, I was working as a part-time collaborator hired by the ESTI at the Château Hotel in Miramar for an event sponsored by RAMSAR, a program of the United Nations. During the coffee break, one of the organizers of that important meeting approached me and asked for a business card. I promised him that I would bring it the following day, for I did not have any on hand at that point. He insisted that I should give him my personal contact information immediately, which I gladly did. He wanted to know if I was interested in interpreting for another event like this one on another island of the Caribbean in a few months. I clarified to him that I was not a full-time worker of the ESTI, but a mere collaborator. That did not pose any problem to him. He stated that he was the one who would pay for those services, and therefore he was entitled to choose his own interpreters.

He was true to his word, for that was exactly what he did. Thus, in July 2008, I traveled with them to the gorgeous French-speaking island of Guadeloupe to interpret at a week-long international event on the protection of marine mammals. This was another important experience, particularly because I had the great opportunity once again, but this time abroad, of sharing the booth with flawless, prestigious ESTI colleagues Nancy Echevarría Urdaneta and Gilberto Bengochea Pascal, whom I love, admire, and respect a lot for being excellent professionals, true paradigms in my ongoing search for increasingly higher levels in the performance of our beloved profession, which, according to scientific research, is considered the second most stressful profession (second only to pilots).

Men and kitchens were incompatible

Born and raised within a patriarchal, rural, male chauvinistic setting with a plethora of taboos and biases of all sorts, I never learned how to cook because there was always somebody, needless to say a female, who would be in charge of cooking for me. I did not want to be labeled as an intruder, a meddler minding somebody else's business, for those words are rather derogatory. Men and kitchens were incompatible in the family and social context in which I lived. Having three sisters of my own in our family, even when our mother passed away, there was always a woman – one of my sisters, my sister-in-law, or our father's new wife – who was in charge of the cooking. When I got married, the same old story was repeated day after day for years on end. Simply put, I always had a woman available in the family who undertook the indispensable job of feeding me. When, for whatever reason, my wife arrived home late from work or needed to overnight at a hospital to look after a hospitalized relative or friend, I had to take myself to the street to buy a pizza or a croquette sandwich because I did not even know how to fry an egg, and I felt clumsy, helpless, and awkward inside the kitchen. That situation of helplessness and culinary illiteracy lasted forty long years.

As a result of my wife's surgery (she had to submit to a second surgical operation as a result of vaginal cystoceles – the aftermath of her second childbirth), I had no choice but to undertake the issue at stake and, with all the dignity I could, learn the cooking ABC's. Listening with undivided attention and implementing the wise pieces of advice from the experience accumulated by my wife, my mother-in-law, my sisters, my female neighbors, coworkers, and friends, I entered the fascinating world of food preparation, which today, thanks to God, I enjoy to the fullest and which provides an occupational therapy that relaxes me and makes me feel useful within our family. I must admit, however, that it was not easy for me to break the ice and start out and that I did not always do a good job cooking. When I spoiled a few dishes, the level of stress associated with cooking triggered a deep anxiety and even caused bad body odor in my armpits. Overly concerned with making sure that everything I cooked was going to be alright, I ended up totally stressed out.

At present, I thoroughly enjoy waking up really early, as I usually do, and fixing a good breakfast for my wife and daughters before they get up. I don't think that I am doing anything extraordinary or noteworthy. I do not want any acknowledgment whatsoever for what I do. I am merely compensating a little bit and servicing an old debt from those long years during which a woman was always in charge not only of securing a plate of food on my table but also of washing it afterwards, too. I received these favors because I had the privilege of having been born male into our macho man society. Even if I cooked for the rest of my life, I could not pay off that old gender debt because for forty years, I have been benefiting from the unfair prerogatives of this male chauvinistic society.

What I enjoy the most when cooking is making the homemade desserts, particularly the cream caramel or baked custard with condensed milk and eggs, the delicious flan that is by far my specialty. My only regret is not having learned how to cook earlier.

I could die in peace

Since my daughters were very little, I instilled in them the love for studying, reading, and nonstop upgrading. I told them every now and then about my concern for their future, and said that the greatest punishment they could give me would be to drop out of school. My greatest dream is to see them graduate as professionals in the specialty of their choice, holding a university degree, so that tomorrow they may be themselves, with capital letters, and not "somebody's wife." I would like them to inspire both respect and admiration for who they are, to never be humiliated before anyone or have to depend on the charity or power of any man. I would like them to assert themselves on their own and always try to shine on the place where they may find themselves.

I have always conveyed to them my insight that knowledge is the most powerful weapon that a human being can have. It is the only thing that cannot be snatched away from us, that is really ours. I insisted so much on this issue that, one day while sitting around the table, they told me not to worry any more. Then they both solemnly promised me that one day they would cover their little five faces photographs, taken when they were merely six months old each – which I had placed on top of my two graduate diplomas – with their respective university degrees. When that day comes, I told them jokingly, I could die in peace. Seeing my daughters professionally accomplished in life would certainly be one of the greatest spiritual satisfactions that I could ever have.

After having attained many unimaginable things in my life, having materialized my dreams and getting way beyond what I expected, I often say that I may die any day now. Although, of course, I would like to enjoy what I have achieved with so much sacrifice and perseverance. I would like to see and enjoy my grandchildren. There are still many things that I would like to learn and do. The educational process stretches from the crib to the grave; at least, that's the way I see it. As long as there is a capable brain, eager and thirsty for information and knowledge, it needs to be nourished. Even if it is just to learn something new, life is always worthwhile. As it is so rightly said, life is always much more, and it should never be used to no advantage because it is one and only.

Times do change indeed! How very true the assertion is that children resemble their times much more than they do their parents. Much as we may try to avoid it, however, one is surprised that "like father, like son." Despite the fact that one always drags inevitable vestiges along from childhood, I have tried to the best of my abilities to educate my daughters and to relate to them in a very different way than my father did to my sisters.

My girls are the best thing that ever happened to me. They are the perfect gift, an everlasting source of joy, satisfaction, pride, and admiration. Both excelled at the top of their classes in school since they were very young and have accumulated noteworthy curricula vitae. They know how to take good advantage of their time, talent, and above all their opportunities in a very intelligent and rational way – a fact that I admire and respect a lot. My greatest concern was to avoid having them go through the experience of either my mother or my sisters. I wanted something better for them. I wanted them to excel, not just to please their daddy or to obey him for that matter, not just because it was expected of them, but rather – and thank God that has been the case – because it was their own need; so, all by themselves, they would set a life goal and would reach it no matter what the cost.

With my daughters in front of the MLK Center in 1995

I have never had to worry about their homework or any other school papers they were supposed to hand in. They have been responsible and studious enough to be in charge of those issues all by themselves. They have never told me "Daddy do this work for me," but rather, "Daddy, give me an idea for what I need to do" or "Daddy, check what I did and tell me what you think about it?" At the parents' meetings I attended, I always received praises from their teachers and professors. For a parent – at least for me – that is of paramount importance and is so gratifying that it makes me feel accomplished from the paternity perspective. Our children's successes in life are part and parcel of our own share of accountability before society at large. Upon bringing them into this world, we should devote ourselves totally to their good with our soul, heart, and life.

Way before they were born, my daughters already had a book as a gift, especially bought for them, zealously kept, and air-tightly sealed in cellophane paper, patiently waiting for them to turn ten years old, when they could benefit from its reading and the wise pieces of advice found within its pages. I am referring to the book *Heart* by the Italian writer Edmundo de Amicis. This is one of the books that most impacted me, so I wanted my children-to-be to read and understand it. That is why, to make sure that would be the case, when the book was still available at the bookstore, I purchased two copies. That was indeed their birthday gift from me when each turned ten years old. I also urged my students to read it, and so they did. After reading this wonderful book with all its valuable universal and imperishable teachings, one grows to love, consider, admire, understand, and respect one's parents and teachers even more.

A valuable initiative

When Wendy and Betsy were in second grade and kindergarten respectively, in the setting of our household, we took on a routine practice that turned out to be a real blessing in terms of the necessary communication within the family bosom. After having taken a basic training workshop at the Dr. Martin Luther King, Jr. Memorial Center on the teaching methodology of Popular Education, it occurred to me happily that I should implement that initiative at dinner time, when the four of us gathered around our table. It was during the most difficult years of the Special Period, and consequently, both the quality and the variety of items on the daily menu were considerably affected. The point was to try to take advantage of those precious moments to the maximum so as to get to know how our children thought and to be able to educate them by inculcating real human values in them at a time in which these latter were crumbling in our society.

The allegedly naïve little game of ours consisted of sharing among the family a couple of personal experiences daily. It was expected that everyone else to listen while each person related one experience from the day that was pleasant to them and explained why that was the case. Likewise, we were expected to share something that we had disliked, providing reasons that justified the feelings that the experience had triggered in us. I recommend from the bottom of my heart to all those who have small children to cheer up and implement such a valuable initiative, as it will contribute greatly to the family framework. Thanks to that habit, we managed to learn many things that were good and bad, funny, sad, worrisome, and incredible; but above all, that became a thermometer, a gauge, in order to objectively know what our daughters thought and how they felt during times of extreme uncertainty and an acute crisis of moral and ethical values. We knew many important things that, otherwise, we would have never known. That routine became such a gratifying time of communication and affection that we would all look forward to it anxiously at dinner time, and to a large extent, it made up for the shortages on the table.

Since I was a boy, as I have already said, I enjoyed reading short stories, learning them by heart, and telling them afterwards. That was another resource I availed myself of during the hard times of the first half the 1990s, when the blackouts were so long that – as comedians used to say – what we had were rather "lightenings" because the blackouts would stretch for up to 16 hours daily. In order to entertain our girls and to make them laugh really hard, taking into account that childhood is short-lived, and due to the fact that we did not know how long that awful situation would last, I would sit on a rocking-chair and have them both sit on my lap – one on each of my thighs – while I told stories. Other times, if it was not too hot, we would go to the bed and there, lying on my back, sandwiched between them, I began to freely unleash my imagination and my most disarranged, witty, and goofy ideas, making up stories of all sorts in which the main characters were our own extended family members, our neighbors, coworkers, school classmates, friends, acquaintances, and churchgoers.

The most nonsensical stories were woven right on the spot during those unforgettable moments of hilarity that we enjoyed to the fullest. Sometimes I started to tell a made-up story and then urged them to follow it up so as to develop their ingenuity, mental agility, and logical thinking. I was not surprised at all when later on in school, they were both the winners at a contest on the writing of unheard stories. Two of their stories were even chosen and published by the 1996 Latin American Agenda, dedicated that year to the literary production of girls all over our continent. What gratifying pride I felt when I had the privilege of holding in my hands that publication in which the stories written by my wonderful little girls appeared! My daughters are the most precious gift that life has granted me. They have indeed given me many satisfactions and have made me the proudest father of the universe. May God bless them forever!

When Wendy and Betsy were in elementary school, they were both selected in 1997 to travel to Germany as members of a children's choir Christmas tour. The choir was to perform in concerts held in German churches. Upon their return, they submitted themselves to the corresponding auditions and music proficiency tests and were enrolled at the Alejandro García Caturla Elementary Music Conservatory, where they were trained in choir conducting. Once graduated, holders of an elementary music level, they decided to apply for the Vladimir Ilich Lenin Exact Sciences Vocational High School Institute, where I had worked during the last nine years of my former career as an English teacher. Both of them graduated there, and thanks to their excellent academic performance, they managed to get the major of their choice. Wendy leaned towards the sciences and studied Industrial Engineering, whereas Betsy, following my own footsteps, opted for letters and was enrolled in Foreign Languages (English and French).

Wendy and Betsy in 2010

I had always asked them to study anything whatsoever that they were truly fond of, but that they should please grant me the satisfaction of showing up at home some day holding a university degree diploma. They have not let me down – just the opposite. Wendy has already graduated with honors, a gold title, and five points in her general academic average. Betsy, in turn, is also about to graduate with honors.

I have systematically visited the Presidential Palace, currently the Museum of the Revolution, for many years as part of the program of scheduled activities for the foreign delegations I work with in my capacity as translator-interpreter. I must admit that history was never my strong suit and that, many times, I felt ashamed when I was unable to answer with clarity, promptness, and accuracy questions that visitors would ask me. Over the course of time, however, little by little, I felt the pressing need of upgrading and updating myself in that regard. At present, thank God, I may be of help as a local guide at the Museum of the Revolution whenever necessary. This has been quite important for my self-esteem. My motivation has been so high that I saw fit to encourage my two daughters, as well, and have trained them both to do the same. Today, they are able to do it with a great deal of love, providing museum tours in English for the delegations

I work with. This fills me with pride, for it is something like enjoying a crop that one painstakingly planted and cultivated for years on end, in order to, finally and right on time, enjoy and harvest the long-expected fruits.

When my daughters were getting closer to the decisive moment of joining the university, I promised them that, if they managed to get the major they wanted, I would teach them how to drive so they could get a driving license upon reaching 18 years of age. This was one more incentive in their personal training for life. And so I did. On their respective summer vacations right after completing high school, I took them to Ciudad Libertad on Sunday afternoons, and there, within the convenient availability of its empty streets, they learned how to drive. When they felt at ease and safe doing it, I took them out into busy streets. Later on, when they were ready, they submitted themselves to the corresponding theoretical and practical exams. Sure enough, they fulfilled their part, and I did mine. Upon turning 18 years old, both had already acquired their well-deserved driving license. Both are also studying at the French Alliance.

My daughters, thank God, have not been slaves of domestic work as my poor mother was. She came into this world to work like a mule and to raise kids. My girls occupy their time by doing a million things that contribute to their personal growth. Because they are young women, they never miss opportunities to go out, take a walk, dance, learn about places, have fun, and hang out with their friends. They live intensely, availing themselves of every single opportunity provided to them because life is always much more. That makes me proud and pleases me as nobody is able to imagine. Only God bears witness that I thank Him on a daily basis for both of them.

Working out the muscles

Even though, as a boy, I played baseball, to tell the truth, I was not a good player. I used to excel more at playing volleyball and in track and field, which I liked a lot. I felt elated the day when we won a volleyball match against another elementary school, and I was the one who set the decisive point at the very last minute when everything seemed to be hopelessly lost. The euphoria of my team was so great that they lifted me up very high and paraded me all over the school sports facilities. In junior high school, I was fond of gymnastics and the exercises we used to practice on the judo mat. Later on, when I joined the boarding school, I focused my attention on common warm-up exercises, doing push-ups, sit-ups, squats, and other free-chest workouts. In the final years of my university training, I began to jog in the mornings after the regular calisthenics and eventually added a few other exercises with the fixed bars and the pumping of weights with a solid iron axle that I managed to get. The point is that I have always enjoyed and needed to do some type of physical workout. With so much sedentary and intellectual work, exercising my muscles and sweating profusely has always been something I have been concerned about and have worked at systematically.

On Sunday, August 24, in the summer of 1996, I was visiting in New York City at the house of a Puerto Rican friend by the name of Franklin Velázquez, who had invited me to join his family for dinner at his place on 44th Street in Brooklyn. I shared with him the fact that I was sleeping very little and very badly, that sleeplessness was giving me a hard time, and that I was already very worried about that unsustainable situation. He saw fit to tell me about the systematic practice of yoga and presented me with my first book on that subject. In order to make sure that I improved the quantity and the quality of my sleep, I was willing to take an inroad into any field whatsoever, and yoga seemed to offer just what I needed.

As soon as I returned from the United States, I thoroughly read that interesting book with a great deal of curiosity, and I gradually started to implement a full session of hatha yoga. The adaptation process to the new exercises was very slow, but the outcomes and the benefits that I began to witness, little by little, were very encouraging. I lost weight and gained flexibility. I started to incorporate āsanas, or yoga postures, as I explored the issue even further. I expanded my bibliography and created my own session, which I called Yogalberto, for I designed it in keeping with my personal needs and interests. To my regular yoga daily session, I added the highly beneficial sun salutations, practicing six rounds of those perfect calisthenics, which I have kept up until the present. I also took a training course on hatha yoga at the premises of the National Theater, which was taught by the celebrated professor Eduardo Pimentel. In November 1999, I had a great opportunity to participate at the Yoga International Festival held in Havana, in my capacity as interpreter. At that event, I learned quite a lot, for it suited me to a T.

I was so motivated because of my personal experience doing yoga that some psychologists in charge of the logistics of a workshop asked me to prepare a theoretical-practical presentation about it for a couples retreat organized in 1998 by the Marianao Ebenezer Baptist Church. It focused on health therapy alternatives. With the kind assistance of my wife, I managed to piece together a handmade booklet, translating information from my specialized bibliography in English and photocopying complementary images. I managed to dictate the theoretical lecture, provide the practical demonstration, and hand out – as an additional courtesy to the participating couples – a copy of that handbook, which I entitled "Yoga and Health." It entailed a great deal of sacrifice, but it turned out to be a rousing success, inspiring many of the people present. When there is something benefiting us personally and we hold the irrefutable evidence of the harvested results, sharing that well-being with others is both a duty and a gratifying experience – at least it is for me. People may take it or leave it – they must choose on their own what is best for them; but at least they are educated; they get the information they need; they open up their horizons; they grow towards new dimensions; and the way I see it, that is the most important thing.

Since I moved to the city on March 31, 1994, I took advantage of the convenience of having a community facility very handy – at walking distance from home – the Jesús Menéndez sports complex, just a couple of blocks away in the already centenarian Pogolotti neighborhood, the first working class community of Cuba. I began running very early every morning, before sunrise, when it was still dark. If there is something I really take pride in, without aiming at any cheap vanity, it is my steel will whenever I set a goal and decide to undertake a task. For years on end, I kept running ten laps around the baseball field, rain or shine, always at the same hour, when cold, and even with painful ingrown toenails in my feet.

Both the physical and the spiritual well-being that I enjoyed after finishing each of those workouts was so gratifying that the personal sacrifice was worthwhile. So as not to be concerned about counting my laps and to really relax and enjoy the exercise, I implemented a reliable technique. After my warm-up, I picked up either ten pebbles or ten twigs and held them in my hands while running. Whenever I passed by the starting point, I dropped them one at a time, and when I ran out of them, I had the clearest proof that I had completed my ten laps.

Unfortunately, I started having problems with one of my knees, and the physician advised me to stop running, claiming that my joints were worn out and that exercise might worsen the situation, which was already irreversible. During the most pressing years of the Special Period, I had designed a twofold wooden seat at my father's carpenter's shop so as to be able to transport my two little girls in my bike to their daycare center. My students used to make fun of that invention of mine, claiming that it resembled several things at a time: an ironing board, a shoe shiner's chair, and a crossbow. The fact is that pedaling on a daily basis long kilometers by bicycle, keeping that inadequate position, slightly uncomfortable, with my legs wide open in a wrong angle, started gradually wearing out the ligaments and the inner cartilages of my knee joints. That, on the one hand, and on the other, the fact that since I was a boy, I suffered from orthopedic disorders – diagnosed with shaft shinbones that were never taken care of properly or corrected by the right orthopedic footwear – are the reasons why, every now and then, I endure an inflammatory and painful crisis that makes me limp and disturbs me even when driving.

I decided to do without the orthopedic shoes due to the lousy quality of their horrible design. My colleagues and my students used to call them *vaquetetumbos* (I bet I will knock you down). A young professor like me would not dare stand in front of a classroom full of teenagers wearing such affront on his feet. It was preferable to bear the pain that would radiate along both my legs whenever I was compelled to stand for a long time, such as when I was on guard duty in school and was required to look after the lunch or dinner process in the school dining hall. Sooner or later, I always ended up leaning against one of the flower pots very discreetly so as to alleviate the pain that tired me out unbelievably.

I did not want to give up and follow a completely sedentary lifestyle without the systematic practice of physical exercises that I have always enjoyed so much. Thus, although I stopped running to obey the medical advice, I started to walk an hour every day instead, traveling in different directions so as not to get bored. I used to leave home before daybreak, and when my wristwatch marked half an hour, I made a U-turn and came back along the same route. Due to the irregularities of the ground, however, with so many potholes everywhere, plus the fact that I was wearing the wrong shoes for such long walks, my joint pains came back once again, which made me feel down and out both physically and emotionally.

Because of the impossibility of running or walking, I started to think of other variants so as not to quit in my struggle to ensure daily physical therapy. I have never given up the session of the sun salutation of hatha yoga. It is simply a series of twelve postures in a slow, dynamic transition from one into the other that strengthens and makes the spine supple, which is vital for a healthy mind in a healthy body. The systematic practice of these exercises facilitates the nervous system's communication between the spine and the brain, expediting the process of action-reaction, stimulus-reply of our central nervous system, which is healthy for any human being and which is of paramount importance for the sort of work that I do – that is, simultaneous interpretation, which requires swift, efficient, and reliable mental agility.

"The third time is the charm" is what people say. In my case, that proved to be right indeed. My daughter Betsy brought home a program of aerobic exercises by the North American professor Leslie Sampson in a DVD format. She told me, "Daddy, I think I found what you have been looking for so long." How right she was! The therapy lasts 45 minutes. It includes a nonstop walk in the same place, tantamount to three miles, while doing a whole bunch of exercises for the arms and legs, adding hand weights deliberately. It has been a blessing to do the routine right in my own bedroom, in front of the TV set, regardless of whether it is raining or cold outdoors.

Let them keep calling me young man

When still very young, one tries long and hard to look older and to give the appearance of maturity; however, when one really matures, then one does whatever it takes to make sure it is not noticed. When I was 14 years old, I hated it when I was referred to as a boy. Why would that be so? It must be because our perspective on age is relative, and it glides away like a cunning snake as we grow older. When one is hardly 20, the future stretches forward as a highway until it fades in the haze or fog. Who really knows what lies ahead along that everlasting foggy road? I firmly believe that youth, at least spiritual youth, is an attitude to life. Nobody grows old just because a given number of years have been lived. The one who grows old is the one who gives up his dreams. You are as young as your faith, as old as your doubts; as young as your confidence in yourself, as old as your fears; young as your hopes, old as your discouragement. Those who want to remain young will do so.

I am still called "young man" every now and then despite my five decades. It is one of the phrases I like to hear most at this age. Why would that be? I guess it has to do with the relativity of age. At the age of 50, I love it whenever people use the sweet words "that young man." It tastes like glory every time I hear it – like music to my ears. The day they stop calling me that, I will start to worry or will resign myself to what belongs to me, no matter what. I will accept the respectable third age with dignity and the charms that it also claims as all the other ages do. Actually, I already have it just around the corner, so to speak. Ten more years to go – that will elapse in the twinkling of an eye – and I will already be getting into it with the spiritual satisfaction of having faithfully fulfilled what was suggested by Martí about planting a tree, engendering a child, and writing a book.

I look younger than I actually am for the following reasons: I have almost no gray hair yet; thankfully, I have never smoked, which I am glad about for I lost my father at the age of 67 due to lung cancer; I have never abused alcoholic beverages, though I like to drink both rum and beer moderately; I have always done physical exercises; and I have not inherited baldness, at least for the time being. That is why people keep on calling me "young man" in spite of my years. Amen!

One day, I was with my daughter Wendy, who accompanied me to the Jamaican Embassy in Miramar, where I was applying for a visa.

One of the female pastors who would be traveling with me, out of sheer curiosity and mischievousness, whispered to a male pastor who happened to be there, "Wow, the interpreter's girlfriend is really young!" The latter smiled and clarified that Wendy was actually my daughter. Another time, when I was with Betsy, my other daughter, at the fair exhibit complex of Expo-Cuba during the Havana International Fair, the mother of one of her friends greeted her in the crowd of visitors while I was waiting for her under the shade of a tree. After checking me out several times as she stood a few meters away from me and looking kind of intrigued, she asked, "Is that your new boyfriend?" Betsy could not help but laugh when clarifying that I was her father. No exaggeration needed. It is true that I still look young, but it is not a big deal.

I DO NOT BELIEVE IN CHANCES

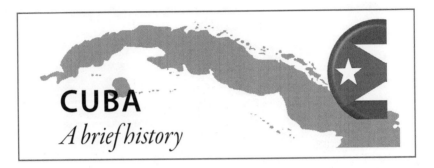

CUBA
A brief history

The Late 2000s: A Better World Is Possible

Although economic reforms of the last decade looked positive, Cubans did not benefit equally. A survey of Havana in 2000 showed that 77 percent of the population had insufficient income to meet their needs.

Older generations remembered Cuba prior to the Revolution; they recalled the headiness of social change and possibility of the 1960s and the relative material stability of the 1970s and 1980s. Their expectations gave the changes of the 1990s and early 2000s a certain anguish. For those who came of age in the Special Period, the early decades seemed a distant chimera. Both those who lived the experiences and those who learned about them had to face contemporary realities that did not live up to revolutionary dreams. In 2002, the US Interests Section in Havana started to promote and support opposition groups in Cuba. In March 2003, there was a wave of arrests of individuals who had accepted gifts and money from the US Interests Section and other organizations. In return for those gifts, they provided information intended to overthrow the Cuban government.

The election of Hugo Chávez in Venezuela in 1998 significantly changed the dynamic of inter-American relations. Cuba had never been quite as isolated as US policymakers suggested. In the Third World and in the non-aligned countries, Cuba was a leader.

In December 2004, Chavez and Castro launched the Bolivarian Alternative for Latin America and the Caribbean (ALBA) as a socialist model for economic integration in the Americas. It was a real challenge to the neoliberal, capitalist integration of the Free Trade Agreement of the Americas (FTAA).

In a bilateral agreement, there was an exchange of Venezuelan oil for Cuban medical and other services. By 2006, the petroleum-for-doctors agreement included Bolivia, too. By 2007, Venezuela was playing the role of great Cuban subsidizer that the former USSR had once played.

In 2006, Fidel Castro announced that, as a result of his illness, he was temporarily ceding his presidency to the first vice president, his brother Raúl. In

February 2008, he declared that he would not seek re-election at the end of his term. The National Assembly unanimously chose Raúl Castro to succeed Fidel as President.

During Raúl's first few months in office, he came up with several economic steps that triggered a lot of commentary domestically and abroad. Access to computers, video cameras, and cell phones – previously restricted – was opened, and Cubans were granted entry to tourist hotels. Renewed emphasis was placed on agriculture and production.

Only months after Fidel ceded his post, Barack Obama was elected as President of the US, promising "change." He announced that he was lifting Bush-era restrictions on Cuban-American travel to the island and on remittances, and he stated that he was ready to discuss both restoring direct mail and drafting a new accord on migration.

While Raúl Castro called for talks between the two governments on all topics, with no preconditions whatsoever, Obama kept on insisting that dialogue would be limited unless Cuba carried out internal reforms. Meanwhile, the global economic decline and falling prices for Cuban exports, along with a couple of devastating hurricanes in 2008, accounted for an economically bleak 2009.

In spite of decades of hardships, a poll commissioned by the *Miami Herald* in 1994 confirmed strong popular support for Fidel Castro's government: 69 percent of Cubans thought of themselves as revolutionaries, socialists, or communists, and 58 percent on balance thought the Revolution had produced more achievements than failures.

Even the special rapporteur of the UN Human Rights Commission, Carl-Johan Groth, said the regime enjoyed "credibility and a margin of confidence in broad sectors of the population far greater than observers have believed." That majority backing needs to be recognized by critics, especially those in the US capital.

We still believe that a better world is possible, no matter what. We cannot give up our dreams, and we need to maintain our struggle at all costs to make sure that the very best is yet to be seen. It could not be otherwise, because hope is the last thing we should lose. The bottom line is that the history of the Cuban Revolution is still unfolding, and the most educated predictions have proven wrong again and again.

We are still alive … and kicking!

I Would Be a Translator Again

He who did not spare his own Son,
but gave him up for us all—
how will he not also, along with him,
graciously give us all things?
Romans 8:32

To talk about my life, my memoirs, I need to speak about the Dr. Martin Luther King, Jr. Memorial Center (CMMLK) to which I owe my empirical training as a translator-interpreter, my entrance into the field of Bible and theology, the opportunity to travel all over Cuba and overseas, the immense privilege of meeting personally and interpreting for important national and international personalities, and many other associated benefits that enabled a radical change in my life right when I needed it most. The Center has been the materialization of my dream. To the Center, its staff, its leaders, and especially to Rev. Raúl Suárez Ramos, its founder and director whom I admire, love, and respect like a father, I will forever be grateful as long as there is a breath of life in me.

Thanks to both the Center and Rev. Suárez, this country boy who is writing his own book today was able to become a translator just as he had dreamed ever since he was a poor teenager. I thank God for each and every one of the blessings I received through this noteworthy institution and its dear staff. I feel a deep loyalty towards the Center and towards Rev. Suárez, in particular, whom I won't be able to let down for anybody or anything in the world. The trustworthiness, the loving care, and the respect I have harvested at the Center are unfathomable. I want to take advantage of this wonderful opportunity to publicly acknowledge the fact that, if today I enjoy certain prestige as a professional, I owe it precisely to the Center, which granted me a great opportunity at a moment when, even though I had enough willingness to spare, I was still far from being a good interpreter.

Along this lengthy path towards my longed -or dream, I have gone through many distressing times, difficult moments, and embarrassments. But, I must admit that the blessings, the gratifications, and the joys I have received and the professional and spiritual accomplishments I have achieved have far outweighed any unpleasantness. As I could not speak about my life without alluding to the Center, for it would obviously be incomplete, it is with sincere love and deep gratitude that I offer the following information, particularly to those who are not sufficiently acquainted with the Center to appreciate its value and relevance. Hence, I provide here a brief historical review of the institution that welcomed me in its bosom back in January 1993, when I arrived with an old borrowed case, crammed with illusions and overflowing with nervousness, the perfect mix to place our hands on the plowshares and not look back, as Suarez likes to say so frequently.

At the beginning of the 1970s, Reverend Raúl Suárez and his late wife, Clara Rodés, arrived at the community of Pogolotti, west of our capital – the first working-class neighborhood of Cuba, centenarian already – in order to carry out their pastoral ministry. It is not a secret that the first few years of the Revolution were not easy for religious people in our country, who, even though they did not suffer from persecutions per se, were greatly discriminated against and limited from many different perspectives.

Upon their arrival in Marianao, they came to realize that something was wrong with the local church they had been assigned to, for it was a virtually white church in the middle of a black community. Most of the black families were practitioners of religions having an African origin. Clarita and Raúl did not feel at ease with that ironic situation and decided to come up with something in order to improve their ministry. In addition, many families, including a good number of pastors, had left the country around that time; therefore, the church was practically empty. They felt, however, that God had not left Cuba, and consequently, their place was here with their church and their people; although, of course, difficult challenges were expected. This married couple of Baptist pastors, facing a huge challenge, with their heads full of dreams and ideas, chose to start doing things and overcoming obstacles so as to achieve their goals, providing a beautiful Christian witness before believers and non-believers alike and demonstrating that many things can be attained when there is enough perseverance and tenacity and above all – a lot of faith.

The Dr. Martin Luther King, Jr. Memorial Center

On April 25, 1987, the Dr. Martin Luther King, Jr. Memorial Center emerged as a fruit of everything that was thought and done up until that historic date. It has been growing in size as well as in the diversity and scope of its work over the years. But initially, what made it famous was its connection with the Pastors for Peace US-Cuba Friendshipment Caravans led by Rev. Lucius Walker, which began to bring humanitarian aid to Cuba in November 1992. Rev. Suárez met Rev. Walker for the first time in Nicaragua, where he took the initiative to invite him to Cuba. The CMMLK became his Cuban partner at a very critical time, from the economic viewpoint, for our island nation, for those were the first and hardest years of the Special Period.

The US-Cuba Friendshipment Caravans were coming from the country that was supposed to be our enemy. It has always been quite clear to Cubans, however, that the disputes between our two nations have been between our governments and not between our peoples. We have never called Americans "gringos," and there is no animosity whatsoever against them as a whole. We have historically shared many common things that bind us together. That is why, when Rev. Lucius Walker arrived in Cuba in 1992 with the first caravan of Pastors for Peace, showing the love and care of the US people for Cubans in one of the greatest gestures of human solidarity ever, he automatically became a beloved hero in our country and was happily welcomed everywhere in our island. He was even received by Fidel Castro himself, who valued his selfless attitude.

It goes without saying that it was a great honor for me to be involved directly as Rev. Walker's interpreter whenever he was in Cuba. The Friendshipment Caravans came intentionally without a license, claiming that if there was a law keeping them from helping their neighbors at a time of need, they wanted to break it. The way they saw it, the US economic blockade against Cuba was unethical, immoral, and not Christian at all. They came once or twice a year with a shipment of love and humanitarian aid after traveling across the United States along various routes, stopping at different cities to collect the aid that people had donated and to educate them about the Cuban reality and the injustice of the US foreign policy towards Cuba – particularly, the embargo. Every time they came, they brought yellow school buses and other vehicles, bicycles, computers, medical equipment, Bibles, powdered milk, wheel chairs, crutches, medicines and disposable materials.

Interpreting for Rev. Raúl Suárez Ramos

I would like to point out that Rev. Raúl Suárez Ramos, our director and my pastor par excellence, considers himself as an "uncomfortable friend" of the Cuban Revolution because, as a true prophet, he denounces and condemns injustice energetically at the right place and time. Just to mention a couple of examples, he was one of the religious leaders who wrote a letter addressed to Fidel demanding a meeting with him so as to complain about the unjust statements the Commander-in-Chief, while in Brazil during the '80s, had made when referring to Cuban Christians. He was also the only member of Parliament who raised his voice courageously to oppose the death penalty when its approval was being analyzed in the bosom of our Parliament.

The CMMLK defines itself as a macro-ecumenical, non-profitable, non-governmental organization, having a Christian inspiration. Its main goal is to accompany the Cuban people and their churches in solidarity and prophetically by means of training for conscious, organized, and critical participation in increasingly more just social projects. It has become the Mecca of popular education in Cuba. It is an alternative educational institution par excellence, which has gained great prestige, not only all over our national territory, but also in the whole world. Our Center has been visited by people from all the continents, eager to partake in academic exchange and to share knowledge – a great diversity of people: from landless peasants in Brazil all the way to popular educators from East Timor near Indonesia. Our Center promotes solidarity not only of the world towards Cuba but also of Cuba towards the world. In our solidarity department, we provide a number of services for foreign delegations that come to Cuba, not as tourists, but rather as students, ready to explore and to know about our reality, our achievements, and our shortcomings. That is why they are not lodged at hotels, in tourist resorts, or in the downtown area of the city. They stay in our own Center, in our neighborhood, so they may be able to witness our community life firsthand and feel closer to the people, the lowly ones.

The CMMLK has the capacity to accommodate 80 people in its 20 rooms. It also provides food services, land transportation, guide-program coordination, and translation-interpretation. Delegations visiting us come from the United States for the most part. They are organized and facilitated by North American organizations that serve as our counterparts. The list includes: Interreligious Foundation for Community Organization-Pastors for Peace, the Center for Global Education, the Mennonite Central Committee, the Chicago Religious Leadership Network on Latin America, EPICA, the Trinity Lutheran Seminary, Witness for Peace, the Latin America Studies Program, and others.

On average, delegations come for a period of ten days and request a tight and varied program of activities, in which there is a combination of lectures, presentations, exchanges, encounters, outings, museum and historical site visits, and city tours, as well as recreational, sports, and cultural activities. They always visit a province other than Havana to get to know the countryside. They go to the beach as well as to churches, cooperative units, schools, hospitals, factories, and social projects of all sorts. Many of the delegations include as part of their schedules visits to the National Assembly of the People's Power, the Ministry of Foreign Affairs, and the US Interests Section in Havana, which fills them with even more questions than the ones they arrived with.

Visitors tell us that getting to know Cuba firsthand, not as a tourist, opens their eyes. From then on, their perspectives on Cuba change radically. They arrive on our island with ideas formed mainly by the mass media in their home countries, where typically almost everything written about Cuba is negative. The good things we do are never written about. The last day of their visit, an evaluation activity is conducted, documenting in writing the individual and group experiences. These forms are well worth reading.

The CMMLK also operates as a disaster relief agency in a coordinated joint effort with foreign NGOs. In the event of any natural catastrophe, such as a hurricane, it requests financial, human, and/or material resources in keeping with needs, so it can reach out with a sympathetic hand in those places where it might be needed most. In collaboration with the government offices at different levels, it is actively involved in social projects such as street lights, housing repair, and construction.

One of the most appreciated community services provided by the CMMLK is the care granted to the third age. Two groups of senior citizens, known as the Psycho-ballet, are examples of what may be achieved with the elderly when there is enough will to join efforts to support the most vulnerable in our society. About 70 seniors, members of the local church and grandparents from the community at large, have joined this wonderful project, which is directed by a couple of psychologists and a dance professor who, as volunteers, provide their support, time, and talents to strengthen the mind, body and self-esteem of these people who, otherwise, could feel increasingly more excluded. The CMMLK also provides them with lunch twice a week and supports them with medicines and other available items as donations. They do physical exercises, carry out all kinds of activities, excursions, and handicrafts. They perform at national and international events held in Havana and in the church liturgy. They live intensely and have developed a strong sense of belonging to their group, making up something like a big extended family.

Another service we provide is the Paulo Freire Documentation Center, a library specializing in socio-theological literature and popular education. About 40 people work full time at the CMMLK. Supporting them is a huge network of collaborators – Cubans and foreigners, believers and atheists, Catholics, Protestants, and practitioners of other religions, as well as volunteers and temporary staff members who are hired for services that are required.

Although we work in many community projects in close connection with governmental agencies, we are an independent NGO, and we do not get any financing from the state. The CMMLK is self-financed and to that aim counts on support from NGOs in many other countries, mainly in Canada and Europe, which fund many of our projects. The Center is also nourished from the revenues it gets from the services provided to visiting delegations.

The Center defines itself as a macro-ecumenical institution welcoming all people of good will, regardless of their creeds, but obviously, it does have a Christian inspiration. It focuses on what people have in common to strive for a better and more just world and not on the differences they might have from their many different perspectives. What really matters is the unity attained within our diversity.

From the structural point of view, the CMMLK is steered by a board of directors made up of a director, a general coordinator, five heads of departments and an administrator. The five departments are: Pastoral and Socio-Theological Training and Reflection, Popular Education and Follow-up of Local Experiences, Solidarity, Popular Communication, Sustainability and Institutional Development.

To sum it up, I may say that the Dr. Martin Luther King, Jr. Memorial Center is a dream come true thanks to the power of faith, goodwill, and the huge desires of a community to do things for the sake of social well-being. It is a real hive of worker bees without lazy drones or queens: a paradigm of what can be achieved thanks to human solidarity and friendship among the peoples of the world. It shows that although financial and material resources are required to materialize dreams, but that human resources – people willing to work and devote themselves to just causes – are most important.

Interpreting for Fidel

On Friday July 31, 2009, I interpreted the speech delivered by Rev. Lucius Walker at a joint political solidarity rally organized by the Cuban Institute of Friendship with the Peoples (ICAP) to celebrate the 40th anniversary of the Venceremos Brigade and the 20th US-Cuba Pastors for Peace Friendshipment Caravan. This event was held at the Flags Forest of the José Martí Anti-imperialist Tribune, right across from the US Interests Section in Cuba. After the event, I was called by María de los Ángeles Pérez, an official from the Office for the Care of Religious Affairs at the Central Committee of the Communist Party of Cuba, who let me know that, at 11:00 AM, I had to be ready at the headquarters of the ICAP on 17th Street in El Vedado because the personal security staff of our Commander-in-Chief, Fidel Castro Ruz, would come at that time to pick up Lucius, and I was expected to interpret for him.

Right at that time, according to the scheduled activities of the Caravan, a meeting would begin with the relatives of the Cuban five, who were behind bars in the United States. I was supposed to be a part of that event, but I was told not to worry about a thing because it had already been taken care of. I was given a mango juice and a ham and cheese sandwich, taken to one of the air-conditioned reception lounges for VIPs, and seated on the comfortable sofas of that compound. I was then told to relax, as it was not known how long the encounter would last. Because it was Fidel, I knew for sure that it would not be brief.

Even though I had interpreted for the Commander before, in brief spontaneous dialogues with Lucius and a few other North American religious leaders that took place in public rallies (such as at the Moncada Barracks in Santiago de Cuba, the José Martí Revolution Square, the Havana International Conference Center, the José Martí Anti-imperialist Square, and the Palace of the Revolution in Havana), this would be the first time that I would do it officially. Fidel, around that time, was almost never seen on TV, and the few times that he was, it was just in pictures and not in videos for he was still convalescing from surgery, which kept him away from his customary life for a long period of time. This situation generated many unfounded rumors and speculations, mainly by the enemies of the Cuban Revolution and of our Socialist process. There were even those who affirmed that, very likely, he had been dead for a while, but that people had not been informed for reasons of security.

Interpreting for Fidel in his own household, at a time in which so many things were spoken about him and almost nobody could see him up close and personal, was a privilege that filled me with joy and pride on one hand, but with nervousness and anxiety on the other. Obviously, we always want to give the very best from ourselves in our professional performance and to leave in our wake a good image about our job. As an interpreter for Fidel, my need to succeed was multiplied exponentially, and I feared that I was not good enough to undertake such a responsibility. But I mustered all the courage I had and decided to do it to the best of my abilities, with all the dignity that such a big commission entailed.

Later, I learned that this visit, one of the very few that Fidel was accepting due to his personal health situation (he was abiding by strict medical instructions) came about when he learned from his brother, Raúl, that on a flight from a rally in Holguín to Havana, Lucius had asked Raúl to please give Fidel a hug and his best wishes for a prompt recovery. Lucius had personally expressed to Raúl his desires to see Fidel, but he was aware that a visit would not be advisable at that time. Fidel, however, when told what Rev. Walker had said, called Caridad Diego, head of the Office for the Care of Religious Affairs and gave her instructions to find a space within the hectic schedule of the Caravan so that he could invite Lucius to his house to hold a friendly dialogue. In this polite way, he wanted to be able to please his dear friend. He was looking forward to seeing him and greeting him personally, as he habitually used to do on each Caravan.

Caridad was the one who suggested that I should be the interpreter for that fraternal encounter, and then Fidel sent for me. Thus, a whole meaningful experience started out, which marked my professional performance as a translator-interpreter. I was able to do something that I never thought I would do. Becoming a translator, my golden dream, was one thing; doing my job simultaneously, an almost unreachable dream, had also been achieved; but interpreting for Fidel, that was not even on my agenda because it was too important for me to be asked to do it. It went far beyond my most ambitious expectations as a professional.

I will never forget the translation-interpretation post-graduate courses at the School of Foreign Languages of Havana University in 1985. The distinguished professors Lourdes Llansó Alzugaray and Isabel Casado Díaz, who were in charge of teaching us, used to tell us a whole bunch of anecdotes about the interpreters who freaked out, totally blocked and paralyzed, due to the nervousness triggered by the sheer idea of being asked to interpret for Fidel. Back then, I was still working as an English teacher at the Vladimir Ilich Lenin Vocational High School, and I thought deep down that I did not really have to be worried about that at all, for surely I would never be expected to do such a thing. Never say, "I will not drink from that water."

We were traveling on board vehicles of the personal security of the Commander, heading towards his residence located at the enigmatic Point Zero, and I could not believe this was really happening to me. As we rode to the expected rendezvous, I was thinking that there were many other colleagues, professional interpreters with outstanding careers and far more experience than I, who, the way I saw it, should be in my place because, even though I did this job as my regular work now, I was self-taught, a totally empirical translator-interpreter, and I was aware that I was neither the best nor the one and only of my kind.

I cannot deny, however – resorting to that quota of personal vanity that we all have, whether we are willing to admit it or not – that I was feeling euphoric. This country boy, still getting rid of some rural attachments, was interpreting for Fidel Castro, himself, right in his own household. How much I would have liked to share that wonderful experience with my parents! How proud it would have made them to know that their little nest egg had managed to reach the very summit of his dreams and had even gone way beyond it! Because, when you come to think about it, after such an experience, what could challenge me more? What else more important could happen to me?

Maybe I was not the fittest to interpret for Fidel, but I was indeed Lucius's interpreter in Cuba. That would obviously relax me to a certain degree because I knew him very well after so many years, and I had the quintessential right of providing him with those services even if the interlocutor was Fidel. Besides that, I am very fond of a phrase that I once heard from a colleague who advised me with a deep sincerity, "Never underestimate yourself; do not ever ask anything from anybody, but whatever you are given, take it, and if you may, choose it!" Certainly, I had not asked for that unfathomable privilege, but if I had been asked, I would, of course, not refuse it.

Other participants in that unforgettable encounter between Fidel and Lucius were Ellen Bernstein, associate director of Pastors for Peace, Rev. Thomas Smith, member of the Board of Directors of that organization, and Caridad Diego from the Central Committee of the Office for the Care of Religious Affairs.

Fidel greeted us all effusively upon our arrival, including me, which I will forever appreciate, for it is quite common for many people, particularly those occupying leadership posts, to overlook interpreters and to take us as if we were one more electronic device facilitating communications. More often than not, they forget that we are first and foremost human beings. Fidel's wife, Dalia Soto del Valle, asked me to sit on a chair by the right side of the Commander, across from his guests. I did not have time to get nervous because I had to concentrate intently on my work. Filled with enthusiasm, he would not stop talking. I had no choice but to simultaneously interpret into English all his multi-topical conversation in real time.

I needed to be so focused – trying to listen, hear, understand, and convey everything at the same time – that my brain could not afford to worry or to busy itself with other issues. Time passed at a dizzying speed. In good Cuban slang, "it went by at a million." Fidel, with his unfathomable wisdom and his gifts as a speaker par excellence, spoke about a whole number of interesting things. Fortunately for me, what he referred the most to was one of the two books written by the President of the United States, Barack Obama, *Dreams from My Father*, the very last book I had finished reading a week earlier. That was not by chance. As it is said in English, "it was meant to be; it was in black and white already." I felt quite at ease translating what I still had fresh in the back of my mind. It turned out to be quite interesting and curious at the same time to know that the book in Spanish that Fidel had in his hands was the one I had finished reading in English the week before, that in his mind he was filtering through the information that I had pondered over and stored in my own mind just a few days earlier.

The meeting lasted two hours and forty minutes. It easily could have extended way longer than that, but the right time arrived for Fidel's prescribed medication, and that was the best of pretexts for us to leave so as not to abuse his generosity. We said goodbye in time for him to rest, as was in keeping with his medical instructions.

As an excellent host, when our farewell time arrived, Fidel invited us to have a group picture taken with him in the middle. One of his five children, Alejandro, was our photographer. To my surprise, when they were getting ready and settling themselves around him, he started to move his head in different directions, asking where the interpreter was. What he said next, I will never forget as long as I live, for I have it engraved and recorded in the deepest part of my mind. He began to praise my job publicly, which I liked on the one hand, particularly because Fidel was the one doing it; on the other hand, I was embarrassed that he was doing it in front all the people present.

He exclaimed with evident admiration, "Wow! He is really good! I did not even realize that there was an interpreter between us. He is very fast." Then he asked me out of a subtle curiosity, "Where did you learn such good English?" In a nutshell, I told him who I was and how I had upgraded myself. He congratulated me once again and told his guests with pride, "That's for you to see the quality of the professionals that we train in our country!" I just could not believe that Fidel was the one who was speaking like that about my person and praising my job. I could die any time from then on. After that, what else but heaven? He also saw fit to be kind enough to send me a copy of the group picture that was taken to perpetuate that historical encounter. I treasure it as the most important picture of my whole lifetime.

At Fidel's house in July 2010 with the Pastors for Peace leaders.
From left: Alberto, Rev. Lucius Walker, Fidel Castro, Ellen Bernstein,
and Rev. Thomas Smith

I thought that would be something like debut and farewell, not because I had done a bad job, but rather, taking into account Fidel's age, his health status, and the fact that what happened was a purely circumstantial meeting. As I had been Lucius's interpreter since the Second Pastors for Peace Caravan in 1993, it was logical to a given extent that I should be the one interpreting for that meeting, but that was it. I was pleased, nonetheless, treasuring that imperishable encounter as a beautiful page of my curriculum vitae and as something to share with my daughters and eventually my grandchildren. Little did I suspect at that point that this meeting would only be the first of other similar experiences.

In late August, hardly a month after that unique opportunity, I got a telephone call from the Central Committee that made me suspect right away that I would be expected to carry out another important job. It was from Caridad Diego's office, and it was limited to asking me only, very likely as a matter of security, if I would be available over the weekend because, very possibly, I would be needed once again. I did not think that it would be about Fidel one more time. I thought it likely that an important church leader was coming from some English-speaking country and they needed me to interpret a meeting at the Central Committee of the Office for the Care of Religious Affairs, as I had done this several times previously. Never did I guess what would happen next.

That very night, I got a second telephone call, this time from the

Head of the Ideological Department of the Central Committee, Rolando Alfonso Borges, who asked me to be ready the following day, first thing in the morning. He told me that a car from the Central Committee would come to pick me up at home. He asked about my address so he could give it to the driver in charge of my transportation. He was the one who let me know that, once again, it would be a meeting with Fidel. He said they needed to know if they could count on the services I provided the previous time with Lucius. Needless to say, I did not hesitate for a second before consenting, asserting that I would gladly do it, which did not relax me at all. I committed the mistake of being too discreet and did not ask him with whom the meeting would be this time. The only thing I knew that night was that I would be taken by car to the house of the renowned documentary maker Roberto Chile. From there, we would all depart together for the appointment that was scheduled for 10:00 AM.

When I hung up the phone, my head was not big enough to accommodate all the questions that were emerging from my ever-growing curiosity as I tried to guess for whom I would have to interpret and about what. Had I known ahead of time, I would have prepared myself slightly better, looking up information, reading, inquiring about the issue to be addressed and the guest in particular. Only one thing I did know for sure, that as we Cubans put it, "it would fall from the tree." This meant that it had to be somebody very important to succeed in arranging an interview with Fidel in the middle of his recuperation. Still, who would that VIP be?

My daughter Betsy understood my anxiety and, knowing me so well, invited me to take a long walk with her in order to help me relax, trying to entertain me mentally on the one hand and to physically tire me out on the other, to make sure I could fall asleep. The following day, I would face once again an enigma I could not yet decipher. For me, worry and sleeplessness have always walked hand in hand, and they have been directly proportional to the dimensions of the concern being addressed. We walked down the streets and avenues of Marianao, chatting cheerfully, trying to guess the celebrated personage I would face in a matter of just a few hours. We had a long walking tour. As soon as I got home, I took a bath as hot as possible to relax my muscles, and fully aware that would not be enough, I took a

3 mg tablet of melatonin, a nighttime dietary supplement, as an aid to help me sleep. It had proven to be pretty effective at other times when I felt high levels of stress.

How naïve of me to think that the long walk, the hot bath, and the sleeping pill were going to fulfill my objective. That may be the perfect combination for other people or under other circumstances, but in my case, it was a total waste of time. I stayed awake with my eyes open, like a fish on a rack, all night long, without sleeping, not even for a second. Thus the day came, and I was still trying, tossing and turning in my bed during the never-ending wee hours. I needed to recover my energies somehow, and I could not give up, concerned about the weariness that would eventually take hold of me. Fortunately, soporifics do not succeed much with me, but stimulants do indeed. I took a cold shower to cheer me up and drank lots of strong black coffee. The combination of cold water, black coffee, and above all my great concern to make sure that everything would work out right and I would not let our Commander down really did work wonders.

Roberto Chile was the one who clarified my uncertainty when he let me know that it was the famous US filmmaker Oliver Stone who was visiting Cuba and would be interviewing Fidel. Back in 1992, Stone interviewed him for his documentary, *Comandante*. We arrived at Fidel's house long before Stone did.

I liked the fact that Roberto Chile showed interest in getting to know me. While the cameramen and technicians were finalizing details about the microphones and lights, he beckoned to me, said hello and engaged himself in a very cheerful conversation during which he asked me many questions about my life, my family, my studies, and my experience as a translator. I was quite impressed by his thorough knowledge about my hometown, Managua. He even spoke to me about new projects in that area.

The interview with Oliver Stone extended over four consecutive hours, and I had to interpret simultaneously most of the time. Fidel was waiting for him with an inch-thick dossier containing all the information he had managed to get about the life and work of this US film director. He had already read all that volume with the voracity that characterized him as a tireless reader. Stone was obviously interested in getting to know about the content of that portfolio bearing his name on its front cover, and Fidel, to the surprise of all present, began to tell him by heart many things that he remembered from his recent reading about the life and work of this important artist of cinema.

Translating for Oliver Stone (second from left) and Fidel (right)

As I expected, Fidel addressed a wide assortment of topics, ranging from literature, politics, economy, filmmaking, history, and religion to international relations, the different US administrations, the Missile Crisis, the mercenary invasion by the Bay of Pigs, the interference of the United States in the Middle East, the new situation in Latin America, relations between Cuba and the Bolivarian Republic of Venezuela, the Cuban Revolution, the environment, the development achieved by science and technology, the danger posed by a preventable nuclear war, along with his assessments of the autobiographical book written by the US President, Barack Obama, *Dreams from my Father*, which he had amply underlined. On the margins of the pages, he had jotted down many remarks.

It was something like speaking with a great walking encyclopedia. Maybe his physical health was still disrupted, but his mental clarity and sharpness were really amazing. About that topic, he commented that now he was doing what he should have done all along and that he never did for reasons we all know about. He was taking very good care of himself, "as a fine rooster," according to the country people, and was abiding by the medical prescriptions to the very letter: eating properly, taking all his medications on time, sleeping six hours a day, doing his physical rehabilitation, including a walk of two kilometers daily, even drinking the exact amount of wine suggested by the physician in charge of him. Now, he had all the time in the world to write his memoirs, read a lot, including all the bulky volume of cable news that he receives every day, watch TV, and enjoy the baseball games that he is so fond of.

When I finally got home after that intense workday, releasing all the tension that had built up and feeling the added relief of having finished that second experience despite not having closed my eyes the night before, I was so physically, mentally, and intellectually exhausted, that a splitting headache took hold of me mercilessly. As if that were not enough for one day, after a few hours, Caridad Diego called me and wanted to know how I had fared, for she was the one who had recommended me the previous time for the meeting that Fidel held with Rev. Walker. She told me that Fidel had called her and that he was very impressed with my job. The awareness that I had not let him down with such a commission was extremely gratifying and would amply compensate for my unbearable headache. Before finishing our conversation, she warned me that I should be psychologically prepared and should not be surprised at all if I were called again sometime later.

I was already relieved of my headache, sitting completely relaxed in my rocking chair in front of the TV set, when my daughter Betsy picked up the phone and told me with a frightened little face that it was for me. It was the head of Fidel's personal security escort who was speaking to me. My heart almost stopped beating when I overheard him say, "Commander, the interpreter is already on the line, whenever you please." I was paralyzed, gripping the telephone as if I had suddenly frozen. Listening to Fidel's voice through my phone handset, right there in the comfort and intimacy of my small apartment, seemed to be science fiction and not a real fact.

He was very kind; he spoke with me for several minutes, thanking me repeatedly for all the work I had done, apologizing for the intensity of that lengthy and tiring workday, and expressing interest in knowing my take on the interview. When I confessed to him that I had been unable to sleep the night before due to my nervous tension, he laughed and told me, "Don't worry. Tonight you will sleep smoothly." He treated me as a father would have done. When I hung up after his caring farewell, the hand I held the phone with was soaked in perspiration. My family was all around me, pricking up their ears and popping out their eyes in disbelief, as if watching a spectacular thriller. We could not believe what had just happened and what all of us had witnessed: Fidel Castro calling me at home to chat.

The third chapter of that unique experience did not take long in appearing. A month later, in September, I got another telephone call from Alfonso at the Central Committee wondering if they could count on my services one more time. They would use the same modus operandi as they did the time before. They would come to pick me up and take me to Roberto Chile's house. It was the same story: I did not know the details and prudently did not ask for security reasons. Chile let me know that this time the guests of the Chief were the celebrated North American artists Harry Belafonte, the singer, and Danny Glover, the actor, both personal friends of Fidel who, taking advantage of their stay in Havana on the occasion of the dedication of a new hall for the traveling showcase of the new Latin American movies, had asked to meet with him.

Belafonte wanted to tape an interview of the Commander as part of a documentary he was making. This time, he came accompanied by his wife and daughter. All combined, they made up a select group of about seven people. That was another long workday of remembrances. Even though it was customary for Fidel to address current issues from all over the world, he emphasized the issue of Cuban internationalist missions in the field of health care because Belafonte's daughter, being a pediatric psychiatrist, could not help but show her keen interest in that regard. This was my third visit to Fidel's home, and being there in the midst of his family, surrounded by his wife, his children, and his grandchildren, still seemed completely unreal and impossible to me.

The pictures taken during the meeting with Oliver Stone were publicized on the Internet and traveled all around the world by way of cyberspace, thanks to modern information and communication technologies, which make the world a small village. Huge distances are no longer communication obstacles at all. Right after that, my friends, relatives, coworkers, colleagues, former students, neighbors, and acquaintances started to identify me gradually, making me out in the pictures on their computer screens. From then on, an unceasing flow of e-mail messages was unleashed, both domestic and foreign, and I received telephone calls and personal questions from many curious people who would congratulate and tease me, reminding me repeatedly of the magnitude of the task I had undertaken. The intelligent country boy, as my first teacher used to call me, had interpreted for the Commander-in-Chief. I don't believe it myself despite the pictures bearing witness to the veracity of the facts.

The late Professor Casanova had not been wrong, when several times, he forecast in the early '80s that I would someday interpret for Fidel. Then, I was just a new graduate, dreaming about becoming a translator-interpreter on some faraway date. How unrealistic and absurd his prophecies had seemed to be back then! How much I would now like to share with him the truth about the event that he had envisioned with so much certainty! Regretfully, a fatal fall on a staircase had put an end to his life some years before. Interpreting for Fidel, several times for that matter, made me conjure up his pleasant memory and thank God one more time for him and for everything he taught me.

If I were born again

Needless to say, I feel quite accomplished professionally. If I were born again, I would be a translator again without the slightest hesitation, despite the sacrifice and the dedication that achieving it entailed. What I enjoy most about my job is that I can never claim that I have reached the summit, and know everything there is to know. If I were to do that, I would be deceiving myself. I used to enjoy teaching quite a lot, and the daily exchange with my students was gratifying. Working with teenagers for years on end always made me feel very spiritually young. However, the time soon arrived when I felt stagnant, under my real capacity, and under-exploited. It was something like functioning at 110 volts while being designed for 220 instead.

The English that I acquired gradually – over the years, in each of the postgraduate training courses I took, plus that which I learned by means of my reading habit, which soon became my hobby – needed greater demands that would compel me to put it to good use. It wasn't until I began to interpret professionally that I realized how much vocabulary I had already mastered, but also all the vocabulary I needed to learn as soon as possible.

Due to the characteristics of my profession, I have to do my job as a translator-interpreter for many different delegations. Their programs of activities are varied, in keeping with the specific interests of each group. This means that I may be interpreting at a sugarcane mill, a hospital, a school, an agricultural cooperative unit, a hotel, a church, a scientific research institute, a factory, a cultural or sports activity, or a specialized museum: that is, in any field of human knowledge. Each specialty has its own characteristic slang and jargon, as well as its own terminology, which provides me with an everlasting challenge. An interpreter who respects himself must upgrade his skills all the time by reading, studying, consulting, looking things up, aiming to broaden his active vocabulary constantly, preparing himself to perform his job with dignity and to meet the expectations of people who are always checking both his work and his expertise.

Ideally, there would be specialized interpreters for the various fields of human knowledge. In fact, there are some available, but they make up a small minority compared to the overwhelming majority who must face great challenges in their everyday experience. Usually, participants at international events are specialists, experts on the issues that will be addressed, and researchers who know the most about the issues. Both the presenters and the listeners paying close attention to them in the audience are knowledgeable about the matter that is being examined because they studied it at the university and use it systematically in their respective work and teaching settings. Bottom line, they know it thoroughly. We interpreters are the channels, the instruments to convey those ideas, the communication tools by means of which the experts make themselves understood. We know the least about the issue in question most of the time. Too many times we are called on the phone and only told the date of the scheduled event and its title, for instance: informational sciences, telecommunications, natural catastrophes, alcohol by-products, neurosurgery, and so forth. Then and there, we are made aware of a certain maxim claiming that, with what we know, maybe a whole book could be written, but with what we don't know, a full library could be filled.

A new concern begins with each event and the immediate action that cannot be put on hold: trying to search for updated information about it, to get acquainted to the best of our abilities in both languages with the acronyms, as well as the names of the organizations, the personalities involved, their respective posts and leadership positions, the history of the event, its backgrounds, the references, the glossaries (if any), containing the most frequently used terminology in that field, et cetera. All those aforementioned things entail long hours of study and personal preparation that are not easily understood by people who are not interpreters. Maybe that is why it is easy for people to criticize, compare, judge, and censor when, for reasons beyond our control, we do not meet all their expectations or simply make a mistake, regardless of how tiny or meaningless it might be. Those are the occupational hazards of our trade, and who buys the cow is also the owner of its calf; therefore, we have no other choice but to accept the bad with the good if we really like what we do, which is my case, no doubts about it. It is the price we need to pay, and I am fully aware of it.

This reflection reminds me of one of so many caravans of Pastors for Peace during a visit to the western province of Pinar del Río. As part of the program of activities, a visit to a livestock-raising center for swine reproduction had been planned. As I was Rev. Lucius Walker's interpreter, I was expected to accompany him to all events, which meant an added stress, for he was the central figure of the caravans and thus the focus of attention the whole time. He was also a very famous person and deeply beloved by Cubans. Since I read the program at the meeting held at the North America Division of the headquarters of the ICAP, I was particularly concerned about this swine facility visit due to the nature of the terminology. A center of that kind is not frequently visited; therefore, the specialized vocabulary had to be studied so as to avoid an unexpected and stressful fiasco, or a sudden shortcoming.

One never knows what word the speaker is going to use, let alone whether you know it in the foreign language or not. Too many times, that is only known right on the spot. It is very unpleasant not to understand or not to know how to interpret a given term that may be key in the expressed idea. At times like that, we need to come up with linguistic miracles in order to be able to get through cumbersome situations elegantly and play a good role in front of the attendees. As part of these foreign visiting groups, there are always bilingual individuals or Cubans who happen to know English and who are actually, even if out of good will, evaluating your performance. This further stresses us, even though we pretend that we cannot care less and that everything is under control.

When we were heading towards the aforementioned swine development center, Rev. Raúl Suárez sat beside me on the caravan bus, and he became very interested in knowing what I was reading with so much attention all along that ride. He was favorably impressed to know that it was a book in English on animal husbandry by Higinio Espino. I was studying the book and reviewing a glossary on livestock-raising terminology, particularly words related to swine. Thanks to my preparation, I managed to cope with the challenge with fluency and assurance. This challenge undoubtedly made me grow as a professional, at least in the eyes of my dear pastor. On several occasions, he alluded to that incident as a clear token of the positive impact it had upon his personal assessment of my performance as an interpreter.

That is why I truly admire and respect any colleague doing his job, regardless of how well or poorly he is achieving it. Only those who interpret are able to understand what is felt with each of these experiences during which, if something is not properly understood, the easiest solution is to blame the interpreter immediately, claiming that it is just a matter of incorrect translation. *The rope always breaks by the weakest part.*

For critical onlookers watching from the relaxed comfort of an armchair, it is easy to identify mistakes, be judgmental, and even think that they might do a better job. Nevertheless, those who are experienced in this never-well-acknowledged profession will know that such is not the case at all. I have learned a lot from colleagues with whom I have had the immense privilege to work in many different places, at all sorts of events both in Cuba and abroad, primarily with my dear colleagues from the ESTI, at the Havana International Conference Center, and also in many other hotels in the city of Havana and other provinces. They have been a real school to me along with my empirical training.

Since I was a boy, I was fond of acting. Even though I never thought to be an actor, I rather liked it as a hobby. In elementary school, when I was hardly a second grader, I played the character of the Enchanted Little Shrimp in the homonymic children's short story found in *The*

Golden Age by José Martí. In junior high, I joined a theater interest club and even wrote a short play that was dramatized. Halfway through the play, on stage with a full audience, I was greatly distressed when the fake moustache that had been stuck over my lips with a burning and aggressive glue from the shoe factory, suddenly broke away. Unbeknownst, I did something quite unforgivable, which triggered peals of laughter from the audience. I turned my back on them while trying to fix it back somehow. As I did not succeed, I could not help but exclaim, "Oh my God. Now what am I supposed to do?" I still had the mike in my hand, so even though the crowd would not see what was going on, they heard perfectly well the amplification of my anguish.

Later on, already at the university, I joined an amateur theater group in which I played a few main characters. For one of them, a 35-year-old engineer in a textile industry, I even had to request authorization from the director of our pedagogical unit to grow my padlock, the traditional goatee on my chin, because the physical characterization of that character required it.

I also have been asked to interpret for many training workshops on playback theater – a modality of improvised, spontaneous theater that emerged in the United States – for Cuban and foreign actors and actresses who have been trained in this performing discipline. Finally, I took a theoretical-practical course in story telling taught by the outstanding professor Mayra Navarro at the Ernesto Lecuona Hall of the Great Theater of Havana. I took part at the Story Telling International Festival Primaveras de Cuentos 2008, defending the short story "Memé" by our unforgettable Onelio Jorge Cardoso. I have enjoyed telling stories at homes for the elderly, community centers, cultural institutions, and within the informal framework of gatherings among family and friends. I have received indescribable energy as feedback from audiences everywhere.

With the gradual accumulation of experience in my capacity as communicator, I have been able to incorporate very useful tools when it comes to speaking in public and using microphones. I think an interpreter is an actor in his own right, and even though the golden rule of interpretation is that we should translate ideas and not words, when it comes to interpreting, we are one more actor, if you will, for our task is precisely that of trying to convey what the speaker has expressed as faithfully as possible. It is not a secret to anybody that people – particularly Cubans – do not speak by using words only. The extra-verbal body language is varied, rich, and unique to each person. If one is limited to transmitting cold, dull words without expressive inflexions and shades of meaning, one is mutilating a good part of the message and the intention of the speaker. That is why I try to place myself as close as possible to orators, making sure, as much as I can, to look at their faces so as not to miss a single detail of their expressions and gestures. I learned that from my colleague Juana Vera, the excellent personal interpreter of our Commander and my paradigm par excellence, whom I have admired a lot since I was very young and started dreaming about doing what she did. I have envied her silently and wholesomely for years on end, thinking all along, as some children tell their role models in life, "When I grow up, I would like to be like you." Even if the mics have already been set on the stage in a given way, Juanita always makes sure to readjust hers, so it allows her to see Fidel's face directly in front of her. After accumulating my own experience, I now understand very well why she has always cared about doing that, though it might go unnoticed by many people.

When interpreting, we should place ourselves in the shoes of the speaker, as we say in English, and try to emulate and act out the people we are interpreting for because, at that point in time, we become their mouth and their ideas. We should approach their true intentions as much as possible, even when we may diametrically disagree with whatever is being stated. It is, of course, far easier and more comfortable to interpret when there is empathy and like-mindedness and when we fully concur with what is said. However, even when it is just the opposite, we need to do exactly the same, for we must covey the speaker's ideas just the way they were said and expressed. At least, that is what I always try to do.

That concept is also valid when it comes to written translation. According to what was stated by the celebrated poet Eliseo Diego, an outstanding personality in our culture, in his book *Conversación con los difuntos*, "A good translation, I think, cannot hope but evoke a similar sensation to that of the original in the new linguistic matter where it has incarnated..."

Maybe I should clarify that the terms translator and interpreter have been wrongly used, at least in our country, where interpreters are usually called translators. The fact is that there is a clear-cut difference between both professions, although they are often carried out by the same individual; that is why the hyphenated name of translator-interpreter for you may be one or the other or both as is the case of the majority in which I am included. The distinction is that translation is meant for written activity, whereas interpretation refers to oral activity.

During the act of interpretation, one stops being oneself and automatically becomes an actor personifying the "character" of the individual for whom one is interpreting; otherwise, even when a good performance was accomplished, it would be something like paraphrasing instead of quoting a given author. The goal is not just having a good command of a foreign language and using it fluently. When the situation gets tough, we need to resort to other strategies, including histrionic ones, to make sure we succeed. That has been my personal experience and something that has never gone unnoticed by those who benefit directly or indirectly from the services I render in this job that I love so passionately. That is why I claim, without any fear of being wrong, that if I were born again, very gladly and willingly, without thinking twice, I would be a translator-interpreter again, for that is definitely, absolutely, and unquestionably my ministry – the craved for and yearned for old dream of this humble, intelligent country boy. Although slightly belatedly, thanks be to God, it became reality.

I WOULD BE A TRANSLATOR AGAIN

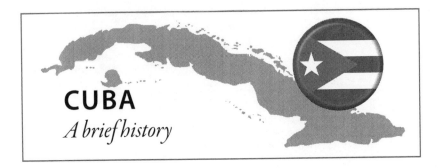

CUBA
A brief history

Welcome to Cuba

Cuba's countryside has always been the cradle of change on our island. Agricultural markets (farmers' markets), which were banned until 1993, are now filled with produce and bustling with vendors and buyers. For the first time, farmers count on strong market incentives and have sped up production.

Land reform has turned 40 percent of all the cultivable land in Cuba over to a new kind of cooperative. There has been a remarkable turnaround in Cuban food production. Through a combination of strategic restructuring by the government, new institutions, creativity, and innovations by farmers, Cuban agriculture slowly, painstakingly, has begun to show signs of new life.

Under the circumstances facing Cuba – the US embargo, loss of trading partners, little international aid, and economic collapse – the most notable accomplishments have been restoring food security, revitalizing the cities with urban agriculture, rebuilding productive capacity based on sustainable practices, and restructuring the agricultural economy without social dislocations.

The relative economic isolation of Cuba and its exclusion from agreements with the International Monetary Fund and the World Bank due to US sanctions paradoxically have strengthened the Cuban government's hand in policy-making.

Thus, Cuba has maintained a nationalist policy towards agriculture –protecting domestic producers from lower-priced food imports and subsidizing different kinds of producers. The government has absorbed the cost of this policy, which has led to unrealistic prices, but the policy has allowed Cuban agriculture to recover from the crisis.

The basic US policy decisions made in the early 1960s have structured US-Cuban relations ever since. The bilateral relationship has experienced many ups and downs, however, including an important relaxation of tensions during the mid-1970s and a marked deterioration of relations during the first few years of the 21st century.

US immigration policy runs a close second to the embargo in sore subjects. In 1966, the US enacted the Cuban Adjustment Act, which grants residency to any Cuban arriving on US shores. Anyone who has ever tried to obtain residency in the US knows what an incredible windfall this is, and people have risked their lives in its pursuit.

The US also promised to issue a minimum of 20,000 visas yearly to Cubans who wished to emigrate, which was the case until 2003 when the George W. Bush administration issued only 500, very likely in an effort to spark another crisis that might be the pretext for military intervention.

In today's Cuban economy, even a strong-willed person must struggle with economic realities in ways that Cubans have seldom experienced. And it has to do so in an environment where social differences are far more prevalent than they were in the past.

There are two primary perspectives about Cuba, at least in the United States. One is the Caribbean image portraying Cuba as an appealing tourist destination with happy, friendly, and carefree people.

The other picture of Cuba is that of a bleak, disintegrating, decaying society with a repressive police state, where people live in dreary fear, keeping all their opinions to themselves, unable to go to church, and hating our historical enemies in the North, who are called "gringos" everywhere but Cuba.

I don't know which of these two notions about my country you may have. To discover the truth, I invite all those who want to learn about Cuba to visit us. But I must warn you before you make this decision that your trip might change your opinion about us and our island. You might even fall in love with our people and our culture.

You might be tempted to come again and again and again. The point is that there is nothing more educational than traveling and seeing and learning firsthand. Whatever brings you to Cuba, you won't find animosity here. You will, rather, be pleasantly amazed by the way you will be welcomed and treated while here.

We are not Paradise, but we are certainly not Hell, either. That much I know. Prove me right by discovering it yourself. You won't ever regret it. I promise. You will be welcomed to my beloved Cuba, my friend, any time!

Epilogue

So, this is my book, which I have written very willingly. I decided that it should comprise only nine chapters, for nine is unquestionably my number: I was born on the ninth day, in the ninth month of the year, and stayed for nine moons in the blessed womb of my dear mother. There might be many more things to talk about in the memoirs of my half wheel, but it would neither be practical nor inviting to the reader to read too thick a book. If I were to live one hundred years and complete my whole wheel with enough mental clarity, maybe then I could be tempted to write my second part.

It is gratifying to share my life by means of these written words. Those who read this book will get to know me better. Writing my memoirs has been the perfect materialization of the wise proverb from our rich popular wisdom claiming that "to remember is to live again." How verily true! In front of my computer, I have laughed like a lunatic. I have also wiped away tears, trying to convey with clarity both the good and the bad moments that I have lived through over my five decades. Filtering that entire emotional load sensitized me about a whole number of subtleties that surprised me very pleasantly. No one knows what the brain is capable of registering and guarding zealously during a whole human lifespan. What affects us, be it good or bad, is engraved indelibly in our "hard disk" and needs to be addressed before an unexpected "virus" may attack and destroy it either partially or totally.

In writing, I did not only deliberately and slowly remember what I have experienced, but I have also had the chance to reread what I wrote so I could improve it, enlarge it, fix it, and rectify it. In the process, I discovered a vast number of details that otherwise would have been easily overlooked. Once I had completed this task, I found it very heartening to sit down and enjoy my work, totally relaxed, just as when a painter or sculptor steps back to double-check that the intended effect was indeed materialized in his work, surprising himself by what he achieved, regardless of all the improvable things that may be left.

Behold here my dream come true at long last, which has gone way beyond my expectations in this exciting translation-interpretation world. Yet, if I were to say that I am already satisfied, I would be lying first and foremost to myself, and I would never ever allow myself to do such a thing. In spite of everything I have achieved during almost twenty years exercising this profession of my dreams, I still feel that there is a long way for me to go in terms of learning, improving, and growing even further in my job. That is the greatest inducement. It nourishes my spirit and my never-ending desire to excel.

Last but not least, the only thing left for me to do is to encourage all of you striving for the sake of your dreams. Never lose heart, no matter what the obstacles, as you pursue your noblest ventures. Continue to hope against all odds.

Once again, I will be forever thankful to God for each and every blessing that He has granted to this country boy who always dreamed of being what he is today, for helping me to defend that long-awaited dream even during the most difficult times, for not letting me lose my faith when I needed it most, and for providing me with the vital energy and stamina to move on in spite of all the obstacles along the way, bearing all along the pride of being a Cuban in these times.

Thank you Lord!

Your eternally grateful translator-interpreter country boy,

Alberto, March 1, 2014

Acknowledgments

I began writing this book by first thanking God for every blessing He has bestowed my life with. I thank Him every single night from my comfortable pillow for each and every one of the things that happen to me on a daily basis, even for those I think I do not deserve because they have been unfair and even cruel at times.

Likewise, I express my heartfelt gratitude to my whole poor family, to all my "guajiros from the green woods," as I used to refer to them with loving care, because in spite of everything, that is exactly what I am, and I am very honored to be one. Deep down in my heart, I firmly believe that the country people are by far the most solicitous, polite, selfless, and hospitable people that may be met, not just in Cuba, but anywhere else in the world.

I dedicate this book to the imperishable memory of my parents, the strong pillars who not only gave us our life, but who also cared about instilling in us deep ethical and moral values since very early on, in the midst of material shortages of all sorts. I dedicate it with a great deal of love also to my two great treasures, my wonderful daughters, Wendy and Betsy, who have filled my life with great emotions and have made me feel the proudest father in the world. I am certain that they will never let me down.

Likewise, may my whole gratefulness reach my faithful wife, Marisol, for her unconditional support. She has stuck with me through thick and thin. I could not possibly have had a better wife. May God forever bless her the way she honestly deserves.

I am grateful to my publisher, Donald Tubesing, who made it possible for my book to be published in English, and to my editor, Susan Rubendall.

To my companions and friends who have won my love, respect, and everlasting gratitude: I thank you for supporting me and advising me through hard times. Particularly, I would like to mention Miguel, Ángel, Aníbal, Carlos, Jorgito, Roly, Mandy, Martica, Nancy, and Vlady. A friend in need is a friend indeed. May God bless them all plentifully because He has already blessed me a lot with them all!

Amen.

Made in the USA
Lexington, KY
05 June 2014